CO-CREATION IN PUBLIC SERVICES
FOR INNOVATION
AND SOCIAL JUSTICE

Edited by
Sue Baines, Rob Wilson, Chris Fox,
Inga Narbutaité Aflaki, Andrea Bassi,
Heli Aramo-Immonen and Riccardo Prandini

I0135779

P

First published in Great Britain in 2024 by

Policy Press, an imprint of
Bristol University Press
University of Bristol
1–9 Old Park Hill
Bristol
BS2 8BB
UK
t: +44 (0)117 374 6645
e: bup-info@bristol.ac.uk

Details of international sales and distribution partners are available at policy.bristoluniversitypress.co.uk

© 2024 Sue Baines, © 2024 Rob Wilson, © 2024 Chris Fox, © 2024 Inga Narbutaité Aflaki,
© 2024 Andrea Bassi, © 2024 Heli Aramo-Immonen, © 2024 Riccardo Prandini

British Library Cataloguing in Publication Data
A catalogue record for this book is available from the British Library

The digital PDF and EPUB versions of this title are available open access and distributed under the
terms of the Creative Commons Attribution-NonCommercial-NoDerivatives 4.0 International licence
(https://creativecommons.org/licenses/by-nc-nd/4.0/) which permits reproduction and distribution for
non-commercial use without further permission provided the original work is attributed.

ISBN 978-1-4473-6716-1 paperback
ISBN 978-1-4473-6717-8 ePub
ISBN 978-1-4473-6718-5 ePdf

The right of Sue Baines, Rob Wilson, Chris Fox, Inga Narbutaité Aflaki, Andrea Bassi,
Heli Aramo-Immonen and Riccardo Prandini to be identified as editors of this work has been
asserted by them in accordance with the Copyright, Designs and Patents Act 1988.

All rights reserved: no part of this publication may be reproduced, stored in a retrieval system, or
transmitted in any form or by any means, electronic, mechanical, photocopying, recording, or
otherwise without the prior permission of Bristol University Press.

Every reasonable effort has been made to obtain permission to reproduce copyrighted material.
If, however, anyone knows of an oversight, please contact the publisher.

The statements and opinions contained within this publication are solely those of the editors and
contributors and not of the University of Bristol or Bristol University Press. The University of
Bristol and Bristol University Press disclaim responsibility for any injury to persons
or property resulting from any material published in this publication.

Bristol University Press and Policy Press work to counter discrimination on grounds of gender, race,
disability, age and sexuality.

Cover design: Lyn Davies
Front cover image: Alamy/Paul Looyen

To the memory of Sue Baines who passed
away as this book was being finalised.
We miss an inspiring colleague and even
better friend (November 2023).

Contents

List of figures and tables

Figures

Tables

Notes on contributors

Heli Aramo-Immonen is Principal Lecturer in the School of Engineering and Business at Turku University of Applied Sciences.

Sue Baines was Professor of Social Enterprise (1956–2023) at Manchester Metropolitan University (MMU), Manchester, UK.

Andrea Bassi is Associate Professor of Sociology at Bologna University, Bologna, Italy.

Judit Csoba is Professor of Sociology in the Department of Sociology and Social Policy at the University of Debrecen.

Chris Fox is Professor of Evaluation at MMU, Manchester, UK.

Giulia Ganugi is Research Fellow at the Department of Economics and adjunct professor at the Department of Political and Social Sciences, University of Bologna, Bologna, Italy.

Jordan Harrison was Senior Research Assistant – Policy Evaluation and Research Unit (PERU), MMU and now works in social and economic consultancy.

David Jamieson is Lecturer in Digital Innovation at Newcastle Business School, Northumbria University, UK.

Hanna Kirjavainen is Senior Lecturer at Turku University of Applied Sciences, Turku, Finland.

Mike Martin is Professor of Enterprise Information Science at Newcastle Business School, Northumbria University, UK.

Inga Narbutaité Aflaki is Senior Lecturer in Political Science at Karlstad University, Sweden.

Riccardo Prandini is Professor of Sociology at Bologna University, Bologna, Italy.

Natalie Rutter is Senior Lecturer in Criminology at Leeds Trinity University, Leeds, UK.

Alex Sakellariou is Lecturer and Researcher at the University of Athens, Athens, Greece.

Florian Sipos is Assistant Lecturer at the University of Debrecen, Hungary.

Hayley Trowbridge is Chief Executive Officer of Peoples Voice Media.

Rob Wilson is Professor of Digital Economy at Newcastle Business School, Newcastle-upon-Tyne, UK.

Acknowledgements

This book is an output the of the EU co-funded Co-creation of Service Innovation in Europe (CoSIE) project. The editors and contributors would like to acknowledge the fantastic work of consortium members, partners in the project who co-created the project, and most importantly the participants in activities of the pilots. The project received funding from the European Union's Horizon 2020 research and innovation programme H2020-SC6-COCREATION-2017 under grant agreement No 770492. www.cosie project.eu.

1

Introduction: Co-creation and the 'sandcastle' problem

Sue Baines, Rob Wilson, Chris Fox, Inga Narbutaité Aflaki,
Andrea Bassi, Heli Aramo-Immonen and Riccardo Prandini

Introduction

Co-creation in the context of public services refers to citizens' contribution to implementing and shaping the services that affect them. It has become an orthodoxy in public policy that is widely accepted as humane and inclusive (Osborne et al, 2016; Bevir et al, 2019). Co-creation has many passionate, committed advocates and appears to be in tune with the times (Brandsen et al, 2018). Despite widespread enthusiasm and support there are also sceptical voices that warn of tokenism and failure to fully recognise imbalances of status and power (Dudau et al, 2019). In this book we present co-creation in a way grounded in practical service dilemmas and lived experience, with a wealth of original evidence from a diverse range of settings and policy domains across Europe. Our primary focus is on human and relational dimensions, at the same time taking an appreciative but critical view of new ways to use digital tools and resources to enable co-creation in public services.

The book is inspired and informed by practical action and original research across Europe. The editors and authors were part of a consortium that delivered a collaborative innovation project, Co-creation of Service Innovation in Europe (CoSIE). CoSIE was one of several projects funded by the European Commission on the co-creation of public services. It was distinctive in its ambition to advance co-creation with citizens who are typically excluded or overlooked. The consortium did this through ten real-life pilots, each working with a different public service and responding with innovations in co-creation to locally determined needs and priorities. Project teams consisting of municipalities, civil society organisations, companies and universities implemented and evaluated the pilots. The CoSIE pilots were implemented successfully, albeit with some surprises and setbacks. Overall, they show that co-creation is possible even in contexts that look highly unpromising, for example, countries where administrative traditions are very top-down, services where providers assume that citizens are 'hard to reach', and even mandated services such as criminal justice and work activation.

Despite notable achievements of the CoSIE pilots at local and sometimes national levels, we recognise that pilots, experiments, demonstrators and the like rarely appear to sustain or expand their promised outcomes (Brandsen et al, 2016). This is why we have come to characterise this approach to policy making as 'sandcastles' washed away by the next tide or kicked over by an incoming political administration or new minister to build their own, leaving little trace. It also allows us to see the problems caused by a 'sandcastle bucket' approach to the adoption of pre-existing interventions from another context which can often struggle in the local conditions and fail to literally take shape in the way they were envisaged.

Co-creation

We take as a starting point the much-cited characterisation of co-creation by Voorberg et al (2015: 1335) as 'active involvement of end-users in various stages of the production process'. This is more a description than a definition and quite broad. Interpretations vary in detail and emphasis but there is common attention to the rights, responsibilities and contributions of people directly affected by services (Brandsen and Honingh, 2018; Bevir et al, 2019). Co-creation echoes the term 'co-production', which has a longer history. Co-production has been described as a practice of reciprocity and mutuality (Boyle and Harris, 2009). It goes to the heart of both effective public services delivery and the role of public services in achieving societal ends such as social inclusion and citizen engagement (Pestoff and Hulgård, 2016). Many practitioners and some commentators use the terms co-production and co-creation interchangeably. In this volume we follow Torfing et al (2019) in making an analytic distinction for the sake of precision. Co-production refers to citizen contributions to the implementation of their services (Osborne, 2018). Co-creation implies that citizens exercise agency to define their goals in order to meet needs they themselves judge to be important. CoSIE adopted a formal definition of co-creation as 'a collaborative activity that reduces power imbalances and aims to enrich and enhance the value in public service offerings' (Fox et al, 2021: 8).

Co-creation necessitates interactions involving a wide range of stakeholders, including citizens, public administrators, community organisations, businesses and educators. Civil society organisations (CSOs) usually have a prominent role. CSOs have tended to be much more aware of co-creation than other sectors and often champion it although co-creation also brings challenges for them. 'Co-creation practices ... mobilize the experiences, resources, and ideas of a plurality of public and private actors in the creation of public solutions' (Torfing et al, 2019: 797). Co-creation, in other words, involves working across many existing divisions not only provider and 'user', but also professions, agencies and sectors with different values, priorities and worldviews.

Social justice, assets and capability

Co-creation is not only about making public services better and more responsive, important as that is. Implicit within it are new roles and responsibilities and, at least potentially, changes in the balance of control. An influential body of work on co-creation from a public administration perspective stresses the interactional logic of public services as *services*, in contrast to the more linear logic of industrial production (Osborne et al, 2016; Osborne, 2018; Peng et al, 2022). We recognise this perspective but our emphasis is different. Rationales for the individual CoSIE pilots overwhelmingly emphasised issues of social justice for people who are marginalised and lack power (although this was not demanded in the funding call). For the editors and authors of this collection, co-creation is essentially a moral endeavour that recognises the legitimate knowledge and lived experience of people who typically have services 'done to' them. This line of thinking is grounded in ideas that emanate from advocacy, capability, human rights and social justice, inspired at least in part by struggles of disabled people for control over the support they need to live independently (Fox et al, 2021). Its moral framework recognises the anthropological dimensions of human beings as 'receivers' (in need of support), 'doers' (capable of action) and 'judges', referring to the idea that citizens are able to say what has value in their eyes, and that this should inform policies and programmes that target them (Sen, 1985; Bonvin and Laruffa, 2018).

Welfare states were founded to combat pervasive evils that beset 20th-century society and to mitigate damage from individual or economic crises (Esping-Andersen et al, 2002; Hemerijck, 2013). Today, many public services are still designed around seeking to fix things for people in the short term (Wilson et al, 2018) and encouraging them to take action that fits the service's priorities, not their own (Fox, 2018). Co-creating public services implies a fundamental rethinking of the role of the welfare state and hence the relationship between individuals and the state (Cottam, 2018). It aligns with asset-based approaches that focus upon people's strengths rather than what is wrong with them (Cottam, 2018; Wilson et al, 2018). All this resonates with an 'investive' turn in social welfare intended to strengthen people's skills and capacities over the course of their lives (Hemerijck, 2015; 2017; Baines et al, 2019). 'Social investment' welfare has been criticised for overemphasising labour market activation and failing to fully address the needs of the most vulnerable (Cantillon and Van Lancker, 2013). Morel and Palme (2017) counter that it should be viewed more holistically in terms of capabilities, thus foregrounding human freedom, democracy and citizenship (Sen, 2001). The strengths and capabilities of citizens are inherent in co-creation. The co-creative pilots highlighted in the second part of this book are all intended in different ways to enhance assets and build capability.

Social innovation

We see co-creation and social justice as intimately linked to another idea that has become firmly ensconced in policy agenda: social innovation. Social innovation mobilises citizens to become an active part of the innovation process (Voorberg et al, 2015). It denotes novel, effective and just solutions that benefit society as a whole (Phills et al, 2008; BEPA, 2010; Marques et al, 2017). Characteristic of social innovations across many contexts is that they 'raise the hope and expectations of progress towards something better (a more socially sustainable / democratic / effective society)' (Brandsen et al, 2016: 6–7).

The idea of social innovation has roots in various traditions and has been described as 'fluid and diverse' (Nicholls et al, 2015: 1). Yet there is some agreement that social innovation coheres around new forms of institutional relationships and collective empowerment, especially of the most marginalised (Moulaert et al, 2013). Social innovations, as much writing on the topic attests, are inherently co-creative in harnessing ideation from diverse communities and fostering new relationships and interactions (Mumford, 2002; Murray et al, 2010; Grimm et al, 2013). New ideas, in short, come from people and relationships (Cottam, 2018). All this is borne out in empirical studies of social innovations across Europe and beyond that highlight co-creative aspects (Evers and Brandsen, 2016; Moulaert and MacCallum, 2019; Oosterlynck et al, 2019).

Social innovation almost invariably has positive and optimistic connotations but real-life examples are not always successful or beneficial (Brandsen et al, 2016; Meijer and Thaens, 2020). Even when they are successful, effective approaches may not be sustained (Brandsen et al, 2016). As with all social innovations, a key challenge for co-creation is how individual examples can go beyond silos and discrete projects, share learning, and evolve into the 'modus operandi' of institutions and societies. As we shall see, social innovation, even with (or perhaps because of) co-creation is harder than we think.

Digital technologies and digital social innovation

Digital technologies are sometime claimed to narrow the gap between service providers and citizens. Social media has the potential to reach groups who do not respond to more traditional methods and there is a prima facie case that such digital resources can help to accelerate co-creation, although evidence is somewhat thin (Lember et al, 2019). Countervailing factors are likely to include the digital exclusion of many people in need of public services and the failure of digital innovations to connect with their life worlds (Jarke, 2020). One of the more recent developments in thinking around the role of digital technologies in social innovation contexts is the emergence of ideas around digital social innovation (DSI; Stokes et al, 2017). Drawing on long-standing traditions of participatory design in civic tech, community informatics and digital civics, DSI has been defined as 'technology that enables greater participation in government or otherwise assists government in delivering citizens services and strengthening ties with the public' (cited in Stokes et al, 2017).

The starting point of DSI is one of foregrounding social issues as opposed to technological artifice, which a recent review (Qureshi et al, 2021) labels as a 'social first' approach where the creation of societal platforms should have primacy over commercial platforms in order to meet collaborative social aims. The second aim of DSI is to maximise the social impact of the application of technology. Key here is the notion of 'techno-ficing', meaning that the utility and affordances of the technical artifacts for the societal or community issues at hand should be geared to the social purpose and not to technological aspirations, which some in the wider community refer to as 'TechforGood' or 'DataforGood'. The final construct from the review is the role of bricolage is defined as the sustainable engagement of local assets to facilitate challenging resource scarcity and social norms to foster innovation (Qureshi et al, 2021).

Optimism regarding DSI potentially addresses the challenge for co-creation in how individual activities can move beyond the 'concreteness' and 'overspecification' tendency of technologies and technologists to enable the scalable and sustainable achievement of social aims of individuals, societies and communities by emphasising the ability to build social platforms and apply technology in its most appropriate form. However, perhaps like the life-cycle of our 'sandcastles', both social innovation and DSI require access to the beach, with lots of space, a relatively predictable tide and local readily available equipment and materials rather than the reality of construction in the middle of a busy street already full of structures and unpredictable movement.

The Co-creation of Service Innovation in Europe project and pilots

The CoSIE consortium was awarded funding from the European Commission Horizon 2020 under a call entitled 'Applied co-creation to deliver public services'. The use of digital technologies in co-creation in the public sector, in particular open data and social media, was one of the key objectives of the programme. All the editors and authors were part of the CoSIE consortium. CoSIE set out with two aims: to advance the active shaping of service priorities by end-users and their informal support networks; and to engage citizens, especially groups often called 'hard to reach', in the collaborative design of public services. This volume seeks to bring a critical edge to these expectations and their enactment, including the role of digital technologies for co-creation. Authors draw on successful and less successful practical efforts to co-opt digital technologies, meeting an urgent need to disentangle promotional hype from genuine co-creative opportunities.

One of the assumptions of the Horizon Programme call reflected in the innovative aspects explored and experimented within the CoSIE proposal and the subsequent project was the unproblematic utility of open data and social media tools as means of supporting co-creation processes with citizens and shaping the design of innovative interventions (Jamieson et al, 2019; Jalonen and Helo, 2020). A number of issues emerged around the problems of these sorts of technologies as a recipe for improving social justice for socially excluded/disadvantaged groups. The possibilities of digital resources in the forms of open data and especially social media proved more limited than originally anticipated. Evidence in specific contexts appears in the second part of this volume. The project level work explored the blending of various stakeholder engagement and interpretative methods (including Community Reporting and Living Labs) as ways of 'assemblaging' or 'bricoluering' elements together to co-create both the practices and the platform infrastructures for implementation of the pilots. Through a DSI lens we saw the majority of pilots adopting a social-first stance with some adopting techno-ficing elements and many moving to bricoleuring processes over the course of the project.

Two cross-cutting approaches were proposed by the project to support the pilots through the process of local deliberations of co-creations and to provide the basis for generating generic reflections on the co-creation for the production of project level outputs, such as the massive open online course and Roadmap. First, Living Labs (living laboratories) are environments that can support public open innovation processes. Originally developed in the 1990s for technological innovation, Living Labs have emerged in the 21st century to foster experimentation and testing of new solutions in public services (Dekker et al, 2020). CoSIE made use of visualisation and animation tools that the Living Labs team based in Newcastle, UK had developed over many years of supporting service innovation and co-creation in complex, multi-agency, cross-sector service environments. As CoSIE progressed, the Living Labs approach evolved into deployment in an online tool, CoSMoS (Jamieson et al, 2020). This digital environment fostered reflective discussions/deliberation about intentions and intervention (strategising); resources and ethics needed to support co-creation (resourcing); value and impact (evaluating); and learning based on variety of evidence sources including experiential knowledge (learning).

Community Reporting is a storytelling methodology that trains and supports citizens to use digital tools to articulate and share their own lived experience stories for research, service development and policy development. It is characterised by: scope for citizens to 'set the agenda'; creating spaces for deliberation to occur between different stakeholders; and providing tools through which effective 'institutional listening' can occur. As part of the CoSIE project, Community Reporting was applied in each of the CoSIE pilots as a tool for co-creation, supporting the innovations being made in the different public services. Community Reporting also enables stories to be mobilised for change as 'a mechanism through which public services can truly reconnect with citizens' (Trowbridge and Willoughby, 2022: 299).

At the heart of the project were the ten pilots. Each CoSIE pilot had different target groups, service needs and local settings. They worked with marginalised, sometimes stigmatised people beset by multiple disadvantages (for example, disability, residence in depleted or remote locations, low income, refugee status). Pilots took place in 'brown field' sites with many other competing or cooperating interests and initiatives. CoSIE did not presuppose a single pathway to co-creation. On the contrary, partners tested and developed diverse platforms and interventions.

The pilot partners had already clearly identified a social need and target groups before the project started. They were at different stages of readiness to act so their inception was arranged in 'waves' which commenced in sequence as follows:

- Wave A: 'Leading' pilots were the readiest to implement co-creation. Each of them had the benefit of learning from earlier co-creative actions in their respective regions or services. They commenced first, in spring 2018.
- Wave B: 'Following' pilots lacked the history of established co-creation that informed their wave A counterparts and were expected to benefit from the leading pilots' experience.
- Wave C: The final group were dubbed 'promising' pilots. Each had identified a significant need and a strong local will to co-create. Wave C pilots were intended to learn from the first two waves.

Finally, methods and tools produced from work done during waves A, B and C were applied in in a test site in the context of inner-city community gardens for citizens and other stakeholder groups in a municipality near Athens, Greece.

There were 24 partners in the CoSIE consortium. Pilots were initiated variously by municipalities, public service agencies, CSOs and companies. Evaluation was undertaken by university partners in each country. The chapters that follow this introduction are informed by evaluative research as well as Community Reporting and events and interactions occasioned by Living Labs. With hindsight, we reflected that the three 'wave' pattern set out in the original plan for the project looked overly neat to fit the complex reality of the worlds of the pilots. There was certainly evidence of mutual learning as intended. However, pilots learned and grew in many ways and the rather linear idea of a knowledge transfer model across the three waves did not capture the actual learning processes.

The CoSIE project was carried out from 2018 to 2021. The ten pilots (and one test site) are listed in Table 1.1 with their partners, and a brief indication of their target groups, overall aims and digital social innovation journey. Despite their many differences, there was a common logic across all of them in commitment to re-envisage and reposition those who are typically the targets of services (that is, have services done to them) as asset holders with legitimate knowledge that has value for shaping service innovations.

Book structure

Following this introduction the book is divided into three parts. The first part takes stock of recent developments in theory and policy. In the second part we draw on our original research to document differences and commonalties of co-creation practice across diverse services and national contexts, highlighting implementation challenges and strategies to overcome them. The final part returns to the metaphor of the 'sandcastle' with reflections on sustainability.

The first part comprises two chapters. In Chapter 2, 'Understanding co-creation: strengths and capabilities', Chris Fox sets out the principles of co-creation in conceptual terms. He presents co-creation as more a moral than a technical or administrative change to business as usual. Taking a stance grounded in lived experience of people who deliver and receive services, Fox argues that human flourishing and the 'good life' must lie at the heart of our understanding of co-creation. He sets the scene for the empirical content (the second part of the book) with a counter to criticism that co-creation (and the so-called 'co-paradigm' more generally) is a fad with little substance. The substance in social justice and legitimate knowledge of people who typically have services 'done to' them, he argues, is real and urgent.

Chapter 3, 'Co-creation as a driver of social innovation and public service reform?', by Andrea Bassi, Inga Narbutaité Aflaki, Heli Aramo-Immonen and Sue Baines, turns to the policy context. The authors draw attention to the intersection of co-creation and social innovation, and review how social innovation has become a prominent policy imperative, especially in the European Union. International evidence is considered that foregrounds co-creative aspects to social innovations. The chapter illustrates the intersection of co-creation and social innovation, using examples from the

Table 1.1: CoSIE sites, target populations and aims

Country	Pilot name and partners	Target population	Main aim	Digital social Innovation process
Italy	Reducing childhood obesity. Health Authority of Reggio Emilia; Lepida; University of Bologna	Families of children in Reggio Emilia diagnosed as overweight or obese	Make a trusted app available as a bidirectional communication channel between families and institutions	Techno-ficing with social-first elements
Sweden	Strengthening social services with co-creation dialogue. Municipality of Jönköping; Karlstad University	Residents of Jönköping with various needs using municipality Personal Assistance (PA) services	Embed co-creation in the PA service (where it lagged behind other disability services in the municipality)	Social-first with minor techno-ficing elements
UK	Personalised services for people with convictions. Interserve Ltd; Manchester Met University	Individuals serving community sentences or released from prison on license	A new more person-centred model of practice in rehabilitative processes	Initially techno-ficing transitioning to social-first during the project
Estonia	Co-designing innovative community-based services. Association of Municipalities of Võru County; Helpfic; Tallinn University	People with disabilities in a remote rural area of Eastern Estonia	Increase citizens' involvement in service design, and challenge the traditional format of social and health care services	Initially techno-ficing transitioning to social-first during the project
Hungary	Self-sustaining villages. Jasz-Nagykun-Szolnok county; University of Debrecen	Households in small, remote settlements beset by social and economic disadvantage	Enable households and communities to build upon their assets and utilise their own resources	Social-first with techno-ficing elements moving to bricoleuring processes
Spain	Empowering Valencian entrepreneurial skills. València Activa; Polytechnic University of Valencia	Citizens of Valencia who have been left behind by the world of work	Co-create a community that inspires and enables people to reduce the risk of entering into a business venture	Social-first with techno-ficing elements

(continued)

Table 1.1: CoSIE sites, target populations and aims (continued)

Country	Pilot name and partners	Target population	Main aim	Digital social Innovation process
Finland	Youth co-empowerment for health and wellbeing through social media. Association of Finnish Local and Regional Authorities; Turku University of Applied Sciences	Young people not in employment, education or training (NEET)	Find new ways to involve NEET young people to increase their participation in society and decrease exclusion	Techno-ficing with social-first elements
Poland	Neighbourhood meeting place for seniors. 'ProPo' Active Senior Foundation; University of Wroclaw	Older residents of a housing estate in the city of Wroclaw	Develop the concept of a common shared space for incubation of ideas and actions on local issues	Social-first with techno-ficing and bricoleuring elements
The Netherlands	No time to waste. Nieuwegein municipality; University of Applied Sciences Utrecht (HU)	Residents of a socially and economically deprived neighbourhood in Nieuwegein	Reinstate lost trust in the relationship between residents and municipal government	Social-first with bricoleuring elements
The Netherlands	Improving services for unemployed people. Houten municipality; HU	Refugees at a long distance from the labour market in the municipality of Houten	Work with job seekers and employers in new ways to improve the job-seeker employer match	Social-first with bricoleuring elements
Greece (test site)	Inner city community gardens. University of Penteion, Athens with the municipality of Aghios Dimitrios	Residents of a suburb with high population density and lack of green space	Access to fruit and vegetables	Social-first and techno-ficing with bricoleuring elements

CoSIE pilots that took place in Hungary, Spain and Estonia. In doing this, it highlights innovations in collaborative forms of governance, professional roles, digital technologies, and the balance of control underpinned by asset-based approaches.

The second part of the book comprises five chapters about putting co-creation into practice. Each chapter draws on original research evidence based on evaluations of one or more CoSIE pilots. Chapter 4, entitled 'Co-creating capacity? Empowerment and learning for front-line workers and organisations', is by Inga Narbutaité Aflaki and Andrea Bassi. They offer new perspectives on front-line managers and workers as potential social innovators, detailing how co-creation transforms their identities, roles and relationships. Reporting from a Swedish municipality in which the CoSIE pilot moved Personal Assistance services for people with functional and cognitive impairments towards co-creation culture, it illustrates co-creative approaches and strategies harnessed to transform disabling narratives. Emphasis is placed on the importance of change conversations and learning dialogues, where collective sense-making about change takes place, and on the role of a facilitator to lead the transformative change. Contrasts and comparisons are drawn with a different service (children's health) in another national context (Italy) to underline key learning regarding approaches and strategies that can help to empower front-line workers as change leaders in asset-based working.

In Chapter 5, 'Co-creating with marginalised young people: social media and social hackathons', Heli Aramo-Immonen and Hanna Kirjavainen focus on young people whose voices are rarely heard. This chapter reports some positive advances in innovation with digital technologies. The aim of the pilot in Finland was to find new practical ways to involve NEET (not in education, employment, or training) young people in co-creation processes to increase their participation in society and decrease exclusion. It did this in a set of short, intensive, activities called hackathons (a name derived from the IT industry), fostering interactions that co-created new, practical ideas. One idea that originated in a hackathon won a nation-wide innovation award and has been adopted and extended across the country. The Finnish pilot also had a specific objective to increase use of social media as a way to uncover unmet service needs of marginalised young people. It extended its reach with a dedicated tool that yielded valuable information about the lives of young people not accessible any other way. This pilot was able to deliver on promises of social media for co-creation when others were not.

Chapter 6, 'Digital technology, stigmatised citizens and unfulfilled promises', by Sue Baines, Jordan Harrison and Natalie Rutter, reports a CoSIE pilot situated within the criminal justice system in England. Building on an earlier proof of concept, this pilot demonstrated that tools originally developed in a social care context can be adapted for people on probation, recognising their assets as well as deficits. As one of several supplementary interventions, work commenced with high hopes on an app intended to promote greater involvement of individuals in their rehabilitation. This was not successful. Social media were entirely shunned by this pilot. A pilot working with residents of an extremely disadvantaged neighbourhood in the Netherlands similarly reported fear and loathing of social media. The chapter concludes with the reflection that digital technology, especially social media, may be unwelcome, inappropriate and even unethical in some service contexts.

Chapter 7 is 'Connecting citizens and services through the power of storytelling' by Hayley Trowbridge. This chapter explores digital storytelling – specifically the Community Reporting methodology – as a tool to connect citizens with services. It reports various ways in which Community Reporting was utilised for co-creation in the CoSIE pilots, focusing on Spain, the Netherlands and Poland. There were challenges of working with digital stories, notably digital exclusion, heavy demands on time and resistance from some powerful stakeholders. Nevertheless, these pilots demonstrate the power of Community Reporting to help develop services in a way that draws upon the existing assets of the people and communities. Recommendations are proposed for practitioners to progress the agenda of storytelling within service design.

This section concludes with Chapter 8, 'Co-governance and co-management as preliminary conditions for social justice in co-creation' by Riccardo Prandini and Giulia Ganugi. Taking a social justice perspective, this chapter proposes a framework for observing which actors are included (or not), and ways they can participate in decision-making. The framework is applied to explore the formation of the stakeholders' community of the pilot in Reggio, Italy. Led by a public health body, the pilot included an exceptionally large and diverse group of internal and external stakeholders but fell short of full participation and empowerment for the most marginalised. This points to a need to develop more 'constitutional imagination'.

The final part of the book (Chapters 9, 10, 11 and 12) looks outwards from individual pilots to develop the theme of navigating towards innovative and more just services across Europe. The authors examine various reusable resources for enhancing and building co-creation to move beyond the tendency for increasingly unsustainable sandcastle building, and seek to cultivate parallel infrastructural approaches which allow us to continue to experiment but also to put that in the context of mutual stakeholder co-creation and learning. We will also explore this in the context of making investments which persist beyond the current political and policy cycle.

In Chapter 9, 'Evaluation and the evidence base for co-creation', Chris Fox, Andrea Bassi and Sue Baines reflect on diverse views of what counts as good information and reliable evidence within the CoSIE project and the wider co-creation field. They consider challenges of building an evidence base for co-creation, recognising that linear, cause–effect relationships between co-creation and outcomes can be elusive given the interconnectedness and complexity of services. They go on to propose a new strategy for evaluation of co-creative interventions in future using relatively recent 'small n' methodologies and designs for impact evaluation.

Chapter 10 is 'Living Labs for innovating relationships: the CoSMoS tool', by David Jamieson, Mike Martin, Rob Wilson, Florian Sipos, Judit Csoba and Alex Sakellariou. The CoSIE project applied Living Labs to support pilots with meeting their goals of service innovation and co-creation through the innovation of relationships. The web-based CoSMoS tool was designed with and for the CoSIE pilots so that stakeholders can be engaged interactively or offline, individually or within a workshop environment. During and after facilitated workshops, pilot team members and stakeholders populated CoSMoS with evidence using input questions and prompts. The chapter shows how the tool was applied in Hungary and Greece. It concludes with reflection on how it served to scaffold reflections and learning on the wide range of social, ethical, moral, organisational and technical challenges of co-creation across different service environments.

Chapter 11 is 'Moving towards relational services: the role of digital service environments and platforms?' by Mike Martin, Rob Wilson and David Jamieson. There is widespread recognition that information and communications systems that support service innovation and delivery should be joined up. Yet it has become clear that 'integrationist' approaches have failed because they are unable to cope with dynamic complexity. Drawing on the applied learning from the CoSIE project, this chapter sets out a third, architectural approach to the creation, operation and governance of collaborative sociotechnical information infrastructures and platforms for service innovation. This 'relational' approach supports mixed economies of provision in which public, private and third sector agencies coordinate to meet multiple and evolving objectives and interests in the delivery of services for people and communities.

In Chapter 12, 'Conclusions: Moving beyond building sandcastles ... long-term sociotechnical infrastructure for social justice', the editors, led by Rob Wilson, summarise the book's central premise. They consider what the future holds for the challenges of co-creation in social service innovation and asset-based working, and what is required to take the approaches described to the next level. This provides a foundation for understanding, analysing, designing, and accounting for services and the environment or ecology they operate in. The chapter explores the paradox of 'concrete elasticity'. This apparent oxymoron denotes 'concrete-ness' in policy and programme planning, delivery and design against the 'elasticity' required for an authentic, sustainable co-creation where real lives and complex public service systems intersect. A new service model is presented that combines context-specific structures with reusable infrastructures able to support and sustain successive initiatives.

References

Baines, S., Bassi, A., Csoba, J. and Sipos, F. (eds) (2019) *Implementing Innovative Social Investment: Strategic Lessons from Europe*, Bristol: Policy Press.

BEPA (2010) *Empowering People, Driving Change: Social Innovation in the European Union*, Luxembourg: Publications Office of the European Union.

Bonvin, J.-M. and Laruffa, F. (2018) 'Human beings as receivers, doers and judges: the anthropological foundations of sustainable public action in the capability approach', *Community, Work and Family*, 21(5): 502–518.

Boyle, D. and Harris, M. (2009) *The Challenge of Co-Production: How Equal Partnerships between Professionals and the Public are Crucial to Improving Public Services*, London: NEF.

Bevir, M., Needham, C. and Waring, J. (2019) 'Inside co-production: ruling, resistance, and practice', *Social Policy and Administration*, 53(2): 197–202.

Brandsen, T. and Honingh, M. (2018) 'Definitions of co-production and co-creation', in Brandsen, T., Steen, T. and Verschuere, B. (eds) *Co-Production and Co-Creation: Definitions and Theoretical Perspectives*, New York: Routledge, pp 9–17.

Brandsen, T., Evers, A., Cattacin, S. and Zimmer, A. (2016) 'Social innovation: a sympathetic and critical interpretation', in Brandsen, T., Cattacin, S., Evers, A. and Zimmer, A. (eds) *Social Innovations in the Urban Context*, Cham: Springer International, pp 3–20.

Brandsen, T., Steen, T. and Verschuere, B. (2018) 'Co-creation and co-production in public services: urgent issues in practice and research', in Brandsen, T., Steen, T. and Verschuere, B. (eds) *Co-Production and Co-Creation: Definitions and Theoretical Perspectives*, New York: Routledge, pp 3–8.

Cantillon, B. and Van Lancker, W. (2013) 'Three shortcomings of the social investment perspective', *Social Policy and Society*, 12(4): 553–564.

Cottam, H. (2018) *Radical Help: How We Can Remake the Relationships between Us and Revolutionise the Welfare State*, London: Hachette UK.

Dekker, R., Franco Contreras, J. and Meijer, A. (2020) 'The living lab as a methodology for public administration research: a systematic literature review of its applications in the social sciences', *International Journal of Public Administration*, 43(4): 1207–1217.

Dudau, A., Glennon, R. and Verschuere, B. (2019) 'Following the yellow brick road? (Dis)enchantment with co-design, co-production and value co-creation in public services', *Public Management Review*, 21(11): 1577–1594.

Esping-Andersen, G., Gallie, D., Hemerijck, A. and Myles, J. (eds) (2002) *Why We Need a New Welfare State*, Oxford: Oxford University Press.

Evers, A. and Brandsen, T. (2016) 'Social innovations as messages: democratic experimentation in local welfare systems', in Brandsen, T., Cattacin, S., Evers, A. and Zimmer, A. (eds) *Social Innovations in the Urban Context*, Cham: Springer International, pp 161–180.

Fox, A. (2018) *A New Health and Care System: Escaping the Invisible Asylum*, Bristol: Policy Press.

Fox, C., Baines, S., Wilson, R., Martin, M., Jalonen, H., Aflaki, I., Prandini, R., Bassi, A. and Ganugi, G. (2021) *A New Agenda for Co-Creating Public Services*, Turku University of Applied Sciences, http://julkaisut.turkuamk.fi/isbn9789522167842.pdf

Grimm, R., Fox, C., Baines, S. and Albertson, K. (2013) 'Social innovation, an answer to contemporary societal challenges? Locating the concept in theory and practice', *Innovation: The European Journal of Social Science Research*, 26(4): 436–455.

Hemerijck, A. (2013) *Changing Welfare States*, Oxford: Oxford University Press.

Hemerijck, A. (2015) 'The quiet paradigm revolution of social investment', *Social Politics*, 22(2): 242–256.

Hemerijck, A. (2017) 'Social investment and its critics', in Hemerijck, A. (ed) *The Uses of Social Investment*, Oxford: Oxford University Press, pp 3–40.

Jalonen, H. and Helo, T. (2020) 'Co-creation of public service innovation using open data and social media: rhetoric, reality, or something in between?', *International Journal of Innovation in the Digital Economy*, 11(3): 64–77.

Jamieson, D., Wilson, R. and Martin, M. (2019) 'The (im)possibilities of open data?', *Public Money and Management*, 39(5): 364–368, https://doi.org/10.1080/09540962.2019.1611240

Jamieson, D., Martin, M. and Wilson, R. (2020) *COSMOS – The Co-creation Service Modelling System* [Software], https://doi.org/10.5281/zenodo.4058570

Jarke, J. (2020) *Co-Creating Digital Public Services for an Ageing Society: Evidence for User-Centric Design*, Cham: Springer International.

Lember, V., Brandsen, T. and Tõnurist, P. (2019) 'The potential impacts of digital technologies on co-production and co-creation', *Public Management Review*, 21(11): 1665–1686. DOI: 10.1080/14719037.2019.1619807

Marques, P., Morgan, K. and Richardson, R. (2017) 'Social innovation in question: the theoretical and practical implications of a contested concept', *Environment and Planning C*, 36(3): 496–512.

Meijer, A. and Thaens, M. (2020) 'The dark side of public innovation', *Public Performance & Management Review*, 44(1): 136–154.

Morel, N. and Palme, J. (2017) *The Capabilities Approach: A Normative Foundation for Social Investment?* Oxford: Oxford University Press.

Moulaert, F. and MacCallum, D. (2019) *Advanced Introduction to Social Innovation*, Cheltenham: Edward Elgar.

Moulaert, F., MacCallum, D., Mehmood, A. and Hamdouch, A. (eds) (2013) *The International Handbook on Social Innovation: Collective Action, Social Learning and Transdisciplinary Research*, Cheltenham: Edward Elgar.

Mumford, M.D. (2002) 'Social innovation: ten cases from Benjamin Franklin', *Creativity Research Journal*, 14(2): 253–266.

Murray, R., Caulier-Grice, J. and Mulgan, G. (2010) *The Open Book of Social Innovation*, London: NESTA.

Nicholls, A., Simon, J. and Gabriel, M. (2015) 'Introduction: dimensions of social innovation', in Nicholls, A., Simon, J. and Gabriel, M. (eds) *New Frontiers in Social Innovation Research*, Houndmills: Palgrave Macmillan, pp 1–28.

Oosterlynck, S., Novy, A. and Kazepov, Y. (eds) (2019) *Local Social Innovation to Combat Poverty and Exclusion*, Bristol: Policy Press.

Osborne, S.P. (2018) 'From public service-dominant logic to public service logic: are public service organizations capable of co-production and value co-creation?', *Public Management Review*, 20(2): 225–231. DOI: 10.1080/14719037.2017.1350461

Osborne, S.P., Radnor, Z. and Strokosch, K. (2016) 'Co-production and the co-creation of value in public services: a suitable case for treatment?', *Public Management Review*, 18(5): 639–653.

Peng, Y., Wu, T., Chen, Z. and Deng, Z. (2022) 'Value cocreation in health care: systematic review', *Journal of Medical Internet Research*, 24(3): e33061.

Pestoff, V. and Hulgård, L. (2016) 'Participatory governance in social enterprise', *International Journal of Voluntary and Non-profit Organizations*, 27(4): 1742–1759.

Phills, J.A., Deiglmeier, K. and Miller, D.T. (2008) 'Rediscovering social innovation', *Stanford Social Innovation Review*, 6(4): 34–43.

Qureshi, I., Pan, S.L. and Zheng, Y. (2021) 'Digital social innovation: an overview and research framework', *Information Systems Journal*, 31(5): 647–671.

Sen, A. (1985) 'Well-being, agency, and freedom', *The Journal of Philosophy*, 82(4): 169–221.

Sen, A. (2001) *Development as Freedom*, Oxford: Oxford Paperbacks.

Stokes, M., Baeck, P. and Baker, T. (2017) *What Next for Digital Social Innovation*, DSI4Europe report. Technical report DSI4EU Project, EU Commission.

Torfing, J., Sørensen, E. and Røiseland, A. (2019) 'Transforming the public sector into an arena for co-creation: barriers, drivers, benefits, and ways forward', *Administration & Society*, 51(5): 795–825.

Trowbridge, H. and Willoughby, M. (2022) 'Debate: re-humanising the system or: how storytelling can be used to bridge the divide between services and citizens', *Public Money & Management*, 42(5): 298–299. https://doi.org/10.1080/09540962.2021.1981014

Voorberg, W.H., Bekkers, V. and Tummers, L.G. (2015) 'A systematic review of co-creation and co-production: embarking on the social innovation journey', *Public Management Review*, 17(9): 1333–1357.

Wilson, R., Cornwell, C., Flanagan, E., Nielsen, N. and Khan, H. (2018) *Good and Bad Help: How Purpose and Confidence Transform Lives*, London: NESTA.

2

Understanding co-creation: strengths and capabilities

Chris Fox

Introduction

The main focus of this chapter is to present a theory of co-creation that has practical applications for those designing, managing and delivering public services. It argues that co-creation in public services is inextricably linked to building people's capabilities and agency so that they can flourish and lead a good life. Thus, co-creation is essentially a social practice that aims to create social value and therefore a theory of co-creation must address normative and ethical issues.

The chapter starts by exploring the concept of co-creation, recognising the different ways in which it is understood and distinguishing it from closely related concepts such as co-participation, personalisation and co-production. Co-creation emerges as far more than just a form of practice to be adopted in the delivery of public services. As such it merits a clear theoretical foundation that can be used to guide policy making and practice. The chapter then moves on to consider how co-creation has been theorised from a public administration perspective, recognising that this is a useful starting point for theory building, but also identifying some limitations and gaps that need to be addressed. In response to these limitations a more holistic, normative theory of co-creation is developed. This starts with the proposition that co-production and co-creation in public services necessitate strengths-based practice to help people exercise agency and build their capabilities in order to live a good life. This raises questions about how individuals can exercise agency and pursue their own goals in life while also co-producing and co-creating public services, and what organisational and system-level conditions are required to promote co-created, strengths-based services that promote human flourishing. The remainder of the chapter addresses these questions.

Co-creation and co-production defined

As Bovaird (2007) notes, by the 1980s, the limitations of traditional public service delivery models had become obvious. One response was to increase people's participation in services with many initiatives designed to give people a larger role as 'customers', give people choice or engage them in various forms of consultation and user research. However, such moves, while potentially increasing people's participation, left managers and professionals to decide on the role given to people who used services (Bovaird, 2007). Co-creation, and the related concept of co-production, promises a more radical split with previous practice. It can be distinguished from classical citizen participation in policy making because it is a more intensive form of citizen engagement where the focus is on joint action (Loeffler and Bovaird, 2016), and because of its focus on 'the output-side of the policy cycle: the provision of public services' (Brandsen et al, 2018: 4).

Co-creation perhaps has more in common with the 'personalisation' of public services. Personalisation can mean many things (Needham, 2011), most simply, that public services respond to the needs of clients, rather than offering a standardised service. This was argued as responding to the end of the age of deference, increasing customisation available in consumer goods and the idea that by designing services for the average, they end up fitting no one (Rose, 2016). Personalisation encompasses a range of new ways of designing services, which can provide both what Leadbeater (2004) describes as 'shallow' and 'deep' approaches. Personalisation can include 'providing people with a more customer-friendly interface', 'giving users more say in navigating their way through services', 'giving users more direct say over how money is spent' and users being 'co-producers of a service' (Leadbeater, 2004: 21–24). In Leadbetter's conceptualisation, deep personalisation 'would give users a far greater role – and also greater responsibility – for designing solutions from the ground up' (2004: 19). This seems to concur with Hampson et al (2013), who argue that co-delivery and co-design go beyond person-centred practice, suggesting that co-creation might be understood as a more radical version of personalisation.

This brings us to the distinction between co-production and co-creation. The terms are often used synonymously (Voorberg et al, 2015; Torfing et al, 2019) but Torfing et al (2019) and Osborne (2018) argue for a distinction to avoid concept stretching. Following work by Alford (2015), Osborne et al (2016) conceptualise four processes of co-production, summarised in Flemig and Osborne (2019) as:

1. 'pure' co-production of the individual service and its outcomes which are intrinsic to any service relationship;
2. the co-construction of the 'lived experience' of service users, their families and communities, as a result of using a public service;
3. the co-design and management of individual service packages; and
4. the co-innovation of new forms of service delivery.

Osborne et al note that while pure co-production (1) and co-construction (2) are often unconscious and involuntary, co-design and co-innovation are conscious and voluntary actions that strive for equal partnership between the service provider and service user. These latter two processes are qualitatively different to the first two and can usefully be thought of as 'co-creation'. Thus, in co-production people who use services take over some of the work done by practitioners but are not necessarily required to be involved in service design (Osborne and Strokosch, 2013), but where this occurs it is often termed 'co-creation'. In co-creation, people who use services, their families and their communities, work with people who manage and deliver services to design, create, steer and deliver services (SCIE, 2015).

What is clear from the discussion so far is that co-creation is far more than *just* a form of public service practice that can be adopted or discarded in response to short-term priorities or for superficial reasons. Co-creation requires those involved in designing and delivering public services to reimagine those services and rethink the relationship between services and citizens. This in turn raises important questions about the role of the state in delivering public services. As Bovaird (2007) puts it in a discussion of a broad concept of co-production that incorporates co-creation:

> This is a revolutionary concept in public service. It has major implications for democratic practices beyond representative government because it locates users and communities more centrally in the decision-making process. Moreover, it sheds light on the way emergent strategies are developed at the front line in public services. Finally, it demands that politicians and professionals find new ways to interface with service users and their communities. (Bovaird, 2007: 846)

All of this illustrates the importance of developing strong theoretical underpinnings for co-creation in public services.

Developing a distinctive theory of co-creation in public services: public service logic and value co-creation

Thinking on co-creation often draws on models developed in the private sector (Brandsen and Honingh, 2018). But our understanding of co-creation in public services cannot simply replicate thinking from the private sector. Osborne and colleagues emphasise the distinctive context and nature of public (compared to private) services and the implications of this distinction for co-creation. Osborne et al (2016) and Osborne (2018) describe the service-dominant, as opposed to product-dominant, nature of public services and their delivery, making an explicit link to concept of service-dominant logic developed by Lusch and Vargo (Osborne, 2006). Osborne gives various examples of this distinctiveness. For private sector service firms, the retention of customers and their repeat business is often key to profitability but for public services 'repeat business' may be a sign of service failure rather than success. Also, the reality of unwilling or coerced customers is often unfamiliar to the for-profit sector, but is common in public services. For-profit firms often have a well-defined customer where public services often have multiple end-users and stakeholders, some or all of whom may have different and often conflicting definitions of a successful outcome of a service.

In a series of papers Osborne and colleagues (Osborne, 2010; 2018; Osborne and Strokosch, 2013; Osborne et al, 2016) draw on public management and service management theory to present a conceptualisation of co-creation and its relationship with co-production which centres on the idea of the 'co-creation of value through public service delivery' (Osborne et al, 2016: 640). The starting point for this conceptualisation is a service-dominant perspective (Lusch and Vargo, 2006), which describes the process through which value is added to any service or product: value is co-created through the transformation of service components at the point of co-production (Osborne et al, 2016). Thus, 'a service does not have any intrinsic value to its users. This value is co-created through co-production' (Osborne et al, 2016: 642).

More recently Osborne (2018) has described public service logic, which draws on an alternative body of work on value co-creation (Grönroos, 1982; 1984). This model has important implications for co-creation in public service organisations. First, it shifts the focus away from the performance as the key metric of successful public services to 'value' being the key metric. Second, it makes it clear that value can only ever be created by the service user with the service delivery organisation in a supporting role. Co-creation is thus 'an interactive and dynamic relationship where value is created at the nexus of interaction' (Osborne, 2018: 225). This is an idea that suggests a fundamental shift of power within public service organisations and a different model of public sector governance (Osborne, 2018). It entails a radical 'democratisation' of public services and a clean break with New Public Management (Brandsen and Honingh, 2018; Osborne, 2018; Torfing et al, 2019). Trust, relational capital and relational contracts act as the core governance mechanisms (Osborne, 2006).

This body of work is helpful in putting co-creation on a theoretical footing, distinguishing public service practice from that in the private sector and explaining how public services create value through co-creation. Importantly, it explains how co-creation is central to public sector governance. This provides a useful counter to some critics who are concerned about idealised narratives of collaboration and empowerment that may not be borne out in the experience of less powerful stakeholders (Crompton, 2018) or who warn of tokenism and failure to fully recognise imbalances of status and power (Bevir et al, 2019).

But the model of co-creation outlined by Osborne and colleagues leaves several dimensions of public service co-creation that need further explication. First, there is the issue of agency in service users. Osborne and colleagues recognise that the reality of unwilling or coerced customers is often unfamiliar to the for-profit sector, but is common in public services. For Osborne (2018) these considerations imply both a need to reconsider the issue of the role of voluntary agency in value creation and to recognise that value creation often has to be negotiated between stakeholders. However, more fundamentally than this, in the for-profit sector it is generally assumed that service users have agency and capabilities that are sufficient for them to engage in the co-creation of services. But this is very often not the case in the public sector and a crucial task for many public services is supporting people to build agency by helping them to build their capabilities.

Second, and relatedly, Osborne and colleagues have relatively little to say about the kinds of practices that can help people build their agency and engage in co-production and co-creation. Voorberg et al (2015) in their widely cited review identify eight factors which affect whether the objectives of co-creation and co-production between public organisations and citizens (or their representatives) are achieved and they separate these according to whether they operate on the organisational or citizen side of co-creation. However, on the organisational side these are fairly abstract characteristics, such as an open attitude towards citizen participation or a risk-averse administrative culture. They do not pinpoint specific practices that support effective co-creation.

Third, and again relatedly, the framework that Osborne and colleagues have developed focuses primarily upon the role of the service user. As they recognise, to date, insufficient attention has been given to the role of the service professional. This is problematic because 'the role of the service professional is equally important – coproduction describes the interactions of both service users and service professionals' (Osborne et al, 2016: 649). More relational ways of working are implied, but what is the motivation for citizens and professionals who engage in co-creation? Both professionals and citizens will have to learn new skills with implications for public bodies that embrace co-creation. More attention needs to be given to the role of learning in co-production, specifically 'how service users and professionals learn to co-produce together effectively and how the lessons of co-production are captured at a service level' (Osborne et al, 2016: 649).

In part the limitations in the theory developed by Osborne and colleagues lie in the fact that it is not a normative argument (Osborne, 2021; Osborne et al, 2021). Drawing on Engen et al (2021), Osborne et al (2021) note 'there is no guarantee that user interaction with public services will always create value for them. Poorly designed or delivered public services may actually have a deleterious impact on service users and detract from their lives (value destruction)' (Osborne et al, 2021: 645). In the remainder of this chapter these limitations are addressed by developing a normative theory of co-creation that starts with the proposition that co-production and co-creation in public services necessitate strengths-based practice to help people exercise agency and build their capabilities in order to live a good life.

Co-creation and strengths-based working

The welfare state was created in the mid-20th century to address a set of issues that were most pressing at that time in a society that looked very different to our own, where mass unemployment was a recurring issue, where life expectancy was lower, years in retirement were fewer, families were more uniform and more patriarchal and public service professionals were more revered. Today's social and economic challenges such as long-term health conditions in ageing populations, social isolation, unaffordable housing or in-work poverty are increasingly complex. But, many public services are still designed in such a way as to fix things for people in the short term or encourage them to take action that fits the service's priorities, not their own (Fox, 2018; Wilson et al, 2018). This is a deficit-based approach that 'leaves people without clarity about the changes they want to make or the knowledge, confidence or support to get there. It often only addresses a single (and often most visible) aspect of people's lives, without taking account of what else is going on' (Wilson et al, 2018: 5).

Co-creation and the related concept of co-production implies that people who are usually the targets of services (that is, have services done to them) have legitimate knowledge that has value for shaping service innovations and resources or strengths that can contribute to service delivery (Fox et al, 2021). For example, Loeffler and Bovaird (2016: 1006) define co-production as 'public services, service users and communities making better use of each other's assets and resources to achieve better outcomes or improved efficiency'. The practice of co-creating public services therefore seems to be tied inextricably to strengths-based practice in the delivery of public services.

Strengths-based practice takes different forms, sometimes drawing on appreciative enquiry or motivational interviewing with people who use services, reflective practice on the part of front-line staff, and approaches such as Local Area Coordination and Asset-Based Community Development in the communities that people live in, all of which are designed to help people take action (Mathie and Cunningham, 2003; Rippon and Hopkins, 2015; Wilson et al, 2018).

Strengths-based approaches (sometimes used interchangeably in the literature with the term 'asset-based' approaches) start from the position that people have assets or 'strengths' and focus on people's goals and resources rather than their problems (Price et al, 2020). They therefore draw together concepts of participation and citizenship with social capital (Mathie and Cunningham, 2003). Thus, Baron et al (2019) note that strengths-based approaches explore, in a collaborative way, the entire individual's abilities and their circumstances rather than making the deficit that brought them to the service the focus of the intervention. Strengths-based approaches do not impose a single, uniform structure on diverse communities. Instead, they support citizens' development of their capacity and their opportunities to exercise agency in undertaking small acts that build meaningful relations.

This raises the question of how individuals can exercise agency and pursue their own goals in life while also co-producing and co-creating public services. To put it another way, what is the balance between individual and social or public value in public services delivery (Osborne, 2018)? This is a question that Osborne acknowledges is not fully answered by the theory of co-creation that he has developed (Osborne et al, 2016; Osborne, 2018).

What is the balance between individual and social value in co-creation?

Osborne et al suggest that public service organisations develop resources to offer to citizens, in the form of public services, and value is the product of co-creation, but 'it is how citizens integrate these resources with their own needs, experiences and expectations that will create value in their lives' (Osborne et al, 2021: 668). Such value includes public service outcomes, but also integrates other elements of value for citizens and society that include satisfaction and wellbeing, whole life experience, capacity for change and societal value (Osborne et al, 2021).

The first question this raises is why citizens are motivated to engage in co-creation and co-production? Some forms of co-production will see individuals receiving private value from the service they receive, and whether acting individually or collectively co-production will be primarily of benefit to themselves (Loeffler and Bovaird, 2016, drawing on Alford, 2002; 2009). But some forms of individual and collective co-production and co-creation will generate collective benefits, sometimes in addition to, or sometimes instead of, individual benefit. This suggests that while some co-creation and co-production might be motivated by extrinsic rewards including sanctions, material benefit and raising esteem, intrinsic motivations that speak more to people's ethics and social values will also be important (Loeffler and Bovaird, 2016, drawing on Alford, 2009).

Co-creation is inextricably linked to strengths-based approaches to service delivery. Strengths-based practice focuses on helping people to achieve their goals and live a good life. Does this imply that value is a subjective, individual judgement? If so, how can we reconcile this with the collaborative and social dimensions of co-creation? To put it another way, what is the balance between individual and social value in co-created public service delivery (Osborne, 2018)? These are not just interesting philosophical questions. The evidence base for co-creation has many examples of co-creation being subverted by particular interests or producing outcomes that are harmful rather than beneficial: the so-called 'dark side' of co-creation (Steen et al, 2018). The strengths-based approach has been criticised for being overly individualistic. Some commentators have questioned whether a focus on individuals comes at the expense of addressing structural causes of the issues that people face and as such strengths-based approaches could be seen as an extension of neoliberal thinking in public service reform (Gray, 2011; Friedli, 2013; MacLeod and Emejulu, 2014; Roy, 2017). Can we therefore develop a normative theory of value that can help us to describe co-creation in public services in a way that explains citizen's motivations to co-create and the balance between individual and social value in co-creation?

Capabilities

The capabilities approach is a normative evaluative framework in which the concept of agency is central. It is referenced in the literature on strengths-based approaches. For example, discussion of capabilities and explicitly the capability approach (Nussbaum, 1988; Sen, 1990) have featured in the approach to strengths-based working or 'radical help' advocated by (Cottam, 2018), who argues that: 'The current welfare state has become an elaborate attempt to manage our needs. In contrast, twenty-first-century forms of help will support us to grow our *capabilities*' (Cottam, 2018: 199; emphasis added). Capabilities thinking also underpins the concept of 'good help' promoted by the National Endowment for Science, Technology and the Arts (NESTA) (Wilson et al, 2018). It is also referenced as an element of value co-creation (Osborne, 2021).

The basic insight behind such a capabilities approach is that acquiring economic resources (for example, wealth) is not in and of itself a legitimate human end (Sen, 1990; 2009). Such resources, commodities, are rather tools with which to achieve wellbeing, or 'flourishing living' (Nussbaum, 1988). Discussing how a capabilities approach takes account of the connections between the internal and the external structural realities of our lives and helps us to address both. Cottam argues that:

> What we can be or do depends on our inner worlds, our beliefs, our self-confidence, our skills and our concrete external realities: where we live, whether we have money, and how we are connected. These internal factors and the wider webs and structures we are part of determine what real possibilities we have in our lives. (Cottam, 2018: 200)

The capabilities approach assumes that each citizen is entitled to a set of basic capabilities, but the question is then, what are these capabilities (Claassen, 2016)? Nussbaum provides a substantive list of ten capabilities based on the notion of a dignified human life (Classen and Düwell, 2013), whereas Sen adopts a procedural approach and argues that capabilities should be selected in a process of public reasoning (Claassen, 2016). But as Claassen (2016) describes, both the substantive objectivist list theory of wellbeing (the Nussbaum approach) and proceduralist reliance on democratic reasoning (the Sen approach) have been criticised and it is not clear what the basic capabilities are that we are all entitled to.

Human needs and the good life

Strengths-based approaches encourage people to exercise agency to define their own goals in order to meet needs that they define as important. But this is not simply about giving people choice. As Fox argues: 'Choice cannot be the organising principle of life. Human beings want and need to organise themselves around the hopes, interests and ambitions for themselves, their family and their community. If they had the choice, people would choose the "good life" above all other things' (Fox, 2013: 2).

Alongside choice, people need a guiding vision of a good life, well lived (Cottam, 2018). If the capabilities approach has its limitations, perhaps this is a promising line of argument for providing a theoretical basis for strengths-based approaches? It aligns with arguments for human rights that draw on concepts of agency and purpose, therefore implying that asset-based approaches and co-creation in public services are not simply desirable, but morally necessary. For example, the neo-Kantian philosopher Gewirth (1978; 1996) shows how the rational individual must invest in society and in social solutions to satisfy their basic needs.

The starting point of his argument is that human action has two interrelated, generic features: *voluntariness* and *purposiveness*. Gewirth goes on to show that the two basic human needs or goals which are required to allow the individual to act are freedom and wellbeing. This is a normative or moral argument. Gewirth shows that, if the individual claims that they have a right to freedom and wellbeing, they must also recognise that all prospective, purposive agents have the same rights, an idea he captures in something akin to a 'golden rule' that he calls the Principle of Generic Consistency. To put it another way, once it is accepted that freedom and wellbeing are basic human needs in the sense that they are preconditions for human action and interaction (Doyal and Gough, 1991), then a moral argument can start to develop which says that freedom and wellbeing ought to be recognised as universal rights and that a failure for other people and wider society to do so is logically inconsistent.

Navigational agency

Recently, these two strands of thinking – the capabilities approach and Gewirth's normative, or moral, theory – have been drawn together. Claassen (2016) recognises the criticisms that have been made of capabilities theory, particularly the challenge of describing what the basic capabilities are that we are all entitled to. Arguing that Nussbaum's substantive list is 'perfectionist' but that Sen's procedural approach to defining capabilities is 'empty' he develops a capability theory of justice which aspires to be substantive but not perfectionist. He does this by following the approach adopted by Gewirth (Claassen and Düwell, 2013) and using a conception of *individual agency* (instead of wellbeing or human flourishing) as the underlying normative ideal to select basic capabilities (Claassen, 2016). Using this approach, basic capabilities are those capabilities people need to exercise individual agency. A particular conception of individual agency is implied, one in which individual agency is necessarily connected to social practices and where basic capabilities are those necessary for individuals to navigate freely and autonomously between different social practices (Claassen, 2016).

Claassen (2018) refers to this as 'navigational agency', whereby people can navigate freely between social practices, at the same time exercising agency and pursuing their own goals in life while also contributing to social practices. For navigational agency people need three sets of core capabilities: empowerment to participate in civil society; a decent level of socioeconomic subsistence; and political participation in democratic decision-making procedures. This is an agency-based capability theory that incorporates a 'dual-level theory of agency, where a person's agency is immersed in their social practices on one level, but is able to transcend these practices on a higher level' (Claassen, 2018: 48).

Navigational agency helps us to explain how and why people engage in co-creation and strengths-based work. It also sheds further light on the practice of co-creation and the organisational and system-level conditions that are required to develop and sustain co-creation. These are discussed in the next section.

What individual, organisational and system-level conditions are required to support co-created, strengths-based services?

At this point we can now start to describe a model of co-creation that starts with interactions between individual citizens as social navigators, considers the role of professionals delivering services and extends to public service organisations and the wider public service ecosystem.

One-to-one work

At the heart of co-creation is the concept of individuals exercising agency and 'agency becomes the normative criterion for the selection of basic capabilities required for social justice' (Claassen, 2018: 1). Individuals co-create with public services to grow their capabilities and create social justice. From a practice perspective the emphasis will generally be on 'pure' co-production of the individual service and its outcomes for the individual. This will include *co-construction* of the 'lived experience' of people who use services, along with their families and communities (Flemig and Osborne, 2019). They will often be unconscious and involuntary ways of working (Flemig and Osborne, 2019) in the sense that they are intrinsic to the exercise of agency by people who use services and occur when the values and practice of co-creation are aligned. Another way to think about this alignment is that the distinction between 'doing' co-creation and 'being' co-creative[1] ceases to be meaningful and the work of co-creation becomes fully relational (Osborne, 2006; 2021) and strengths-based.

The move from 'doing co-creation' to 'being co-creative' implies a particular mindset for staff who deliver services and managers and organisational leaders who support them. Work will be strongly relational. Key markers of relational work are skills and values such as empathy, listening skills and good communication. Less emphasis will be placed on activity and more reflection and reflective practice will be of great importance (Needham and Mangan, 2016). This will have implications for how the performance of staff co-creating services is understood and measured.

Relational work that is strengths-based and draws on the resources of people who access services will also require front-line staff to also be effective social navigators (Claassen, 2018).

They will be more outward looking, working across organisational boundaries. Professional co-creators and co-producers must, themselves, be effective social navigators able to work with service users and professionals from other organisations (Mortensen et al, 2020). However, this can be challenging, particularly for professions that exhibit a high level of technical and procedural knowledge, for example, surgeons, nurses, teachers and probation officers who are all depositaries of a set of standardised knowledge that they apply to each individual case. They operate following what has been defined as 'inward look' (Boyle and Harris, 2009) and they sometimes have difficulties in adopting an 'outward look', where they recognise and value lay knowledge and the resources of the people they work with. This is a problem for organisations that want to move towards strengths-based and co-created ways of working where staff will need to operate an 'outward look' to deliver complex interventions that are social and not technical (Mortensen et al, 2020).

Organisational context

The literature on co-creation/co-production is usually oriented to the role of users/clients in the process of service design. There is a systematic underestimation of the role, tasks and responsibilities of professionals in the co-creation and co-production processes (Osborne and Strokosch, 2013; Hannan, 2019; Mortensen et al, 2020). Osborne and Strokosch (2013) describe this as one of the main weaknesses of scientific studies on the topic. Mortensen et al (2020) consider the challenges facing front-line staff. They argue that co-production creates a break with the former roles of front-line staff as either the providers of services to passive clients or customers, instead giving them the role of the 'professional co-producer' expected to motivate and mobilise service users' capacities and resources. Mortensen et al argue that these 'professional co-producers' are often subject to multiple pressures as they handle top-down and bottom-up expectations simultaneously as well as potential horizontal pressures stemming from the expectations of staff from other organisations.

New approaches to recruitment, training and personal development will be needed: creating the new 'professional co-producers' will be challenging. It may well start with value-based recruitment practices, but also implies new approaches to staff training, different ways of assessing workers' development needs and different understandings of how 'cases' are managed with new connections and divisions of labour. Reflective practice is likely to be central to the new, relational way of working. As part of the process of reflective practice, professional co-producers will have to 'unlearn' previous practice and make a conscious break with previous value systems that shaped their prior professional training and practice (Mortensen et al, 2020). Either intentionally or unintentionally, this can sometimes take the form of 'trained incapacity'. This will require considerable organisational support involving rethinking organisational processes and structures. For example, training and development might rely more on coaching and mentoring and less on formal training sessions (Needham and Mangan, 2016). Innovation in front-line services and the flexibility to respond to people's changing needs will require a learning organisation where there is a strong learning culture, a commitment to experimentation and monitoring data is used for reflection rather than target-based performance management (Lowe et al, 2021).

Developing and embedding these practices will require the reconfiguration of organisational structures, processes and values. A model that can address some of the challenges associated with the move to strengths-based working is to move towards self-managing teams (Laloux, 2014), defined by Vregelaar (2017: 4) as 'groups of interdependent individuals that can self-regulate their behaviour on relatively whole tasks'. Vregelaar (2017) identifies the advantages of self-managing teams as: bringing more flexibility; increasing quality of work life; reducing absenteeism and employee turnover; increasing job satisfaction; and organisational commitment. There are clear overlaps between the concept of more autonomous professionals working as part of a self-managing team and strengths-based, co-created work with service users.

While one-to-one work will often have characteristics of co-production as much as co-creation, public bodies will also invest in the *co-design* and management of individual service packages and the *co-innovation* of new forms of service delivery (Osborne et al, 2016; 2021; Flemig and Osborne, 2019; Osborne, 2021). This implies that people with lived experience will be involved in service design whether in one-off exercises, or as part of the governance arrangements for public bodies.

Public service ecosystem context

The social challenges that investment in co-creation often addresses are increasingly complex and traditional public services often look ill-suited to address them. The most common response to these challenges has been New Public Management (Hood, 1991). Customers and consumers of public services, guided by their self-interest, tend to be passive with only a limited role in shaping public services. They might sometimes take on the role of co-producers, empowered by market mechanisms to substitute for market failures (Strokosch and Osborne, 2018), but in this scenario co-production is primarily about driving efficiency rather than creating social value.

An understanding of co-creation in terms of public service logic and value co-creation implies a different understanding of public sector governance. Osborne and colleagues have written extensively about New Public Governance (NPG) (Osborne, 2006; 2010) which is grounded in 'the reality of public service management in an increasingly complex, fragmented and interdependent world' (Osborne, 2018: 225) and recognises that top-down policy making and faceless, impersonal public services are out of step with people's expectations in the 21st century. NPG has co-creation at its heart. It assumes both a plural state, where multiple interdependent actors contribute to the delivery of public services, and a pluralist state, where multiple processes inform the policy-making system (Osborne, 2006). In this version of public governance, trust, relational capital and relational contracts act as the core governance mechanisms rather than the market (Osborne, 2006). The model also has implications for public service ecosystems (Osborne, 2021; Osborne et al, 2021) which are implied in NPG and 'move us beyond the transactional and linear approach associated with NPM, towards a relational model where value is shaped by the interplay between all of these dimensions and not least by the wider societal context and the values that underpin it' (Strokosch and Osborne, 2020: 436).

Relational work that is strengths-based and supported by front-line staff who are effective social navigators will be more outward looking with 'professional co-producers' expected to motivate and mobilise service users' capacities and resources and work across organisational boundaries to do so. This will require flatter organisational structures, based on networks rather than hierarchies, with porous organisational boundaries where knowledge can flow easily between organisations and new innovative solutions can be developed both within and across organisations.

Conclusion

As co-creation becomes more significant in public service design and delivery it is clear that it is far more than just a form of public service practice that can be adopted or discarded at will. Embracing co-creation requires a reimagining of public services and a rethink about the relationship between public services and citizens. A clear theory of co-creation is thus important.

This chapter started with the most developed body of theoretical work on co-creation, which has been elaborated as part of the NPG model. In this model public services do not have any intrinsic value to their users. Instead value is co-created with people who use services. However, while this is a useful framework for thinking about the role of co-creation in public service reform it has relatively little to say about what practices service professionals should adopt to help people build their agency and engage in co-creation, how organisations should be organised to support those professionals and what the balance between individual and social value in public services delivery should be. In part this is because these are normative questions and NPG is not intended to be a new paradigm of public service delivery or normative and prescriptive (Osborne, 2010).

In this chapter a normative theory of co-creation is developed in which co-creation and strengths-based working are understood to be two sides of the same coin and the role of public services is to help people grow their capabilities. However, there are different approaches to identifying what capabilities citizens are entitled to. Recent work by Claassen addresses this issue and he develops the concept of 'navigational agency' whereby citizens can both act autonomously and pursue their own version of a good life, while also being embedded within and navigating between social practices in which they must cooperate with others (Claassen, 2018). This in turn helps us to identify a set of practices that citizens, professionals who deliver services and the public bodies can adopt to support navigational agency. These practices help show how people and organisation can move from 'doing' co-creation to 'being' co-creative.

Note
[1]   Mann (2021), in her exploration of person-centred care, argues that effective person-centred care involves a meshing of principles and practice: ways of both 'doing' person-centred care and 'being' person-centred. I am grateful to her for this metaphor.

References
Alford, J. (2002) 'Why do public-sector clients co-produce? Toward a contingency theory', *Administration & Society*, 34(1): 32–56.

Alford, J. (2009) *Engaging Public Sector Clients: From Service Delivery to Co-Production*, London: Palgrave.

Alford, J. (2015) 'Co-production, interdependence and publicness: extending public service dominant logic', *Public Management Review*, 18(5): 673–691.

Baron, S., Colomina, C., Pereira, T. and Stanley, T. (2019) *Strengths-based Approach: Practice Framework and Practice Handbook*, London: Department of Health & Social Care.

Bevir, M., Needham, C. and Waring, J. (2019) 'Inside co-production: ruling, resistance, and practice', *Social Policy and Administration*, 53(2): 197–202.

Bovaird, T. (2007) 'Beyond engagement and participation: user and community coproduction of public services', *Public Administration Review*, 67(5): 846–860.

Boyle, D. and Harris, M. (2009) *The Challenge of Co-Production: How Equal Partnerships between Professionals and the Public are Crucial to Improving Public Services*, London: New Economics Foundation.

Brandsen, T. and Honingh, M. (2018) 'Definitions of co-production and co-creation', in Brandsen, T., Steen, T. and Verschuere, B. (eds) *Co-Production and Co-Creation: Definitions and Theoretical Perspectives*, New York: Routledge, pp 9–17.

Brandsen, T., Steen, T. and Vershuere, B. (2018) 'Co-creation and co-production in public services: urgent issues in practice and research', in Brandsen, T., Steen, T. and Vershuere, B. (eds) *Co-Creation and Co-Production: Engaging Citizens in Public Services*, Oxford: Routledge, pp 1–6.

Claassen, R. (2016) 'An agency-based capability theory of justice', *European Journal of Philosophy*, 25(4): 1279–1304.

Claassen, R. (2018) *Capabilities in a Just Society*, Cambridge: Cambridge University Press.

Claassen, R. and Düwell, M. (2013) 'The foundations of capability theory: comparing Nussbaum and Gewirth', *Ethical Theory and Moral Practice*, 16(3): 493–510.

Cottam, H. (2018) *Radical Help: How We Can Remake the Relationships Between Us and Revolutionise the Welfare State*, London: Little, Brown and Company.

Crompton, A. (2018) 'Inside co-production: stakeholder meaning and situated practice', *Social Policy and Administration*, 53(2): 219–232.

Doyal, L. and Gough, I. (1991) *A Theory of Human Needs*, London: Macmillan.

Engen, M., Fransson, M., Quist, J. and Skålén, P. (2021) 'Continuing the development of the public service logic: a study of value co-destruction in public services', *Public Management Review*, 23(6): 886–905.

Flemig, S. and Osborne, S. (2019) 'The dynamics of co-production in the context of social care personalisation: testing theory and practice in a Scottish context', *Journal of Social Policy*, 48(4): 671–697.

Fox, A. (2013) *Putting People into Personalisation: Relational Approaches to Social Care and Housing*, London: Respublica.

Fox, A. (2018) *A New Health and Care System: Escaping the Invisible Asylum*, Bristol: Policy Press.

Fox, C., Baines, S., Wilson, R., Jalonen, H., Aflaki, I., Prandini, R., Bassi, A., Ganugi, G. and Aramo-Immonen, H. (2021) *A New Agenda for Co-creating Public Services*, Turku: Turku University of Applied Sciences.

Friedli, L. (2013) '"What we've tried, hasn't worked": the politics of assets based public health', *Critical Public Health*, 23(2): 131–145.

Gewirth, A. (1978) *Reason and Morality*, Chicago: University of Chicago Press.

Gewirth, A. (1996) *Community of Rights*, Chicago: University of Chicago Press.

Gray, M. (2011) 'Back to basics: a critique of the strengths perspective in social work', *Families in Society*, 92(1): 5–11.

Grönroos, C. (1982) 'An applied service marketing theory', *European Journal of Marketing*, 16(7): 30–41.

Grönroos, C. (1984) 'A service quality model and its implications', *European Journal of Marketing*, 18(40): 36–44.

Hampson, M., Baeck, P. and Langford, K. (2013) *By Us, For Us: The Power of Co-Design and Co-Delivery*, London: Nesta.

Hannan, R. (2019) *Radical Home Care: How Self-Management Could Save Social Care*, London: RSA.

Hood, C.C. (1991) 'A public management for all seasons?', *Public Administration*, 69(3): 3–19.

Laloux, F. (2014) *Reinventing Organisations*, Brussels: Nelson Parker.

Leadbeater, C. (2004) *Personalisation through Participation: A New Script for Public Services*, London: Demos.

Loeffler, E. and Bovaird, T. (2016) 'User and community co-production of public services: what does the evidence tell us?', *International Journal of Public Administration*, 39(13): 1006–1019.

Lowe, T., French, M., Hawkins, M., Hesselgreaves, H. and Wilson, R. (2021) 'New development: responding to complexity in public services—the human learning systems approach', *Public Money & Management*, 41(7): 573–576.

Lusch, R. and Vargo, S. (2006) *The Service Dominant Logic of Marketing*, New York: M.E. Sharpe.

MacLeod, M. and Emejulu, A. (2014) 'neoliberalism with a community face? a critical analysis of asset-based community development in Scotland', *Journal of Community Practice*, 22(4): 430–450.

Mann, G. (2021) *Care Relationships in Social Interventions: A Critical Realist Analysis*, PhD thesis, Manchester Metropolitan University.

Mathie, A. and Cunningham, G. (2003) 'From clients to citizens: asset-based community development as a strategy for community-driven development', *Development in Practice*, 13(5): 474–486.

Mortensen, N., Brix, J. and Krogstrup, H. (2020) 'Reshaping the hybrid role of public servants: identifying the opportunity space for co-production and the enabling skills required by professional co-producers', in Sullivan, H. and Dickinson, H. (eds) *The Palgrave Handbook of the Public Servant*, London: Palgrave, pp 937–953.

Needham, C. (2011) 'Personalization: from story-line to practice', *Social Policy & Administration*, 45(1): 54–68.

Needham, C. and Mangan, C. (2016) 'The 21st-century public servant: working at three boundaries of public and private', *Public Money & Management*, 36(4): 265–272.

Nussbaum, M.C. (1988) 'Nature, function and capability: Aristotle on political distribution', *Oxford Studies in Ancient Philosophy*, 145–184.

Osborne, S.P. (2006) 'The new public governance?', *Public Management Review*, 8(3): 377–387.

Osborne, S.P. (2010) 'Introduction: the (new) public governance: a suitable case for treatment', in Osborne, S.P. (ed) *The New Public Governance? Emerging Perspectives on the Theory and Practice of Public Governance*, Oxford: Routledge, pp 1–11.

Osborne, S.P. (2018) 'From public service-dominant logic to public service logic: are public service organizations capable of co-production and value co-creation?', *Public Management Review*, 20(2): 225–231.

Osborne, S.P., Nasi, G. and Powell, M. (2021) 'Beyond co-production: value creation and public services', *Public Administration*, 99: 641–657. https://doi.org/10.1111/padm.12718

Osborne, S.P. and Strokosch, K. (2013) 'It takes two to tango? Understanding the co-production of public services by integrating the services management and public administration perspectives', *British Journal of Management*, 24(51): 31–47.

Osborne, S.P., Radnor, Z. and Strokosch, K. (2016) 'Co-production and the co-creation of value in public services: a suitable case for treatment?', *Public Management Review*, 18(5): 639–653.

Osborne, S.P., Powell, M., Cui, T. and Strokosch, K. (2021) 'New development: "appreciate–engage–facilitate"– the role of public managers in value creation in public service ecosystems', *Public Money & Management*, 41(8): 668–671,

Price, A., Ahuja, L., Bramwell, C., Briscoe, S., Shaw, L. and Nunns, M. (2020) *Research Evidence on Different Strengths-Based Approaches within Adult Social Work: A Systematic Review*, Southampton: NIHR Health Services and Delivery Research Topic Report.

Rippon, S. and Hopkins, T. (2015) *Head, Hands and Heart: Asset-Based Approaches in Health Care: A Review of the Conceptual Evidence and Case Studies of Asset-Based Approaches in Health, Care and Wellbeing*, London: Health Foundation

Rose, T. (2016) *The End of Average: How We Succeed in a World that Values Sameness*, New York: HarperOne.

Roy, M.J. (2017) 'The assets-based approach: furthering a neoliberal agenda or rediscovering the old public health? A critical examination of practitioner discourses', *Critical Public Health*, 27(4): 455–464.

SCIE (2015) *Co-Production in Social Care: What It Is and How To Do It*, SCIE Guide 51, London: SCIE.

Sen, A.K. (1990) 'Development as capability expansion', in Griffin, K. and Knight, J. (eds) *Human Development and the International Development Strategy for the 1990s*, London: Macmillan, pp 41–58.

Sen, A.K. (2009) *The Idea of Justice*, London: Allen Lane.

Steen, T., Brandsen, T. and Vershuere, B. (2018) 'The dark side of co-creation and co-production', in Brandsen, T., Steen, T. and Verschuere, B. (eds) *Co-Production and Co-Creation: Engaging Citizens in Public Services*, London: Routledge, pp 284–293.

Strokosch, K. and Osborne, S.P. (2018) *Literature Review on Public Service Reform Models*, COVAL, https://www.co-val.eu/public-deliverables/

Strokosch, K. and Osborne, S. (2020) 'Co-experience, coproduction and co-governance: an ecosystem approach to the analysis of value creation', *Policy & Politics*, 48(3): 425–442.

Torfing, J., Sørensen, E. and Røiseland, A. (2019) 'Transforming the public sector into an arena for co-creation: barriers, drivers, benefits, and ways forward', *Administration & Society*, 51(5): 795–825.

Voorberg, W.H., Bekkers, V. and Tummers, L.G. (2015) 'A systematic review of co-creation and co-production: embarking on the social innovation journey', *Public Management Review*, 17(9): 1333–1357.

Vregelaar, T. (2017) *Identifying Factors for Successful Self-Managing Teams: An Evidence-Based Literature Review*, essay.utwente.nl/72758/1/Vregelaar_ten_BA_BMS.pdf

Wilson, R., Cornwell, C., Flanagan, E., Nielsen, N. and Khan, H. (2018) *Good and Bad Help: How Purpose and Confidence Transform Lives*, London: NESTA.

3

Co-creation as a driver of social innovation and public service reform?

Andrea Bassi, Inga Narbutaité Aflaki,
Heli Aramo-Immonen and Sue Baines

Introduction

Co-creation has come to the forefront of policy as an innovative way of planning, managing, delivering and assessing public services, especially in the fields of social care, health, education and housing. Although far from universally applied, it has powerful support and many committed champions. Co-creation implies but goes beyond making public services more responsive to the needs and wishes of individuals and communities. It means that people often thought of as 'users', 'targets' or 'beneficiaries' have knowledge and experience that is of value for shaping service innovations. As the Co-creation of Service Innovation in Europe (CoSIE) pilots progressed, engaged with diverse stakeholders and began to share their learning, it became more prominent and explicit across the project that co-creation can only be said to take place when people no longer have services 'done to' them. The mantra of disability activism, 'nothing about us without us', gained traction in the consortium.

Following the conceptual exposition of co-creation in Chapter 2, this chapter highlights its advance in public policy and emphasises the association of co-creation with social innovation. Innovation means new ideas that are put into practice (Hartley, 2014). Social innovation is specifically about human needs (Brandsen et al, 2016; Marques et al, 2017). The idea of social innovation has been stretched in many directions and is sometimes accused of conceptual imprecision (Pol and Ville, 2009; Grimm et al, 2013; Jenson, 2015). Nevertheless, there is some agreement that core features include forging new relationships and enhancing assets and capabilities (Moulaert and MacCallum, 2019). The next two sections of this chapter comprise policy-focused discussion of co-creation and social innovation. Then we introduce examples from the CoSIE pilots of co-creative innovations in different public services in three countries, Estonia (social care), Hungary (improving household economies) and Spain (business start-up support for citizens adrift from the world of work). Across these examples we note common themes under which co-creation and social innovation intersect: shifting the balance of control; innovations in (co-)governing; roles of professionals; and extended or adapted the usage of digital technologies.

Co-creation in policy

Co-creation has gained support from international organisations including the Organisation for Economic Co-operation and Development, the World Bank and the European Commission, as well as regional and national governments (Torfing et al, 2021). The European Commission has high expectations of co-creation to enhance citizens' rights, meet people's real needs and stimulate democratic participation (European Economic and Social Committee, 2022). Many calls within the Horizon 2020 and Horizon Europe research and innovation programmes feature co-creation (Timonen and Lolich, 2021). The CoSIE project responded to a call under 'co-creation for growth and improvement' that sought to foster co-creative innovations in public services on the basis that top-down models no longer meet citizens' expectations.

In this book we distinguish 'co-creation' from the longer established 'co-production' as discussed in Chapter 2. We concur with Torfing et al (2019), who show why a distinction is useful for policy as well as theory with an image of rungs on a co-creation ladder, evoking older versions of a ladder of citizen participation for the enhancement of democratic influence (Arnstein, 1969). The co-creation ladder denotes upward progress from limited forms of 'co-production' where end-users contribute to production and delivery but not to service design, planning or decision-making. We recognise, however, that 'co-production' in a more inclusive sense is in use especially in the English-speaking world. A recently published 'co-production handbook' with a largely (but not exclusively) UK focus, for example, sees the essential elements of co-production as both citizen action and citizen voice (Loeffler and Bovaird, 2021a). This version of 'co-production' would come high up on the co-creation ladder.

Various elements and sub-elements have been defined through the 'co' prefix. Brandsen and Pestoff (2006) recognise three different modes of cooperation between citizens and the public sector, which they call co-governance, co-management and co-production. Co-governance refers to the planning of public services and policy formulation. Co-management means interactions between different kinds of organisations such as citizens' associations and agencies of the state, primarily on policy implementation. Co-production, according to Brandsen and Pestoff (2006), operates at the delivery level when citizens produce their own services. Adopting a micro level of analysis, Nambisan and Nambisan (2013) discern distinct types of active contributions by citizens to public services:

- Ideator: citizens can conceptualise novel solutions to well-defined problems.
- Explorer: citizens can identify, discover, and define emerging and existing problems.
- Designer: citizens can design and/or develop implementable solutions.
- Diffuser: citizens can support or facilitate the adoption and diffusion of public service innovations and solutions.

Loeffler and Bovaird (2021b) specify four 'cos': co-commissioning, co-design, co-delivery and co-assessment. Co-assessment, sometimes called co-evaluation, denotes participants involved in a process of assessment and improvement throughout the life of a service, intervention or project. It is likely to supplement and enhance other 'co' elements rather than follow on after them.

Early iterations of CoSIE attempted to draw upon the wide-ranging literature to position the different 'co'-elements within an overarching, rather linear framework. Experience from the CoSIE pilots showed that that co-creation is not linear and does not map neatly onto phases, stages or similar (Wiktorska-Święcka, 2021). Rather, it is better viewed as a 'constellation' through which various aspects and 'co' practices emerge. This is visualised in Figure 3.1

Policy interest in co-creation varies across different countries and service contexts. At the outset of the CoSIE project, Sakellariou (2018) led a

Figure 3.1: The constellation of 'co' elements

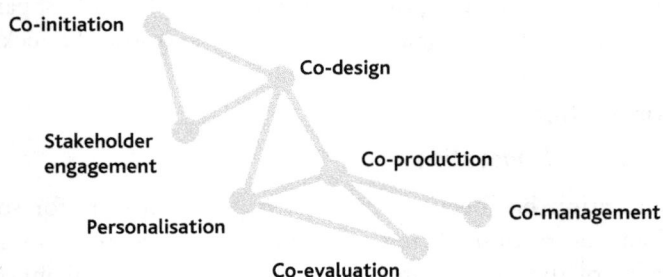

Source: CoSIE (2021)

review of co-creation in the ten participating countries from which two categories emerged:

1. Those in which co-creation was relatively developed (Finland, Sweden, Italy, the UK and the Netherlands).
2. Those in which co-creation was underdeveloped or on its first steps (Spain, Hungary, Poland, Greece and Estonia).

In the first group the environment for co-creation was favourable both at national and institutional levels. In Sweden, for example, the CoSIE pilot was implemented in the context of a legislative framework that obliged state providers of disability services to design them under a co-creative method. Before CoSIE began, the Social Services Department of the municipality of Jönköping was already undergoing a programme of transformation based on active dialogues with citizens. The pilot in Jönköping worked with Personal Assistance, which for various reasons (see Chapter 4) was lagging behind other municipal social services in co-creation. In the UK, co-creation (often entitled co-production) has been institutionalised and required by government agencies. For example, statutory guidance for English local authorities on social care stipulates a requirement for co-production, 'when an individual influences the support and services received, or when groups of people get together to influence the way that services are designed, commissioned and delivered' (Department of Health & Social Care, 2016). There are also highly vocal advocates in civil society (The Social Care Institute for Excellence, 2022).

In the second group of countries co-creation was not on the political agenda when CoSIE commenced but there was sometimes interest from civil society. In Estonia, for example, co-creation was rarely heard in the context of public services although the government used the term 'engagement' to denote taking account of the views of people whom decisions affect. Co-creation was quite widely advocated by Estonian non-government organisations, often directly associated with social innovation. In Poland, on the other hand, co-creation was barely recognised at all and there was a lack of concepts encouraging the involvement of stakeholders, particularly end-users, in public policies (Sakellariou, 2018; Wiktorska-Święcka, 2021).

Social innovation

The need for social innovation

Social innovation has been prominent in policy agenda for somewhat longer than co-creation, dating in its present-day form from the latter two decades of the 20th century. The challenge of social innovation is unavoidable for contemporary society increasingly beset by the great issues relating to the search for subjective and intersubjective wellbeing, and at the same time marked by a continuing economic crisis and legitimacy of the state. In other words, meeting societal challenges calls for innovation. The European Economic and Social Committee (2016; 2022), representing socio-occupational interest groups and civil society to the European Union, sees social innovation as essential to boost participation by members of the public and civil society. Evers and Ewart (2021), drawing on a wealth of applied research across Europe, support this stance with the observation that co-production (or co-creation) should be framed as a form of social innovation in order to become a vehicle for democratising social services.

Innovation is a multidimensional concept that refers to the implementation of new ideas, processes or products, with advantages for businesses and beneficial externalities for society (Committee of the Regions of the European Union, 2015). In industrial and commercial innovation bridging the gap between designers and users of new products and services is a common theme. Firms or individual consumers who modify or develop products have become an increasingly important source of innovations that may be commercialised (Von Hippel, 2005). The influential notion of open innovation urges businesses to seek commercial success by inviting customers to co-create with them (Chesbrough, 2011). In creative industries, for example, customers can supply the firm with innovative ideas and help them respond to market needs (Czarnota, 2017). More generally, firms that are successful innovators pool skills and obtain access to external knowledge (Pittaway et al, 2004). In short, commercial and public sector variations on innovation have in common the opening up of innovation processes to a broader range of people and organisations (Baines et al, 2022).

Social innovation has come to feature almost as prominently as technological innovation in EU policy (Sabato et al, 2017). In the words of José Manuel Durão Barroso (2011), then President of the European Commission, 'Europe has a long and strong tradition of social innovation: from workplaces to hospices, from the cooperative movement to micro-finance'. The upsurge of attention towards social innovation is seen in the many research and innovation projects on social innovation themes that have been carried out by partnerships of scholars and researchers from numerous European institutions with funding from the European Commission. The Bureau of European Policy Advisers (BEPA), directed by Agnès Hubert, in a well-known report proposed social innovation as a key to the relaunch of economic and social development in Europe. BEPA offered the following influential and often quoted definition: 'Social innovations are innovations that are social in both their ends and their means. Social innovations are new ideas (products, services and models), institutions or ways of working that simultaneously address social problems (more effectively than existing approaches) and create new social relationships or collaborations' (BEPA, 2011).

Social investment

Another closely associated set of policy agenda coheres around the idea of 'social investment' (Morel et al, 2012; Hemerijck, 2013; 2015; 2017; Smyth and Deeming, 2019). Social investment refers to the idea that spending on welfare should be treated as a form of 'investment' to improve human capital, combat intergenerational disadvantage, and enhance long-term prospects for economic and social participation (Hemerijck, 2013). Emanating from comparative social policy, it came to the fore with increasing recognition that welfare models originating in the mid-20th century were becoming less and less adequate (Esping-Andersen et al, 2002). Citizens face new social risks, including precarious labour markets, in-work poverty, changing family forms, poor work–life balance, rapid technological development and obsolete skills (Esping-Andersen et al, 2002; Hemerijck, 2013). Measures and instruments associated with social investment are intended to strengthen people's skills and capacities over the life course. The European Commission (2013: 3) stated that 'social investment policies reinforce social policies that protect and stabilise by addressing some of the causes of disadvantage and giving people tools with which to improve their social situations'.

Social investment has become influential but also generated criticism for being less pro-poor than more traditional social policy (Cantillon and Van Lancker, 2013) and moving away from entitlements and rights (Deeming, 2016). Hemerijck (2017: 12) counters that social investment emphasises 'concrete needs and capabilities for social participation and inclusion'. This is elaborated by Morel and Palme (2017), who draw upon Sen's (2001) conceptual framework on human freedom and human capabilities to make links with social justice and democratic development. In their analysis the normative building blocks of social investment include 'enhancing political citizenship by increasing possibilities for active participation' (Morel and Palme, 2017: np). From this viewpoint, social investment shares core principles with co-creation, most notably recognising people as assets and building human capacity. Social investment is a future-oriented perspective that aligns with social innovation because it emphasises a need for non-standard answers to non-standard risks (Baines et al, 2019).

Traditions of social innovation

Social innovation is a surprisingly old notion in the Western world. Ayob et al (2016) trace its sociological heritage back to the 19th century and Moulaert et al (2017) find even earlier antecedents. Until the 20th century, however, its meanings were often pejorative, associated with religious heresy or societal revolution (Moulaert et al, 2017). According to Ayob et al (2016), the first academic journal article to mention social innovation referred to a description of planation slavery as a social innovation. Nevertheless, social innovation has illustrious precursors such as Joseph Schumpeter in economics and Gabriel Tarde in sociology. Schumpeter (1950) elaborated the concept of creative destruction as the property of the entrepreneur who represents the engine of the capitalist economic system. The influence of Schumpeter informs present-day thinking about innovation and entrepreneurship in business and technology. Tarde discerned a phase of rupture with respect to the normal process of social imitation and has influenced later ideas on the diffusion of innovations (Howaldt et al, 2015).

The phrase 'social innovation' in its modern sense appears to have been born towards the end of the 1980s in the European cultural context, starting from the seminal work of the German sociologist Wolfgang Zapf (1989) who introduces it in a substantial essay to identify a new class of innovations and distinguish them from the others (in particular those with a prevalent technological character). Social innovation has been applied to many fields, including urban renewal, territorial economic development, social use of communication and information technologies, and processes of deliberative participation (Bassi, 2011; Grimm et al, 2013). At an international level, four main schools of thought and theoretical approaches to social innovation can be found:

1. The approach of French-speaking Canada that developed through the works of scholars and researchers who group themselves around the Centre de recherche sur les innovations sociales in Montreal – Quebec, founded by sociologist Benoît Lévesque towards the end of the 1980s (Klein et al, 2009; Klein and Harrisson, 2010; Klein and Bellemare, 2011; Klein and Roy, 2012).

2. Urban renewal and development studies, represented by a series of research projects funded by the European Commission from the 1990s, and which see the French-speaking Belgian Frank Moulaert as the main scholar (Moulaert et al, 2013; Moulaert and MacCallum, 2019).

3. The approach of sociology in Germany and Austria associated with the legacy of Schumpeter. The Sozialforschungsstelle Dortmund, ZWE der Technische Universitaet in Dortmund is a centre of excellence and the ZSI researcnicholsh centre in Vienna (Zentrum fuer Soziale Innovation) also refers to this trend (Zapf, 1989; Howaldt and Schwarz, 2010; Franz et al, 2013).

4. Finally, and most recent, is the Anglo-Saxon approach that has developed mainly in private non-profit study centres and think tanks such as the Young Foundation and NESTA in the UK, in particular under the direction of Geoff Mulgan. In spring 2006 a group of researchers belonging in various capacities to the Young Foundation published an influential research report with the evocative title *Social Silicon Valleys: A Manifesto for Social Innovation* (Young Foundation, 2006). From an

academic point of view, the main references are to the Skoll Center for Social Entrepreneurship in Oxford and the group of scholars who gather around the *Stanford Social Innovation Review* of the Center on Philanthropy and Civil Society of Stanford University, California (Mulgan, 2006; 2019; Phills et al, 2008; Murray et al, 2010; Nicholls and Murdock, 2012). The work of Mulgan and colleagues influenced European public debate (Barroso, 2011). However, their approach has been described as 'quite Anglo-centric' with rather less attention to inequalities and democratic deficits than European scholars such as Moulaert (Horgan, 2020: 244).

Examples of social innovation from CoSIE pilots

All CoSIE pilots were concerned with fostering more effective solutions to persistent problems by innovation in ways to incorporate the knowledge of people affected by services. In this section we illustrate the intersection of co-creation and social innovation, drawing on examples from the CoSIE pilots that took place in Hungary, Spain and Estonia. We highlight the following dimensions:

- Shifting the balance of control, underpinned by asset-based approaches.
- Innovative roles and relationships between professionals and citizens.
- Governance innovations or relations between organisations.
- Innovative/extended use of technologies (information and communications technologies).

The CoSIE pilot in Hungary set out to improve household livelihoods in small villages beset by multiple disadvantages. In the short term, the intention was to enable families to utilise their own resources of household economy (including human resources, equipment and natural resources) to empower them in taking greater control over their lives. In the longer run, the aim was to improve the local economy in disadvantaged rural areas. The process resulted in innovation on several dimensions. Besides a conceptual innovation, it evidenced a 'process innovation' with *shifting the balance of control* where the targeted marginalised families and individuals with limited resources took responsibility for designing and implementing their own household economy plans. The innovative pilot actions facilitated rural communities to co-design local projects, choosing their own economic activities and sharing their efforts and resources. This was a sharp departure from what has gone before (Csoba and Sipos, 2022).

At the same time, co-creation required *innovation in (co-)governing* service development by taking into use new operational mechanisms of (direct) local democracy and shifting the roles of the local mayors and coordinators towards mobilising the household economies. Such joint engagement of citizens, public professionals and political leaders in co-creation targeting the same goals was a bold innovation in Hungary with its paternalistic traditions and high level of centralisation. Local leaders commented in the early stages of the pilot that people in the villages had grown accustomed to a feeling of helplessness in the face of paternalistic traditions and welfare dependency. Citizens and local leaders started gradually recognising that they were major sources of knowledge, ideas, experience for making the support services work, and that their informal networks were valuable assets. The pilot co-created opportunities for innovative solutions that also strengthened community integration. As a result of the piloting efforts, a novel community-based public services model was established aiming to improve the local economy (Csoba and Sipos, 2022). Its success directly fed into a new national programme where applicants get extra points during the evaluation of their bid for demonstrating co-creation.[1]

The CoSIE pilots draw attention to the *innovative roles of professionals* especially in relation to citizens in receipt of services. This is important because it has been somewhat underdeveloped in much thinking about co-creation (Osborne and Strokosch, 2013; Hannan, 2019). Pilots in Sweden (Chapter 4) and the UK (Chapter 6) provided bespoke coaching sessions with elements of action learning that demonstrably increased service practitioners' capacity to deploy new tools and skillsets. The pilot in Valencia, Spain known as Co-Crea-Te aimed to improve the lives of citizens who find themselves adrift from the working world by providing them with tools to engage in business start-up projects. This pilot illustrates how co-creation can require professionals to discard cherished assumptions. As one team member reported, when people at a distance from the labour market were asked what they wanted from entrepreneurial training they said they did not want entrepreneurial training, there was already plenty of it around and it did not help them. As a result of hearing this, he reported that "our preconceived ideas came tumbling down around our ears."

Co-Crea-Te embraced the idea of *acompañamiento* – meaning that co-creation can be supported with the help provided not only by professionals, but also by people in receipt of services themselves. It was one of several pilots that drew attention to a need for greater emphasis on lived experience either for professionals themselves or others as part of their teams. The overall aim of the Co-Crea-Te pilot was to bring about a systemic change in the way public services were being delivered by providing a safe, stable and supportive environment, in terms of both a physical and digital co-working space, for people with few or no resources to find means of economic self-sufficiency. The co-working space (Co-Crea-Te) provided participants with several collaborative activities, including workshops, mentoring and pitching sessions.

Co-creation has also been made effective through innovations in governance involving new ways for public organisations to interact in a multiple actor context. This involved establishing new relationships with and between agencies and authorities, and bringing together organisations and groups with different values and priorities, sometimes attempting to bridge long-standing historical contradictions. A good example is the Estonian CoSIE pilot in Vorumma county, a very remote, sparsely populated area with few services and many disadvantaged residents. As a vehicle for co-creation this pilot adapted the format of the 'hackathon', a well-established means to facilitate innovation through intensive, fast-paced collaboration in small groups, originally by prototyping in the IT sector. IT hackathons are very popular in Estonia. The pilot challenged the traditional top-down decision processes by bringing together many different stakeholders (municipalities, non-government organisations, entrepreneurs, community leaders, vulnerable people who used services, and fellow citizens) to promote co-creative solutions to experienced local needs (Toros et al, 2020).

Co-creation sometimes incorporates technological models including those developed in the private sector (Brandsen and Honingh, 2018). Some CoSIE pilots *extended or adapted the usage of digital technologies in innovative ways*. How this was done successfully with marginalised young people in Finland is explained in detail in Chapter 5. Technology-inspired hackathons as used in Estonia might seem at first sight a poor fit with the emphasis on inclusion and social justice. Yet, the CoSIE pilot there adapted the hackathon format in combination with the welfare ethos to improve collaboration between professionals and citizens in public service innovation. This pilot evidences that the fast pace is not suitable for everyone, but many practical measures can enable more people to take part (for example, accessibility logistics, mentor support, appropriate communication). 'Social hackathons' successfully mobilised people in Vorumma from diverse backgrounds – including individuals with disabilities – to co-create new services or innovative solutions to local community needs (Kangro and Lepik, 2022). The hackathons generated 35 project ideas. Twenty continued as citizen initiatives or as co-operation between different service providers. Six of them reached a level to scale up to a local or even regional service. According to the participants, understanding the many different perspectives of problems was one of the biggest benefits of the hackathons. Perhaps more importantly, there was also evidence of movement towards a new public sector culture where experiments and their spaces are favoured, locally and nationally (Kangro and Lepik, 2022). The pilot won the most inspiring initiative of 2019 award from the president of Estonia. Soon after, social hackathons were rolled out nationally.

The prospect of open data appears to match the principles of co-creation (Jalonen and Helo, 2020). CoSIE planned activities that, according to the formal Description of Action, would include 'identifying open data sources, if relevant, to support the co-creation nature of the project'. A few pilots identified some relevant sources of open data that informed the assessment of local needs while others deemed the quality and granularity of available datasets to be inadequate. Only two pilots, those in Spain and Estonia, managed to find ways to involve open data in co-creative processes with stakeholders. In Estonia the pilot team, in consultation with the main analyst of the Estonian Statistical Office, collected a wealth of accurate, up-to-date information and prepared a profile of the county in which the most important statistical characteristics of wellbeing were presented in visual form. This profile was introduced into the social hackathons and participants were expected use it to prove the importance of the problem they were trying to solve. In Co-Crea-Te open data were introduced during open days when the co-working space opened its doors to reach out to local business and neighbourhood associations. This was done with an element of gamification, making use of the city's open data portal.

In addition to its imaginative if limited adoption of open data, Co-Crea-Te in Valencia was one of the most prolific users of social media in CoSIE. The level of on-line activity throughout the duration of the pilot was extremely high and this was mostly due to independent and largely unguided actions from citizens participating in the co-working space. Digital technologies including the website, blognotes, Twitter, Facebook, LindedIn, YouTube, Slack and Trello were run by the pilot participants themselves. The technology was a leveller and gave participants a feeling of belonging. The transfer of power to them occasionally proved to be a source of tension with public service organisations. In this way Co-Crea-Te saw shifting of the power balance between service users and providers.

Conclusion

This chapter reviewed the book's core themes of co-creation and social innovation from a policy perspective. It then turned to the intersection of co-creation and social innovation in practice, briefly introducing three of the CoSIE pilots to illustrate ways it is possible to mobilise the knowledge of people who receive services and nurture their participation in service innovation. This proved to be so even in contexts that looked highly unpromising with people unused to having their voices heard. The pilots in Spain, Estonia and Hungary as discussed in this chapter achieved social innovations that made a difference to local people and their services. The ambitions of CoSIE extended beyond this, to embed co-creation and inspire change much more widely. The pilots in Hungary and Estonia began to move beyond implementing ideas in a specific setting to fulfil those ambitions. We return to the theme of scaling in Chapter 12.

Note

1 The link to the call for proposals with the co-creation methodological guide developed by the management of the CoSIE project can be viewed (in Hungarian) at: https://tef.gov.hu/wp-content/uploads/2020/10/Családi-portaprogram-pályázati-felh%C3%ADvás-szociális-földprogram-pályázati-felh%C3%ADvás.pdf

References

Arnstein, S. (1969) 'A ladder of citizen participation', *Journal of the American Planning Association*, 35(4): 216–224.

Ayob, N., Teasdale, S. and Fagan, K. (2016) 'How social innovation "came to be": tracing the evolution of a contested concept', *Journal of Social Policy*, 45(4): 635–653.

Baines, S., Bassi, A., Csoba, J. and Sipos, F. (2019) *Implementing Innovative Social Investment: Strategic Lessons from Europe*, Bristol: Policy Press.

Baines, S., Wilson, R., Narbutaité Aflaki, I., Wiktorska-Święcka, A., Bassi, A. and Jalonen, H. (2022) 'Editorial: innovating "co-creative" relationships between services, citizens and communities', *Public Money & Management*, 42(5): 295–297.

Barroso, J. (2011) *Social Innovation Europe Initiative*, https://ec.europa.eu/commission/presscorner/detail/en/SPEECH_11_190

Bassi, A. (2011) *Social Innovation: Some Definitions*, Boletín del Centro de Investigación de Economía y Sociedad – CIES N° 88 – March.

BEPA (2011) *Empowering People, Driving Change: Social Innovation in the European Union*, Luxembourg: Publications Office of the European Union.

Brandsen, T. and Pestoff, V. (2006) 'Co-production, the third sector and the delivery of public services', *Public Management Review*, 8(4): 493–501.

Brandsen, T. and Honingh, M. (2018) 'Definitions of co-production and co-creation', in Brandsen, T., Steen, T. and Verschuere, B. (eds) *Co-Production and Co-Creation: Definitions and Theoretical Perspectives*, New York: Routledge, pp 9–17.

Brandsen, T., Evers, A., Cattacin, S. and Zimmer, A. (2016) 'Social innovation: a sympathetic and critical interpretation', in Bransden, T.A., Cattacin, S., Evers, A. and Zimmer, A. (eds) *Social Innovations in the Urban Context*, Cham: Springer International Publishing, pp 3–20.

Cantillon, B. and Van Lancker, W. (2013) 'Three shortcomings of the social investment perspective', *Social Policy and Society*, 12(4): 553–564.

Chesbrough, H. (2011) *Open Services Innovation: Rethinking Your Business to Grow and Compete in a New Era*, San Francisco: Jossey Bass.

Committee of the Regions of the European Union (2015) *Fostering Innovation at Regional Level: Lessons from the European Entrepreneurial Region (EER) Experience*, http://bookshop.europa.eu/en/fostering-innovation-at-regional-level-pbQG0415264/

CoSIE (2021) *Roadmap: The CoSIE Constellations for Co-Creation in Public Services*, https://cosie.turkuamk.fi/arkisto/roadmap/index.html

Csoba, J. and Sipos, F. (2022) 'Politically-driven public administration or co-creation? On the possibility of modernizing public services in rural Hungary', *Public Money & Management*, 42(5): 314–322.

Czarnota, J. (2017) *Co-Creation, Innovation and New Service Development: The Case of Videogames Industry*, New York: Routledge.

Deeming, C. (2016) 'Rethinking social policy and society', *Social Policy and Society*, 15(2): 159–175.

Department of Health & Social Care (2016 [updated 2022]) *Care and Support: Statutory Guidance*, https://www.gov.uk/government/publications/care-act-statutory-guidance/care-and-support-statutory-guidance

Esping-Andersen, G., Gallie, D., Hemerijck, A. and Myles, J. (2002) *Why We Need a New Welfare State*, Oxford: Oxford University Press.

European Commission (2013) *Towards Social Investment for Growth and Cohesion – Including Implementing the European Social Fund 2014–2020*, COM (2013) 83 final, Brussels.

European Economic and Social Committee (2016) 'Opinion of the European Economic and Social Committee on social innovation, networking and digital communication (own initiative opinion)', *Official Journal of the European Union*, https://eur-lex.europa.eu/legal-content/EN/TXT/PDF/?uri=CELEX:52014IE4902&from=IT

European Economic and Social Committee (2022) *Co-Creation of Services of General Interest as a Contribution to a More Participative Democracy in the EU*, TEN/772-EESC-2022, https://www.eesc.europa.eu/en/our-work/opinions-information-reports/opinions/co-creation-services-general-interest-contribution-more-participative-democracy-eu

Evers, A. and Ewart, B. (2021) 'Understanding co-production as a social innovation', in Loeffler, E. and Bovaird, T. (eds) *The Palgrave Handbook of Co-Production of Public Services and Outcomes*, Cham: Palgrave Macmillan, pp 133–153.

Franz, H.-W., Howaldt, J. and Hochgerner, J. (eds) (2013) *Challenge Social Innovation Potentials for Business, Social Entrepreneurship, Welfare and Civil Society*, Berlin: Springer.

Grimm, R., Fox, C., Baines, S. and Albertson, K. (2013) 'Social innovation, an answer to contemporary societal challenges? Locating the concept in theory and practice', *Innovation: The European Journal of Social Science Research*, 26(4): 436–455.

Hannan, R. (2019) *Radical Home Care: How Self-Management Could Save Social Care*, London: RSA.

Hartley, J. (2014) 'Eight and a half propositions to stimulate frugal innovation', *Public Money & Management*, 34(3): 227–232.

Hemerijck, A. (2013) *Changing Welfare States*, Oxford: Oxford University Press.

Hemerijck, A. (2015) 'The quiet paradigm revolution of social investment', *Social Politics*, 22(2): 242–256.

Hemerijck, A. (2017) 'Social investment and its critics', in Hemerijck, A. (ed) *The Uses of Social Investment*, Oxford: Oxford University Press, pp 1–28.

Horgan, D. (2020) '*Social innovation: how societies find the power to change*, edited by Geoff Mulgan, Bristol: Policy Press, 2019; *Advanced introduction to social innovation change*, edited by Frank Moulaert and Diana MacCallum, Cheltenham: Edward Elgar Publishing, 2019', *Social Policy & Administration*, 55(1): 243–245.

Howaldt, J. and Schwarz, M. (2010) *Social Innovation: Concepts, Research Fields and International Trends*, Sozialforschungsstelle, vol 5, Dortmund: TU Dortmund.

Howaldt, J., Kopp, R. and Schwarz, M. (2015) *On the Theory of Social Innovations: Tarde's Neglected Contribution to the Development of a Sociological Innovation Theory*, Weinheim: Beltz Juventa.

Jalonen, H. and Helo, T. (2020) 'Co-creation of public service innovation using open data and social media: rhetoric, reality, or something in between?', *International Journal of Innovation in the Digital Economy*, 11(3): 64–77.

Jenson, J. (2015) 'Social innovation: redesigning the welfare diamond', in Nicholls, A., Simon, J. and Gabriel, M. (eds) *New Frontiers in Social Innovation Research*, London: Palgrave Macmillan, pp 89–106.

Kangro, K. and Lepik, K.-L. (2022) 'Co-creating public services in social hackathons: adapting the original hackathon concept', *Public Money & Management*, 42(5): 341–348.

Klein, J.-L. and Harrisson, D. (2010) *L'innovation Sociale. Emergence et effets sur la transformation des sociétés* [Social innovation. Emergence and effects on the transformation of societies], Québec: Presse de l'Université du Québec.

Klein, J.-L. and Bellemare, G. (2011) *Innovation Sociale et Territoire. Convergences théorique et pratiques* [Social Innovation and Territory. Convergence theoretical and practical], Montréal: Presses de l'Université du Québec.

Klein, J.-L. and Roy, M. (2012) *Pour une nouvelle mondialisation: le défi d'innover* [A New Globalization: the challenge to innovate], Montréal: Presses de l'Université du Québec.

Klein, J.-L., Fontan, J.-M., Harrisson, D. and Lévesque, B. (2009) *L'innovation sociale au Québec: un système d'innovation fondé sur la concertation* [Social Innovation in Quebec: an innovation system based on consultation], Cahiers du CRISES, Collection Etudes Théoriques, no ET0907 mai 2009.

Loeffler, E. and Bovaird, T. (eds) (2021a) *The Palgrave Handbook of Co-Production of Public Services and Outcomes*, Cham: Palgrave Macmillan.

Loeffler, E. and Bovaird, T. (2021b) 'User and community co-production of public value', in Loeffler, E. and Bovaird, T. (eds) *The Palgrave Handbook of Co-Production of Public Services and Outcomes*, Cham: Palgrave Macmillan, pp. 32–57.

Marques, P., Morgan, K. and Richardson, R. (2017) 'Social innovation in question: the theoretical and practical implications of a contested concept', *Environment and Planning C*, 36(3): 496–512.

Morel, N. and Palme, J. (2017) 'A normative foundation for the social investment approach?', in Hemerijck, A. (ed) *The Uses of Social Investment*, Oxford: Oxford University Press, pp 278–286.

Morel, N., Palier, B. and Palme, J. (eds) (2012) *Towards a Social Investment Welfare State? Ideas, Policies and Challenges*, Bristol: Policy Press.

Moulaert, F. and MacCallum, D. (2019) *Advanced Introduction to Social Innovation*, Cheltenham: Edward Elgar.

Moulaert, F., MacCallum, D., Mehmood, A. and Hamdouch, A. (eds) (2013) *The International Handbook on Social Innovation: Collective Action, Social Learning and Transdisciplinary Research*, Cheltenham: Edward Elgar.

Moulaert, F., Mehmood, A., MacCallum, D. and Leubolt, B. (eds) (2017) *Social Innovation as a Trigger for Transformations: The Role of Research*, Luxembourg: Publications Office of the European Union, https://ec.europa. eu/research/social-sciences/pdf/

Mulgan, G. (2006) 'The process of social innovation', *Innovations: Technology, Governance, Globalizations*, 1(2): 145–162.

Mulgan, G. (2019) *Social Innovation: How Societies Find the Power to Change*, Bristol: Policy Press.

Murray, R., Caulier-Grice, J. and Mulgan, G. (2010) *The Open Book of Social Innovation*, London: NESTA.

Nambisan, S. and Nambisan, P. (2013) *Engaging Citizens in Co-Creation in Public Services: Lessons Learned and Best Practices*, Washington: IBM Global Business Services.

Nicholls, A. and Murdock, A. (eds) (2012) *Social Innovation: Blurring Boundaries to Reconfigure Markets*, New York: Palgrave Macmillan.

Osborne, S.P. and Strokosch, K. (2013) '"It takes two to tango?": understanding the co-production of public services by integrating the services management and public administration perspectives', *British Journal of Management*, 24(S1): S31–S47.

Phills, J.A., Deiglmeier, K. and Miller, D.T. (2008) 'Rediscovering social innovation', *Stanford Social Innovation Review*, 6(4): 34–43.

Pittaway, L., Robertson, M., Munir, K., Denyer, D. and Neely, A. (2004) 'Networking and innovation: a systematic review of the evidence', *International Journal of Management Reviews*, 5–6: 137–168.

Pol, E. and Ville, S. (2009) 'Social innovation: buzz word or enduring term?', *The Journal of Socio-Economics*, 38(6): 878–885.

Sabato, S., Vanhercke, B. and Verschraegen, G. (2017) 'Connecting entrepreneurship with policy experimentation? The EU framework for social innovation', *Innovation: The European Journal of Social Science Research*, 30(2): 147–167.

Sakellariou, A. (2018) *Rapid Evidence Appraisal of the Current State of Co-creation in Ten European Countries*, https://storage.googleapis.com/turku-amk/ 2019/04/rapid-evidence-appraisal-of.pdf

Schumpeter, J.A. (1950) *Capitalism, Socialism and Democracy*, New York: HarperCollins.

Sen, A. (2001) 'The fear of freedom', in Pelagidis, T., Katseli, L.T. and Milios, J. (eds) *Welfare State and Democracy in Crisis: Reforming the European Model*, Aldershot: Ashgate.

Smyth, P. and Deeming, C. (2019) *Reframing Global Social Policy: Social Investment for Sustainable and Inclusive Growth*, Bristol: Policy Press.

The Social Care Institute for Excellence (2022) *Co-Production: What It Is and How to Do It*, https://www.scie.org.uk/co-production/what-how

Timonen, V. and Lolich, L. (2021) *SoCaTel White Paper*, https://ec.europa.eu/research/participants/documents/downloadPublic?documentIds=080166e5d8be332f&appId=PPGMS

Torfing, J., Sørensen, E. and Røiseland, A. (2019) 'Transforming the public sector into an arena for co-creation: barriers, drivers, benefits, and ways forward', *Administration & Society*, 51(5): 795–825.

Torfing, J., Ferlie, E., Jukić, T. and Ongaro, E. (2021) 'A theoretical framework for studying the co-creation of innovative solutions and public value', *Policy & Politics*, 49(2): 189–209.

Toros, K., Kangro, K., Lepik, K.-L., Bugarszki, Z., Sindi, I., Saia, K. and Medar, M. (2020) 'Co-creation of social services on the example of social hackathon: the case of Estonia', *International Social Work*, 65(4): 593–606.

von Hippel, E. (2005) 'Democratizing innovation: the evolving phenomenon of user innovation', *Journal für Betriebswirtschaft*, 55: 63–78. https://doi.org/10.1007/s11301-004-0002-8

Wiktorska-Święcka, A. (2021) 'Co-creation of public services in the European Union: concepts, approaches and practice', *Polish Political Science Review*, 9(2). DOI: 10.2478/ppsr-2021–0009

Young Foundation (2006) *Social Silicon Valleys: A Manifesto for Social Innovation: What It Is, Why It Matters and How It Can Be Accelerated*, London: The Basingstoke Press.

Zapf, W. (1989) 'Über soziale Innovationen' [About Social Innovations], *Soziale Welt*, 40(1–2): 170–183.

4

Co-creating capacity? Empowerment and learning for front-line workers and organisations

Inga Narbutaité Aflaki and Andrea Bassi

Introduction

This chapter offers new perspectives on front-line managers and workers as potential social innovators, detailing how co-creation transforms their identities, roles and relationships. Taking its point of departure in the *metaphor of a sandcastle* the chapter illustrates how in different national contexts achieving readiness for co-creation, rather than building sandcastles, requires new approaches to governing the collaborations across professional and organisational boundaries and managing cultural change. The chapter also highlights how service professionals and first-line managers work with reconceptualising their roles and relationships in welfare services to achieve greater social justice for the targeted individuals. It argues how co-creating meaningful service value may take much more in terms of efforts and time than pure organisational, administrative or technical changes which are rather seen as the outcomes of an (ongoing) shift in the approaches and mindsets about service delivery and management.

Reporting from a Swedish municipality in which a Co-creation of Service Innovation in Europe (CoSIE) pilot moved personal assistance (PA) services for people with functional and cognitive impairments towards co-creation culture, it illustrates co-creative approaches and strategies harnessed to transform disabling narratives. Emphasis is placed on the importance of change conversations and learning dialogues, where collective sense-making takes place, and on the role of facilitators to lead the transformative change. Touching also on an Italian pilot engaging families, civil society, and managers and service professionals in addressing a complex child obesity issue, the authors draw attention to key findings and learnings regarding co-creative strategies of managers and front-line professionals as change actors and approaches to facilitate such asset-based working.

The shifting roles of managers and professionals

The expanding literature on facilitating public service co-creation is still heavily focused on the citizen side which has consequences for understanding the role of the public sector in sustaining co-creation culture (Bassi and Fabbri, 2022). The literature that dwells on public governance, management and co-creation highlights the role of senior or mid-management and elected politicians in leading the change (Gioia and Chittipeddi, 1991; Lüscher and Lewis, 2008; Iveroth and Hallencreutz, 2016; Torfing et al, 2016; Sörensen and Torfing, 2022) or increasingly digitalised platforms and techniques to support co-creation (Jalonen and Helo, 2020). Meanwhile, the changes required in professional identities, roles and relationships of those actors in public or private organisations, whose interactions with citizens are crucial for co-creating or co-destroying the service value, are still largely overlooked. The role of service professionals or front-line managers when shifting service cultures to co-creation is often taken for granted, leaving a major gap in the literature (Osborne and Strokosch, 2013; Bassi, 2022). Empirical studies of the strategies of service professionals and lower level managers and the support provided by senior management in such a systemic change (Torfing et al, 2016; Narbutaité Aflaki, 2021) are still scarce.

Co-creation entails a distinct perspective and a major shift regarding roles and guiding principles in public service design, delivery and improvement by focusing on collaborative logics. As discussed in Chapter 2, a body of theoretical work associates co-creation with New Public Governance (NPG), although the argument in this book is that co-creation is in principle a new normative approach to public service delivery and as such requires rethinking the NPG as a new paradigm (see also Ansell and Torfing, 2021). NPG, with its focus upon inter-organisational relationships and trust, is seen as a reaction to shortcomings of New Public Management (NPM), which during the 1980s and the 1990s overruled (at least partially) older traditional public administration (TPA) (Hartley, 2005). NPG integrates some of the key principles of the alternative models such as striving for fairness under TPA and cost efficiency under NPM. Co-creation logic thus reinterprets, expands and shifts some of the key principles guiding public services. This leaves public managers and professionals with new tasks and a complex set of sometimes competing principles to guide their relations to citizens but also peers, democratically elected decision makers and other stakeholders. No wonder it has encountered some resistance.

Table 4.1 provides a synthesised overview of how the roles of public managers and professionals and the ethical principles for their engagement shift across the three models of governance and public management, TPA, NPM and NPG. For example, *fairness* under TPA implies service user treatment through standardised solutions, while NPM translates

Table 4.1: The role of public servants in different models of public governance and management

Key concepts	Traditional public administration	New public management	New public governance
	Public goods	**Public choice**	**Public value**
Role of public professionals	Implementation of professional standards, rule adherence, delivering	Achievement of pre-set objectives	Value co-creators, facilitators, enablers
Role and tasks of public managers	Commanders: managerial planning and process control by the formal rules and legal authority	Efficiency and market maximisers: managerial control over professionals via predefined goals and customers' wishes	Explorers: meta governance, coordination, facilitation
Professional–client relation	Top-down, one-directional relationship	Output-oriented management, performance measurement	Collaborative relationship based on user empowerment and interdependence between public, private and non-profit actors
Service users	Passive consumers	Rational customers	Co-producers (prosumers)
Principles of engagement	Fairness/equal treatment, transparency, effectiveness, efficiency, professional knowledge and discretion	Efficiency/cost reduction, specialisation, competitiveness, short-term perspective, goal-achievement	Social justice, inclusion, participation, influence, deliberation, power balancing, innovativeness, transparency, meaningfulness, professional engagement, long-term perspective
Principles of accountability	Accountability to decision-makers	Accountability to client satisfaction	Accountability to citizens (as service users)

fairness into services tailored to specific individual or group needs in market-like interactions. While elements of co-creation can be found in NPG and TPA (Ansell and Torfing, 2021), expanded co-creation under NPG transgresses pure methodological knowledge and implies rethinking relationships towards citizens in service delivery. On a deeper level, this requires transforming the mindsets of service workers/professionals and their managers. These actors are 'street-level bureaucrats', meaning individuals with the power to exercise discretion over daily decisions affecting citizens' lives. Understanding co-creation requires awareness of how interactions between service workers, their peers, other stakeholders and citizens may affect service production process and its outcomes, and subsequently the value associated with those.

The insight that value is co-created with the citizen in an ongoing circular process and through multiple interactions related to different service 'stages' or aspects (see Table 4.1) – from assessment, design or redesign to changes in service delivery – turns on its head the self-perceptions or identities of street-level bureaucrats. This includes their sense of power or powerlessness, responsibilities and roles in implementing this cultural shift. Yet, pressures for change without adequate support might also evoke alienation or resistance. Co-creation overall entails a new approach and value priorities in managing the necessary organisational adaptations.

Notwithstanding expectations of the 'magic' of co-creation (Ansell and Torfing, 2021), the behaviours and practices of first-line managers and professionals may reflect the attitude that their role is to provide value 'for' the citizens as end users. This way of thinking is tightly interlinked with TPA and NPM and relies on what has come to be called as the public sector dominant logics (Osborne, 2018). These professional patterns are often highly engrained, not least due to the prevalent incitement systems based on *prioritising professional expertise* and *vertical accountability* lines towards senior managers and elected representatives. Particularly in highly technical services, such as health or social care, increasingly, the service value is associated with technical knowledge. This includes handling big data generated based on simplified algorithms from citizen interactions with services (Falk, 2021). Also, while service professionals and care workers enjoy the trust placed upon them by service users, they also have to cope with their interventions being assessed against legal requirements of standardised services and predefined policy goals or organisational objectives. Both these aspects make services more 'inward looking' and prevent openness for lay or citizen knowledge (Boyle and Harris, 2009; Bassi, 2022). What is more, that may challenge the professional ethics and the need for adequate discretion, in turn effecting de-professionalisation (Taylor and Kelly, 2006) and alienation (Tummers, 2012).

It is often forgotten that expectations of particular roles and relationships also need to be meaningful to the policy-implementing professionals and managers (Narbutaité Aflaki and Lindh, 2021). For example, when policies rhetorically put the citizen in the centre but service delivery practices are guided primarily by economic rather than relational values this may result in a value clash and professionals and managers start alienating themselves from their true professional ethical standards (Tummers, 2012). When they lack meaning and experience threat to their power or fear becoming 'redundant' (Narbutaité Aflaki and Lindh, 2021), service professionals and first-line managers may resist the new relational logics of co-creation. This is because no matter how strictly professionals are governed by new service values and goals, they still retain some power – derived primarily from their professional knowledge (Lipsky, 1980) – over the operational values and tasks in implementing policy and service reforms (Taylor and Kelly, 2006). In sum, when new policies for citizen inclusion and influence in decision making or co-determination, or similar terms associated with co-creation, offer little guidance and resources for implementation there is a risk that street-level bureaucrats will get alienated and neglect implementing policy goals.

In reality, co-creation is being introduced to an organisational world inhabited by a hybrid governance and management logics to various degrees incorporating principles from NPM and TPA. In such contexts, all manager levels are crucial for leading and facilitating a shift to co-creation culture. The stance and decisions of senior public managers and elected politicians have a major role in legitimising and sense-making about such a shift with mid and first-line managers and service professionals who undertake major transformation work and grapple with their identities. The senior management are crucial in, for example, shifting service focus from short-term to long-term impacts and from overemphasising formal rule adherence to greater citizen role in service input and meaningful output. This includes transforming the use of information and communication technologies (ICT) to enhance collaboration with citizens (Torfing et al, 2016) and abilities to work with moving targets rather than set goals. They may also undertake key leadership roles to forge organisational silos or stakeholders together in a joined learning process.

Mid- and first-line managers are core actors in implementing cultural change (Alvesson and Sveningsson, 2015; Narbutaité Aflaki and Lindh, 2021). Being seen as the last chain to implement change, first-line managers are expected to undertake leadership or facilitation towards the implementing professionals providing support and guidance, while mid-managers provide legitimacy and support to first-line managers. Sometimes such facilitatory

Table 4.2: The activities and principles underpinning co-creation

Policy/service development dimensions	Civil society actors and citizens	Public administration actors	Principles	Roles
Co-initiation Co-design	Users', clients' organisations	Mid- to first-line management	Inclusion, fairness, social justice	Assessing needs, designing services
Co-governance	Civil society organisations	Politician, senior management	Democracy, participation, influence, power balancing, sense-making, consensus	Decision-making about goals, tools and principles
Co-management	Civil society organisation representatives	Senior-management, mid-management	Effectiveness, efficiency, negotiation	Organising and managing services
Co-production/ co-implementation	Citizens, users, clients	First-line management, front-line workers and professionals	Innovativeness, effectiveness, efficacy	Delivering services
Co-evaluation	Non-public actors involved in service delivering	Mid-management and front-line workers and professionals	Meaningfulness, accountability, transparency	Learning about service improvement
Maintenance Scaling	All non-public actors (stakeholders)	Front-line workers and professionals, mid-management	Sustainability, replicability/ transferability	Implementing learnings, sharing insights

roles are delegated to neutral actors outside the organisations to help structure the processes and bring in fresh perspectives.

Co-creation of value may take place at all policy or service development stages, and along several dimensions such as governance, management or maintenance. Table 4.2 provides an overview of what roles (tasks and activities) public managers and professionals usually engage in from the perspective of a co-creative logic, and what are their underpinning principles.

In what follows, we exemplify with two cases from Sweden and Italy how public organisations and service networks or ecosystems may go about supporting the transformation towards co-creation culture in a way that is meaningful and sustainable, and how managers and professionals perform their new roles and tasks (Italy) and grapple with sense-making about them (Sweden).

Engaging first-line managers in cultural change: evidence from Sweden

In this section, we illustrate how a transformative cultural change towards co-creation in service delivery might be facilitated within a municipal organisation, a key social service provider, by shifting management approach and strategies to empower managers and professionals at the street level. Jönköping municipality, Sweden, a partner in the CoSIE project and home for circa 120,000, inhabitants serves as an example. Since 2012, its social services reform programme, and particularly disability services covering 2,098 users and circa 1,400 permanent staff, have been the targets of cultural change. In our longitudinal study conducted during 2018–2020 we sought to disclose the theory of cultural change where the municipal organisation has taken a systemic grip to empower the street level in co-creating social service value. The study has been conducted in the Disability Services Department and especially PA services and relied on participant observations (9), interviews with managers (34) and document analysis. Importantly, it studied how first-line managers were sense-making of the cultural change and testing new practices in a pilot action facilitated by a hired action researcher.

The Jönköping case stood out in the CoSIE project with its favourable legislative and policy environment. The national legislation and policy aspirations since 1993 have been increasingly geared towards enhancing service users', especially those with various impairments, influence in social service delivery. This has contributed to initiating a major shift in the discourse about people with physical or psychosocial impairments by allowing them greater influence in local service delivery with the aim of creating more meaningful and valuable interventions to promote their autonomy and wellbeing. Nevertheless, the reform still faced challenges in securing user participation and influence at the start of the CoSIE project.

Jönköping municipality has been strategically selected to illustrate a case of long-standing organisational commitment to enhance social service value by working with constant improvements through dialogues with lower level management and users. Such commitment is an outcome of years of systematic developmental work with strategic management reform called DIALOGEN (the Dialogue), supported by municipal political boards. Economic austerity and raising citizen awareness of their democratic rights to influence individual social service delivery have also fuelled the necessity of the reform. Since 2012, the organisation has been striving to find ways to support especially its first-line managers in leading their personnel towards a culture of service improvements and innovations that are meaningful for citizens. Disability services require regular interactions with citizens assisted by the services thus providing apt opportunities for co-creation. Yet, co-creation is especially demanding due to individual varieties of physical or cognitive impairments and there was confusion about its practical implementation or sometimes lack of acceptance among both street-level professionals and citizens. By 2018, after several years of extensive work on service improvement, the commitment to the reform and co-creative culture among lower level managers and street-level professionals was still uneven. The senior management has learned that the key challenge is that of shifting the mindsets of first-line managers and personnel in the context of pressing service circumstances, including relatively low pay and low status of care workers, a tendency not to stay in the jobs for long, and the isolated nature of their day-to-day work based in the homes of service users. Through piloting service improvement cases senior managers came to realise that it had to do with strengthening the *incitements* and *competencies* at the street level, which required both building on the already existent tacit knowledge and de-learning, as well as continuously adjusting organisational recourses to support new practices. Next, we consider some key support strategies illustrated with the studied piloting case.

First, senior management has had a key role in reframing overall *social service culture* towards more citizen-oriented and health-promoting values, marking a shift from a culture more heavily reliant on professional judgement. The senior management did not believe that purely reorganising roles and responsibilities will be sufficient for implementing a cultural change. Instead, they actively and persistently engaged in intra-organisational dialogues to convey the key role of citizen-centred values and started to rely on a supportive, more trust-based management style across all managerial levels (see Ferlie and Ongaro, 2015). They put much effort into reframing the engrained transactional approach to service production with the dominant narrative of street-level professionals seen as 'solely responsible for satisfying service user needs' towards a more interactive, relational approach. This included abandoning a user identity as a passive recipient with very limited, sporadic and uneven participation and influence in service implementation decisions for an identity as a more active service co-creator whose knowledge, experiences, abilities, networks and other resources are to be used, where appropriate, within the set legal boundaries, to enhance service value.

The senior management steering took a shape of meta- or transformative governance (Torfing et al, 2016), by either initiating or *supporting platforms for multiple dialogues* on change initiatives across the manager levels and individual departments, sometimes including citizens. The early manager dialogues have led towards a series of organisational and service improvements that were selected from circa 1,500 ideas, although far from all of those instantly/ directly dealt with value co-creation with citizens.

Additionally, the senior management did implement several major reorganisations. One of those was abandoning multi-layered hierarchy, and *delegating more power* and responsibilities to first-line managers in implementing the reform intentions. First-line managers and their personnel were seen as the ultimate change actors in the strategic steering towards co-creative culture. These managers were to set the operational goals for their service units (guided by the DIALOGEN overarching goals of meaningful, coherent and innovative services) and contribute in selecting their assessment criteria. Such management logics required that ideas for testing service improvements stemmed from the initiatives of first-line managers and their personnel. This way, senior management engaged circa 200 first-line managers not only in implementing but also in co-governing and co-managing the cultural shift towards co-creation.

To illustrate, in our studied PA services the senior management has approved of initiating a service improvement that evolved from dialogues among mid-managers for the PA service unit and the first-line managers. The pilot was focusing on health promotion as a service value to be co-created with users. The senior management has further chosen to support the entrepreneurial mid-manager acting as change leader in initiating a sense-making with the 17 first-line managers about what changes could be necessary, why and how they could be achieved. This was a journey to be primarily undertaken jointly by the 17 managers who, in turn, had to further explore it with their personnel.

As part of this strategy the senior management allocated resources to *pedagogical development* to support first-line managers and service personnel in the entire Disability Services Department. These pedagogical professionals could, for example, assist with dialogical approach when planning or implementing services in citizens' homes; for more overarching service improvements they helped to organise focus group interviews or participatory chain dialogues with groups of citizens and professionals and assisted the communication of feedback between these groups until an agreement is reached.

In the Jönköping pilot, senior management allocated resources for manager meetings and hired an experienced dialogue facilitator, a researcher with a solid professional background in social service management and organisational development. The researcher proved to be a valuable support, within given resource and organisational limitations. She applied action research principles to help structure and advance the learning dialogues among first-line managers towards their chosen improvements whose need was clearly voiced among service users. Additional pedagogical resources were used to explore the voices and lived stories of the service users, mostly in small focus groups, following sound ethical principles. A key driving principle in reforming services was a 'salutogenic' perspective (Antonovsky, 1996), according to which any service improvements were to be guided by an assessment of their coherence, that is, if change is seen as understandable, meaningful and possible to implement. The action researcher applied similar principles that she expected first-line managers to apply in their dialogues with personnel – the deep listening, disturbing the established narrative, and providing new evidence and perspectives while at the same time recognising their capabilities and resources. It was cultivating a more open and supportive culture with positive examples from their own reality and the support they received from exploring selected literature with the facilitator in study circles that had mainly helped to initiate and sustain a healthful transformation in their narrative. The dialogues and group work with desired changes offered new insights about available organisational resources and strategies to deploy those, including broader competence development tools.

While the senior management actively engaged in sense-giving (Gioia and Chittipeddi, 1991) by laying out the overarching goals, strategies of the reform and co-creative principles, they also adopted *a learning approach*. They had opened up to the fact that initiating piloting changes faced some resistance among implementing first-line managers and personnel. Examples from studied housing or PA indicate that at the early pilot stage far from all first-line managers were comfortable with leading their personnel through the landscape of change. As a group they felt stuck in a disabling narrative about their identities and roles in supporting co-creation on a daily basis, their powerlessness or hindrances presented by inadequate administrative routines, resources, and failures in attracting and retaining qualified personnel. In the case of our pilot, by way of consulting with employed action researchers the senior management came to understand change among front-line workers and managers as largely dependent on their joint sense-making processes (Alvesson and Sveningsson, 2015), where some facilitation from engaged researchers has been appreciated.

A major challenge for first-line managers was seeing themselves as capable change leaders while often being new to the job, working with service changes and being accountable to each other primarily in small fragmented teams, managing sense-making with constantly rotating personnel groups and with limited possibilities to support them from a distance in users' homes. The regular dialogues over a year resulted in drawing and committing to joint change vision, exposing their perceptions, fears and vulnerabilities to each other in a larger assistance services group and, gradually, by sense-making together, rediscovering their strengths and abilities, new ways to support each other. The joint sense-making with support from action research and drawing upon open deliberation and joined study circles has contributed in shifting towards a more empowering narrative (Narbutaité Aflaki and Lindh, 2021). These are all examples of co-designing, co-managing and co-implementing micro- or service-level changes.

The co-creation discourse and DIALOGEN reform basically reflected the implementation of 'old', legally established users' rights of participation and self-determination. However, an important part of resistance was due to the street-level professionals facing a dilemma with their identities – was co-creation about de-professionalisation or re-professionalisation? In our pilot, after a series of joinet dialogues the first-line managers have come to the conclusion that co-creation does not imply letting the user with impairments decide in all legally approved assistance matters, which to them signalled a 'let go' attitude towards the user or de-professionalisation. Instead, allowing user influence in co-creating service value requires a delicate balancing between the professional approach and enacting the user's right to influence her own autonomy and wellbeing, an approach described as 'responsible care mentality'. Re-professionalisation was understood as identifying service design or delivery situations with attentiveness to a user's opinion or choice and encouragement of user participation and influence. Their joined understanding of co-creation could be paraphrased as a collaborative approach allowing to openly question: 'With whom and how can I figure out how personal assistance [services] can be meaningful and useful in user's everyday life?' As a result, acting as change actors, they looked over and simplified the language used in communicating with users, strengthened collaboration on user cases, and introduced more dialogue-based meeting routines, starting with those for first-time service users.

By the end of the pilot, the major concerns of the first-line managers remained sustaining their joint learning dialogues and scaling out such dialogues to their personnel groups, which, given constant personnel rotation, was perceived as a never-ending journey. There was, however, a greater appreciation among managers at all levels that shifting organisational culture and routines on a daily basis requires time, persistence and relevant resources and strategies to support and engage lower managers and care workers in sense-making and providing feedback. Overall, piloting micro-level changes was presumed to be a ground for learning and gradually effecting systemic change. Such half-evolutional, half-steered change, however, was a time-consuming process. When the pilot ended, the cross-unit learning from it was still embryonic, with remaining unclarities in responsibilities and challenges in prioritising between the organisational aims.

Our findings indicate, nevertheless, that the systemic grip of the service management reform in Jönköping municipality has created a momentum towards an organisational culture and professional ethos accommodating greater user influence. The strategic and facilitatory role of senior management and the change leadership at the front line has not been finally shaped, if it ever will be, and the testing and learning is ongoing.

Co-creating an app for the prevention of childhood obesity: evidence from Italy

The Italian pilot in the CoSIE project was about innovative service contributions in preventing and reducing the incidence of childhood obesity in the territory of the Reggio Emilia, a municipality in the Emilia-Romagna region in the north-east of Italy. By the start of the pilot, Reggio Emilia already had an ongoing multilevel and multi-target programme for the prevention and management of childhood obesity known as 'Bimbi Molto in forma' (BMInforma). This was aimed at linking health promotion and primary prevention (building an environment where healthy choices are easier) with secondary prevention (counselling and motivational interviews with overweight children) and the treatment of obesity complications (multidisciplinary team interventions for obese children).

The major CoSIE pilot objective was implementing, with the help of researchers from University of Bologna, new co-creation strategies to improve and develop the BMInforma programme and to strengthen the collaboration networks in the various areas of prevention and treatment of childhood obesity. One of these innovative strategies was the co-creation of a digital tool, an app, as a response to the obesity epidemic among children and young people. For more detail about this app (named 'BeBa'), see Box 4.1.

Box 4.1: The BeBa app

Besides professionals, BeBa targeted the family members of children aged 0–13 to facilitate parent–pediatrician collaboration on the prevention of overweight and childhood obesity, promote healthy eating behaviours, and provide motivation to exercise. BeBa is based on the idea of nudging, where each completed action provides a score and parents can see the progress of each child. The parent can mark two of the activities as 'carried out', namely, participation in a suggested physical activity and after making a proposed recipe. An essential condition for its use and its effectiveness is that the data provided by the app have a value for families as they come from an authoritative source. The app creators ensured transparent and responsible information sharing in line with the ethical requirements of the Italian National Health System. Children's wellbeing is powered by an existing backend service management system to which an easy-to-use interface has been associated with a user management function, intended for those who need to enter, modify and update the information in the various sections and functions of the app. The parent has the right to activate geolocation in order to receive information relating to the initiative in their local area. The app does not collect any personal data of the parent and very generic anonymous information about a child.

BeBa was created and later put to test by the pilot partners Lepida (a publicly owned private agency that provides ICT services for the Regional Health Service) and the Reggio Emilia health authority (AUSL), with the support of the University of Bologna. The development of the app engaged numerous stakeholders operating through a series of topic-specific working groups. Contributors included service professionals, the local Institution of Schools and Nursery Schools, the health authority's sports medicine service, sports associations, and the company running school catering services. The meetings of the working groups were numerous and lasted a year or sometimes longer. The functionalities of the app were designed and developed from the information collected from these groups, clearly indicating collaborative cross-sectoral and cross-organisational co-creation by active players committed to the prevention of childhood obesity in the entire Emilia-Romagna region. Chapter 8 returns to this pilot and examines in depth co-governance across the diverse plurality of actors. Here we focus on the perspective of the main front-line professional group, in this case paediatricians.

There was of course some resistance, especially at the beginning of the Italian pilot, from the paediatricians, to getting involved in co-creation of the app due to the fear of additional workload. Initially, they showed some disappointment towards their senior managers for getting involved with this and many other European Union projects without being asked about their interest or capacities, as well as for lack of monetary incentives especially in terms of compensating for the extra time that they had to spend on the realisation of these projects. Finally, the resistance was also fuelled by perceived insufficient sharing and learning from the results of these projects that were often retained at the central level in the structure. In the pilot, these resistances were gradually overcome thanks to the contributions of two female paediatricians who acted as 'informal leaders' due to the high reputation and esteem they held among the professional community. They played the role of catalysts and bridges between the paediatricians and the pilot leaders, facilitating a two-way communication and helping to convince even the more sceptical ones of the value in testing co-creation within the frame of the CoSIE project: "Communicating with people you do not know and with whom you are not used to work is tiring but what you do in this way of working makes the difference" (paediatrician, Italy).

The Italian case clearly showcased the challenge of joining several professions and professional and lay knowledge and in a fruitful dialogue. The dialogue succeeded in being sustained for over a year largely thanks to the ability of the leader of the project to motivate the actors and create a welcoming climate for dialogue, where he avoided putting his formal authority above the others, but acted as a peer and, by active and deep listening, allowed other professionals, managers and laymen to step in and make their perspectives visible.

Additionally, any time that there was a disagreement among different positions in the professional community and inside the bureaucracy structure, the research team acted as a buffer, able to absorb the tensions and to reduce the potential of conflict among the actors involved. The researchers contributed with 'scientific legitimacy' for the choices made by the steering committee concerning the choice of the service, methodology adopted and the tools employed during the project, given the high reputation rank of the University of Bologna among the health professionals. Moreover, the researchers introduced the European dimension and possibilities to compare the pilot co-creation experiences with those of the other nine project countries, which was particularly appreciated by senior and middle managers. The fact that the facilitated dialogues took place in a neutral arena ('Luoghi di prevenzione'), Emilia-Romagna Center for the Training of Social and Health Care Workers, made it easier to open up for more power equilibrated dialogues.

Overall, the Italian pilot, similarly to the Swedish one, illustrates professional resistance or at least confusion when facing co-creative norms and roles. Creating platforms for joined and fair deliberation and self-reflection, and engaging trustworthy and change-motivated facilitators seem to be a key mechanism to lower resistance and increase engagement. Such platforms, in turn, require top management and political decision makers who are supportive of experimentation.

Conclusion

We can summarise the key elements that emerged from the project empirical analysis, here exemplified by the Swedish and Italian pilot cases, as facilitatory in improving the propensity of front-line managers and street-level professionals to engage in co-creation processes:

1. *Involving* middle managers, front-line managers and service professionals from the very early phases in the co-design of the service innovations or improvements.
2. *Shifting lower manager roles and responsibilities* from pure administrative to leadership tasks, such as by delegating power in setting operational goals, assessment criteria.
3. *Establishing a system of incentives* in order to motivate public managers and professionals to engage themselves in the co-creation activities by self-selection and building an enabling organisational/administrative environment. For example, allowing flexible working time schedules, creating monetary incentives (allocating additional time and resources); providing the needed technical tools; helping to recruit the right competences; and easing the administrative burden to free more time for development and learning.
4. *Finding* someone with high reputation or authority and knowledge who is capable to act as a *process catalyst and/or facilitator* both inside his/

her professional community in sense-making about the cultural change, and in a bridging role across professions, service units or organisational boundaries. This is especially imperative in highly professionalised human services (such as healthcare or social services).

5. *Supporting* street-level professionals in their role as reflective practitioners and key change agents, and lower level managers as change leaders *with appropriate pedagogical training* on collaborative and co-creative approach, preferably by engaging community stakeholders and concerned citizens.

The CoSIE project results show that street-level professionals may be involved in various co-creation stages beyond co-implementation and maintenance, including initiation, governance and management (see Table 4.2). Indeed, for co-creation logics to be implemented and sustained it is not enough to involve one managerial level, rather, the change has to transpire all the way through organisational hierarchies and across organisational silos and boundaries. Yet, any attempts to govern towards co-creation may fail unless front-line managers and professionals are motivated or feel that they have some freedom and support to explore their identities and shape roles, and that the change is meaningful. It seems that front-line managers and professionals' motivation, rather than their purely formal roles, provides a good start for building a common ground, while support from senior managers and politicians justifies the efforts and enables the longer-term sustainment. A good way to prepare for the new roles proved to be, in line with earlier arguments, the need to develop a culture of learning (Torfing et al, 2016). This was achieved by designing platforms for dialogue and support to help to continuously reflect, sense-make about changing service aims, principles, roles and their translation into practice.

In conclusion, embedding co-creation as an integral part of the professional and front-line manager approach in an organisational culture or service system that still partly operates under a mixture of TPA and NPM logics needs to be seen as a process in making, or a metaphorical 'train journey'. The destination of the journey is shifting to adapt to constantly changing political, social and economic dynamics and service demands. Cultural change is challenging, it often faces resistance, involves backward steps, and takes time and consistency. It requires political courage and top-management guidance and support in prioritising values and goals.

References

Alvesson, M. and Sveningsson, S. (2015) *Changing Organisational Culture*, London: Routledge.

Ansell, C. and Torfing, J. (2021) *Public Governance as Co-Creation: A Strategy for Revitalizing the Public Sector and Rejuvenating Democracy*, Cambridge: Cambridge University Press.

Antonovsky, A. (1996) 'The salutogenic model as a theory to guide health promotion', *Health Promotion International*, 11(1): 11–18.

Bassi, A. (2022) 'The unintended consequences of co-creation in public services: the role of professionals and of civil society organizations', *Public Money & Management*, 42(5): 302–303.

Bassi, A. and Fabbri, A. (2022) 'Co-production paradigm: threat or opportunity for social economy?', in Bance, P., Bouchard, M.-J. and Greiling, D. (eds) *New Perspectives in the Co-Production of Public Policies, Public Services and Common Goods*, Liège: CIRIEC, pp 99–123. http://doi.org/10.25518/ciriec.css3chap5

Boyle, D. and Harris, M. (2009) *The Challenge of Co-production: How Equal Partnerships between Professionals and the Public are Crucial to Improving Public Services*, London: NESTA.

Falk, P. (2021) 'Towards a public sector data culture: data as an individual and communal resource in progressing democracy', in Concilio, G., Pucci, P., Raes, L. and Mareels, G. (eds) *The Data Shake: Opportunities and Obstacles for Urban Policy Making*, Cham: Springer, pp 35–45.

Ferlie, E. and Ongaro, E. (2015) *Strategic Management in Public Service Organisations*, London: Routledge.

Gioia, D.A. and Chittipeddi, K. (1991) 'Sensemaking and sensegiving in strategic change initiation', *Strategic Management Journal*, 12(6): 433–448.

Hartley, J. (2005) 'Innovation in governance and public services: past and present', *Public Money and Management*, 25(1): 27–34.

Iveroth, E. and Hallencreutz, J. (2016) *Effective Organizational Change: Leading through Sensemaking*, London: Routledge.

Jalonen, H. and Helo, T. (2020) 'Co-creation of public service innovation using open data and social media: rhetoric, reality, or something in between?', *International Journal of Innovation in the Digital Economy*, 11(3): 64–77.

Lipsky, M. (1980) *Street-Level Bureaucracy: Dilemmas of the Individual in Public Services*, New York: Russell Sage Foundation.

Lüscher, L.S. and Lewis, M.W. (2008) 'Organizational change and managerial sensemaking: working through paradox', *Academy of Management Journal*, 51(2): 221–240.

Narbutaité Aflaki, I. (2021) 'Implementing co-creation as a policy norm in Sweden: steering strategies for a robust organisation', *The Polish Political Science Review*, 9(2): 89–106.

Narbutaité Aflaki, I. and Lindh, M. (2021) 'Empowering first-line managers as change leaders towards co-creation culture: the role of facilitated sensemaking', *Public Money & Management*. https://doi.org/10.1080/09540962.2021.2007636

Osborne, S.P. (2018) 'From public service-dominant logic to public service logic: are public service organizations capable of co-production and value co-creation?', *Public Management Review*, 20(2): 225–231.

Osborne, S. and Strokosch, K. (2013) 'It takes two to tango? Understanding the co-production of public services by integrating the services management and public administration perspectives', *British Journal of Management*, 24(S1): S31–S47. https://doi.org/10.1111/1467–8551.12010

Sörensen, E. and Torfing, J. (2022) 'The three orders of public innovation: implications for research and practice', *Nordic Journal of Innovation in the Public Sector*, 1(1): 35–52.

Taylor, I. and Kelly, J. (2006) 'Professionals discretion and public sector reform in the UK: revisiting Lipsky', *International Journal of Public Sector Management*, 19(7): 625–642.

Torfing, J., Sørenssen, E. and Røiseland, A. (2016) 'Transforming the public sector into an arena for co-creation: barriers, drivers, benefits and ways forward', *Administration and Society*, 51(5): 795–825.

Tummers, L. (2012) 'The policy alienation of public professionals: the construct and its measurements', *Public Administration Review*, 72(4): 516–525.

5

Co-creating with marginalised young people: social media and social hackathons

Heli Aramo-Immonen and Hanna Kirjavainen

Introduction

This chapter focuses on insights from a pilot conducted in Finland. The Finnish Co-creation of Service Innovation in Europe (CoSIE) pilot, 'Youth Co-empowerment', was targeted to young people not in employment, education or training (so-called NEETs). The rationale behind the pilot was the importance to gain understanding about their situations and challenges, as well as to pilot new ways to involve them in society.

The numbers of young NEETs are remarkable in the Western societies. In Finland, among 20–24-year-olds, there were approximately 38,000 NEET young people in 2018, 11.8 per cent of the whole age group (Valtioneuvosto, 2019). The challenges these young people are facing relate to unemployment, lack of education, mental health problems, lack of hobbies, bullying, inability to act and loneliness (Halme et al, 2018), as well as to the cross-generational nature of disadvantage, stemming from the parents' lack of social, cultural and material resources (Erola et al, 2017). However, NEET is by no means a homogeneous group but consists of a myriad of sub-groups including substance abusers, those with different kinds of mental disabilities, and the socially withdrawn. Thus, the term 'marginalised young people', although widely used, is problematic as it simplifies the matter too much (Aaltonen, 2016).

The starting point of the Finnish CoSIE pilot was to amplify the young people's own voice, as too often professionals, researchers and other adults speak on their behalf. The project team aimed to tackle this problem by hearing opinions directly from young people using three different methods: digital storytelling, social hackathons and social media. The multifaceted nature of the target group supported the need for several approaches because providing only one kind of co-creation method, especially traditional ones emphasising the ability to form and voice one's opinions and preferences, disfavours those with mental or physical disabilities or social problems (Brandsen, 2021).

The pilot undertook needs analysis consisting of earlier research, discussions with relevant actors and Community Reporter interviews. Community Reporting is a digital storytelling method (for more detail see Chapter 7). It has proved useful for the needs assessment phase of projects in public service co-creation, enabling people to tell authentic stories about their lives and experiences (Keller et al, 2019; Trowbridge and Willoughby, 2020). The interviews were implemented by university students, who used their own networks to contact the target group and approached young people on the streets of Turku to gain true insight from them. The most important findings were that the sense of purpose and meaning and a well-structured identity are key issues protecting young people from marginalisation. Many interviewees were content with the public services even though they had not been able to help them. Almost all brought up their loneliness and the need for informal peer contacts.

Social hackathons and encountering training

Hackathon – a term derived from 'hack' and 'marathon' – has roots dating back 50 years, to programming at the Massachusetts Institute of Technology (Zukin and Papadantonakis, 2017). During the 1990s the phenomenon evolved into IT-community-wide two-day co-creation events between project managers, graphic and interface designers. Contemporarily, hackathons spread beyond the conventional tech world to educational, creative, social, corporate and government sectors due to their inclusiveness – the so-called 'come-one-come-all ethos' (Briscoe and Mulligan, 2014; Kienzler and Fontanesi, 2017; Zukin and Papadantonakis, 2017; Suominen et al, 2018).

Traditionally business hackathons incorporate the feature of innovation in team level 'coopetition' (meaning concurrent collaboration and competition) as well as 'pitching', which refers to condensed verbal presentation (Briscoe and Mulligan, 2014; Suominen et al, 2018). Hackathons have recently spilled over also to the educational sector, providing a promising methodology for teaching fuzzy front end of innovation in higher education institutions. Educational hackathons, as one particular focus area of hackathons, have not yet been thoroughly researched beyond the IT industry (Porras et al, 2018; Suominen et al, 2018). Social hackathons are distinct from business and educational hackathons. The focal stage of a social hackathon is co-creation.

Social hackathons typically utilise the inclusiveness of the method and mitigate the competitive edge. Co-creation in social hackathons has a special meaning. Co-creation, as we understand it, is around collective innovation, trialling and experimentation. It involves, engages and is led by citizens and people who use services. Therefore the assignment in social hackathons is coming among the users themselves, not from service providers.

According to Suominen et al (2018), the innovation process generally includes four phases of which idea generation is considered the first one (Salerno et al, 2014), also called the fuzzy front end of innovation (Koen et al, 2001). Experimentation, continuous exploration and exploration, for example, is regarded one of the focal innovative competences, which needs to be strengthened, especially in static and rule-based environments (Bozic Yams, 2017), like public service production in the traditional way. However, exploitation of an individual's own resources and capabilities requires cooperation with others (Aramo-Immonen et al, 2015). In social hackathons, co-creation, at its best, emerges in dialogue between users and public service providers. Initiative, however, should come from the user side.

The social hackathon in practice

In the Finnish pilot, the main aim was to find out new ways and methods for involving NEET young people in co-creation processes, in order to increase their participation in the society. The rationale was the importance to understand better the many shades of marginalisation and, thus, find purposeful ways to reach and include the young people outside the system into public service design and delivery. During the project, our understanding of the target group's multifaceted nature became even more profound than before and, thus, it was clear that several approaches needed to be piloted in order to make the group of young participants more various and enabling more diverse voices to be heard (see Brandsen, 2021). Probably the most important method tested during the pilot was a *social hackathon*, implemented twice in the spring of 2019 in the city of Turku. The form of the hackathon was altered from its original counterpart, as they lasted only one day each. The duration was decided because we anticipated that it would be difficult to get young people and professionals to commit to a long-lasting endeavour.

In line with Lember (2018), social hackathons used in the pilot represented both a method of co-creation as well as a source for co-creation initiatives. They were attended by young people and Turku city officials and front-line workers, as well as by professionals from several non-government organisations (NGOs), the employment office, Ohjaamo youth guidance centre, a vocational school and the social insurance institution of Finland. The actual ideating and developing work were done in small groups, which the participants were divided into after a short activity aimed at them getting to know each other better and make the atmosphere more relaxed and safe. These groups consisted of both young people and professionals and one project team member who facilitated the process. The participants found the arrangement, which enabled an equal standing for young people and professionals alike, especially inspiring.

'We [young people and professionals] set ourselves in the same boat, instead of adults always telling how young people should act. We got input and encouragement from each other. I got the feeling that I could do more of this. I learned about myself and about my work. The events [the pilot arranged] were learning opportunities.' (Leader of Vamos NGO in Turku)

The group work started with empathising activities, as the participants were presented with a fictitious case. In this 'ice breaking' example, young people's situations were described, including their specific problems and ambitions. These cases were based on the profiles created earlier in the project after the Community Reporting interviews. The decision to utilise these profiles was made, so that the young people did not feel any pressure to open up about their personal situations and problems. They were naturally allowed to do that if they so wished. Indeed, many expressed themselves very openly about their past challenges and how have they been able to overcome them during the case discussions.

These groups were given a task to anticipate the challenges, ambitions and aims that the young people described in the case might have, and what kind of activities could help the young person move forward. Based on this, groups were asked to formulate a beneficial goal, which would enable the young people to achieve their aims. After this, groups carried on with brainstorming different kind of ideas, with which the decided goal could be achievable. Next, they selected one of the ideas and finally proceeded with formulating a concept of the solution they considered the best possible option. At the end of the workshop, groups built a prototype with Lego blocks, pitched it to others and received feedback in a supportive and positive atmosphere.

We chose to have as participants mainly young people who had overcome the most difficult times in their lives, as we found this to be a more sound solution ethically. These young people were also better able to contribute as they were more capable of analysing their own path and the factors that had influenced their choices and situations and, also, what had helped them personally. The pilot team was conscious of the safety of the young participants who opened up about their own lives in the workshops and offered them the opportunity to talk hypothetically through the profiles, which proved successful. Most of the young people said they could recognise themselves and their peers in the profiles.

The project team was impressed by the skills, enthusiasm and openness of the young participants: especially since we were told repeatedly by professionals at the beginning of the pilot how difficult it would be to attract young people to join co-creation activities. Fortunately, this proved wrong and demonstrated that the young people are actually very capable and willing to participate, if the method is suitable and the topic is important for them: "Everything was new to me. Creating a new thing was a new process for me. The idea phase, creativity. Plenty of new things" (young person involved in the pilot process). The project team got plenty of good ideas and concepts from the hackathons, such as new kinds of meeting points, mobile apps about services with augmented reality, and mobile games increasing one's social capability.

The encountering training

Turku University of Applied Sciences (UAS) took responsibility for implementing one of the ideas: a course on how professionals should encounter a young client. This idea stemmed from young people's personal experiences of how professionals focus on the computer instead of them during the appointments, are not mentally present, and have prejudices or express a sense of hurry and haste. The course was co-created with Turku UAS lecturers, university students and an NGO called Tukenasi and this NGO's youth development panel. The training is revolutionary because it is not only developed but also led by young people who have experience of difficult situations and service usage.

The course aims for the professionals to learn to reflect better one's own ways of working, to learn to encounter the young client individually and with genuine interest, and to learn how to provide services flexibly, according to young people's individual needs. The training begins with an independent self-reflection questionnaire about how the participant perceives their own encountering skills, followed by workshop activities done in small groups, which are steered by young people. Themes these workshops cover are the courage to ask, how the young client truly is, the courage and ability to trust the experiences they tell without prejudices, and the sensitivity to notice the potential need of help behind the 'mask' the young people might have built.

The training course has won an innovation award from the Finnish National Children's Foundation, ITLA, in a competition that searched for innovative ideas on how to get children and young people heard in the decision-making processes. It is sustained by Tukenasi NGO, who has been awarded a grant to continue the training and develop it even further. Several actors, such as the cities of Turku and Helsinki and trade unions, have bought this training and it has been implemented both on-site and online. Turku UAS or Tukenasi do not benefit from this training, but the young trainers were recompensed for their time. Organisations are able to order this training from the website www.kohtaamiskoulutus.fi. Moreover, Turku UAS, together with the University of Turku, has created a one-credit massive open online course about how to encounter young people as clients. In addition to being open to everyone, this course has been included in several curricula in the social and educational field.

'The encountering training is great. Young people have been genuinely able to develop things. The pilot was ideal model for co-creation already at the idea phase and especially at the implementing phase. The product is a step forward; there is truly results from this work. We have proceeded quite far: hearing [young people] is common but they don't have the access to actually do things. Usually young people are tools to adults; this is turned around in the final product. Young people were able to do genuine influencing work.' (Youth worker from Tukenasi NGO in Turku)

'It has been fantastic to get to influence the surrounding society. Something that you wouldn't have believed you would be able to do.' (Young person involved in the pilot process)

Social media for co-creation

Social media can be defined as a group of internet-based applications that build on the technological and ideological foundations of Web 2.0 and that enable the creation and sharing of user-generated content (Kaplan and Haenlein, 2010). Social media are often referred to as applications that are either fully based on user-generated content or in which user-generated content and the actions of users have a significant role in increasing the value of the application or the service (Kangas et al, 2007). A large number of social media application categories have been identified in the literature: wikis (for example, Wikia and Confluence), blogs (for example, WordPress and Blogger), microblogs (for example, Twitter), social networking sites (for example, Facebook, Instagram, LinkedIn, Yammer, Socialcast), discussion forums (for example, phpBB), open or private communities (for example, Jive, Lithium community platform), content-sharing sites (for example, YouTube, SlideShare, Flickr, and Pinterest), social office tools (for example, Google Docs), social bookmarking (for example, Delicious), mashups (for example, Google Maps), and virtual social worlds (for example, Second Life) (Jussila et al, 2015). Understanding how social media facilitates the exchange of knowledge in the co-creation context is vital in order to manage digital public service innovation processes. The social media creates both great opportunities and benefits for knowledge sharing, new knowledge creation and, as a result, platforms for co-creation. However, at the same time, social media creates new challenges for information and knowledge risk management (Väyrynen et al, 2013; Aramo-Immonen et al, 2016).

Jussila and Aramo-Immonen (2016) conducted a longitudinal study among Finnish university students between 2012 and 2016. The results of the survey brought understanding on the perceived social media risks originating from internal (personal) sources and involving sociological, psychological and cognitive barriers. They identified 34.5 per cent sociological barrier-based risks, 34.5 per cent psychological and 13.8 per cent cognitive barrier-based risk, but only 10.3 per cent technical barrier-based sources. In frequency order among top ten risks of all 128 findings were 33.5 per cent sociological barrier-based risks, 16.4 per cent technical, 7 per cent psychological and 6 per cent cognitive barrier-based risks. The most perceived risk was technical barrier-based information security, in other words, fear of losing personal information due to technological failure. In the group of social barrier-based risk were privacy issues, perceived reputation and public image, intellectual property right risks, and fear of spreading incorrect information and information misuse, for example.

As a part of the CoSIE project, Turku UAS developed a cloud-based software application called Luuppi, to lower the threshold for researchers and developers to use social media as data. Social media served to reach those who did not want to participate in traditional workshops. Almost all Finnish young people use social media channels. The Luuppi app enabled real-time retrieval of social media data as well as the visual and interactive presentation of the results of the analyses. It was used together with artificial intelligence for analysing messages published in Hikikomero, an anonymous chat room that is part of the Ylilauta discussion forum, dedicated to depressed and socially withdrawn people, who face challenges with social interaction (see Jalonen et al, 2021).

Social media utilisation in practice

Digital technology was used in CoSIE pilots in different ways to support the co-creation activities. We shall take a closer look at how this was done the Finnish pilot among 'hard to reach' young people. One example of a social media tool used was the Jodel platform where the focus group members were reached in the Finnish context. The Finnish pilot used data and information and communications technology (ICT) tools in three levels: scanning and creating context; classifying data with the Luuppi tool; and manually analysing collected data. Topic modelling and machine learning algorithms were used (Jalonen et al, 2021). In addition, locally available digital technologies (for example, mobile phone videos) and ICT (for example, email and various chats) were used to support conversations and relationship-building and to gather and share lived experience stories.

Different Finnish national open data sources were used to gather knowledge about the pilot city's young people and also about wellbeing management in the city of Turku. Social media data was curated in order to highlight different points of views from the target group (the Ylilauta Finnish discussion board and image form and a particular imageboard, Hikikomero). The Finnish pilot produced a dataset of lived experience stories.

It was learned that social media can have a more powerful effect than one single case indicator and social media and case indicators combined are a good way to understand the reality of 'hard to reach' young people. It was evidenced that in order to increase understanding, we need to acknowledge valuable information about the bottlenecks experienced in the co-creation system (for example, via social media data). Utilising this information, fine-tuning of the service can be done in public administration communications. Social media data offers powerful direct feedback because of its anonymity. Social media is one channel to reach young people but not better than the direct face-to-face connection through friends or trusted partners like NGOs. However, social media and the open data should be involved strongly in the planning phase of co-creation projects.

Data are sometimes hard to gather and use. Social media data are not easily locatable to one particular source, such as a city or service. The data are often on the national level. The quality of the social media data is a question mark because they are anonymous. Still, it offers powerful direct feedback. Today, social media is more and more based on pictures and not so much on text. Therefore, new ways to analyse are needed. It is difficult to know the right social media channels to find the target groups. In the different channels there are different sub-groups. During the CoSIE project, Jalonen et al (2021) summarised the potential of digital technology use in co-creation as follows:

> The current research illustrates that digital technologies can be used to capture large datasets, creating the big picture and framing the data in a meaningful way. The use of social media discussions in the co-creation of public services is also in line with the OECD's (2019) policy recommendations, which emphasize, among others, dialogue between government and citizens and the active collection of civic feedback. However, many managerial tasks need to be prioritized to harness the full potential of digitality, which includes, but is not limited to, acquiring technological expertise, the creation of dynamic and agile organization cultures, encouraging personnel to experiment and boldly applying new and innovative approaches to reach the unreachable with new tools. (Jalonen et al, 2021: 809)

Conclusion

Young people are willing and able to participate and innovate public services more suitable for their needs, if the method is right and they deem the theme important. One of the problems has been that vulnerable young people have traditionally been seen through problem-based lenses and have been excluded from co-creation possibilities as they are considered to be 'too fragile'. Recently, the focus has shifted more to strengths and assets, not dismissing potential risks and challenges but rather seeing them as a part of young people's social habitat (Sanders and Munford, 2014).

Contemporary society, with COVID-19, war in Europe and global warming, contributes to young people's malaise with inequality and polarisation, uncertain prospects for the future and high pressures to succeed. Thus, it is more pressing than ever to try to find ways to reach young people, especially as they are not interested in traditional forms of participation in co-creation but seek new ways of activism to support and promote the subjects they consider important.

References

Aaltonen, S. (2016) 'Challenges in gaining and re-gaining informed consent among young people on the margins of education', *International Journal of Social Research Methodology*, 20(4): 329–341.

Aramo-Immonen, H., Jussila, J.J. and Huhtamäki, J. (2015) 'Exploring co-learning behavior of conference participants with visual network analysis of Twitter data', *Computers in Human Behavior*, 51(Part B): 1154–1162.

Aramo-Immonen, H., Jussila, J.J., Ilvonen, I. and Helander, N. (2016) 'Perceived risks in social media use: a longitudinal study among university students', in García-Peñalvo, F.J. (ed) *TEEM '16: Proceedings of the Fourth International Conference on Technological Ecosystems for Enhancing Multiculturality*, New York: Association for Computing Machinery, pp 777–780.

Bozic Yams, N. (2017) 'Integrated model of innovative competence', *Journal of Creativity and Business Innovation*, 3(2005): 140–169.

Brandsen, T. (2021) 'Vulnerable citizens: will co-production make a difference?', in Loeffler, E. and Bovaird, T. (eds) *The Palgrave Handbook of Co-Production of Public Services and Outcomes*, Cham: Palgrave Macmillan, pp 527–539.

Briscoe, G. and Mulligan, C. (2014) 'Digital innovation: the hackathon phenomenon', *Creativeworks*, 6: 1–13.

Erola, J., Kallio, J. and Vauhkonen, T. (2017) Ylisukupolvinen kasautuva huono-osaisuus Turussa ja muissa Suomen suurissa kaupungeissa [Multi-generational accumulation of disadvantage in Turku and other large cities in Finland]. Turun kaupunki, tutkimuskatsauksia 2/2017 [Finnish research report], https://www.turku.fi/sites/default/files/atoms/files/tutkimuskatsauksia_2-2017.pdf

Halme, N., Hedman, L., Ikonen, R. and Rajala, R. (2018) Lasten ja nuorten hyvinvointi [Wellbeing of Children and Young People]. Kouluterveyskyselyn tuloksia. Työpaperi 15/2018. Terveyden ja hyvinvoinnin laitos, Helsinki [Working Paper, Institute of Health and Welfare], https://www.julkari. fi/handle/10024/136748

Jalonen, H., Kokkola, J., Laihonen, H., Kirjavainen, H., Kaartemo, V. and Vähämaa, M. (2021) 'Reaching hard-to-reach people through digital means: citizens as initiators of co-creation in public services', *International Journal of Public Sector Management*, 34(7): 799–816.

Jussila, J.J. and Aramo-Immonen, H. (2016) 'Experienced risks in social media use – longitudinal study among university students', in Gómez Chova, L., López Martínez, A. and Candel Torres, I. (eds) *Proceedings of the 8th International Conference on Education and New Learning Technologies*, Barcelona: IATED Academy, pp 1255–1260.

Jussila, J., Kärkkäinen, H., Aramo-Immonen, H., Ammirato, S., Felicetti, A.M. and Della Gala, M. (2015) *Social Media Applications in External B2B Transactions: An Empirical Analysis of the Finnish Technology Industry*, IFKAD2015 Bari, 10–12 June.

Kangas, P., Toivonen, S. and Bäck, A. (2007) *'Ads by Google' and Other Social Media Business Models*, Espoo: VTT Technical Research Centre of Finland.

Kaplan, A.M. and Haenlein, M. (2010) 'Users of the world, unite! The challenges and opportunities of social media', *Business Horizons*, 53(1): 59–68.

Keller, J., Virág, T. and Trowbridge, H. (2019) 'Mapping diversity in our neighbourhoods: crossing of two research methods', in Keresztély, K., Barthel, M. and Scott, J. (eds) *Voicitys – Voices of Diversity – Connecting People and Policies for More Integrated Neighbourhoods in European Cities*, Berlin: Comparative Research Network, pp 20–42.

Kienzler, H. and Fontanesi, C. (2017) 'Learning through inquiry: a global health hackathon', *Teaching in Higher Education*, 22(2): 129–142.

Koen, P., Ajamian, G., Burkart, R., Clamen, A., Davidson, J., D'Amore, R., et al (2001) 'Providing clarity and a common language to the "fuzzy front end"', *Research Technology Management*, 44(2): 46–55.

Lember, V. (2018) 'The increasing role of digital technologies in co-production and co-creation', in Brandsen, T., Steen, T. and Verschuere, B. (eds) *Co-Production and Co-Creation: Engaging Citizens in Public Services*, London: Routledge, pp 115–127.

Porras, J., Happonen, A., Khakurel, J., Knutas, A., Ikonen, J. and Herala, A. (2018), 'Hackathons in software engineering education – lessons learned from a decade of events', in *SEEM '18: Proceedings of the 2nd International Workshop on Software Engineering Education for Millennials*, Gothenburg: Association for Computing Machinery, pp 1–8.

Salerno, M.S., Gomes, L.A.D.V., Silva, D.O., Da, Bagno, R.B. and Freitas, S.L.T.U. (2014) 'Innovation processes: which process for which project?', *Technovation*, 35: 59–70.

Sanders, J. and Munford, R. (2014) 'Youth-centred practice: positive youth development practices and pathways to better outcomes for vulnerable youth', *Children and Youth Services Review*, 46: 160–167.

Suominen, A.H., Jussila, J., Lundell, T., Mikkola, M. and Aramo-Immonen, H. (2018) 'Educational hackathon: innovation contest for innovation pedagogy', in Bitran, I., Conn, S., Huizingh, K.R.E., Kokshagina, O., Torkkeli, M. and Tynnhammar, M. (eds) *Proceedings of the 2018 ISPIM Innovation Conference*, Stockholm: Lappeenranta University of Technology (LUT) Scientific and Expertise Publications.

Trowbridge, H. and Willoughby, M. (2020) 'Connecting voices, challenging perspectives and catalysing change: using storytelling as a tool for co-creation in public services across Europe', in Scott, J. (ed) *Cross-Border Review*, Budapest: European Institute of Cross-Border Studies – Central European Service for Cross-border Initiatives (CESCI), pp 59–72.

Valtioneuvosto (2019) Koulutuksen ja työn ulkopuolella olevat (NEET) nuoret, katsaus tilanteeseen ja toimenpiteisiin [Overview of the situation and measures for young people not in education and work (NEETs)], https://valtioneuvosto.fi/documents/1410845/4449678/Koulutuksen+ja+ty%C3%B6n+ulkopuolella+olevat+%28NEET%29+nuoret%2C+katsaus+tilanteeseen+ja+toimenpiteisiin/51231944–1fc0–ef0b–fc7a–afc6c975b010/Koulutuksen+ja+ty%C3%B6n+ulkopuolella+olevat+%28NEET%29+nuoret%2C+katsaus+tilanteeseen+ja+toimenpiteisiin.pdf

Väyrynen, K., Hekkala, R. and Liias, T. (2013) 'Knowledge protection challenges of social media encountered by organizations', *Journal of Organizational Computing and Electronic Commerce*, 23(1–2): 34–55.

Zukin, S. and Papadantonakis, M. (2017) 'Hackathons as co-optation ritual: socializing workers and institutionalizing innovation in the "new" economy', in Kalleberg, A.L. and Vallas, S.P. (eds) *Precarious Work*, Bingley: Emerald Publishing, pp 157–181.

6

Digital technology, stigmatised citizens and unfulfilled promises

Sue Baines, Jordan Harrison and Natalie Rutter

Introduction

This chapter reports and reflects on largely unfulfilled promises with regard to the adoption of digital technologies for co-creation. The main empirical focus is co-creation extended to a domain where it appears extremely unpromising, namely criminal justice. The aim of the Co-creation of Service Innovation in Europe (CoSIE) pilot in the UK was to help people on probation become more active participants in their own rehabilitation, build on their strengths and thus embed elements of co-creation in probation. The pilot partner was one of the private sector Community Rehabilitation Companies (CRCs) then contracted to deliver probation services in England for people deemed 'low to medium risk'. The pilot was known as 'My Direction' and took place in the city of Hull in the north of England.

My Direction drew upon learning from social care (Fox and Marsh, 2016) and an earlier small-scale 'proof of concept' pilot in which the university and pilot partner had tested different elements of person-centred practice and co-produced working (Fox et al, 2018). It attempted to include a technological element in the form of a mobile phone application. Although this was only one aspect of the pilot it is the main focus of this chapter, reflecting the commitment of CoSIE to explore digital resources for co-creation as fully as possible. We also consider use of social media and turn briefly to a CoSIE pilot in the Netherlands where it similarly proved hard to take advantage of digital promises. This was a pilot called 'No Time to Waste' in a neighbourhood in the municipality of Nieuwegein, near Utrecht. The neighbourhood faced multiple social problems and residents felt ignored and stigmatised.

Following this introduction, we position My Direction and its digital aspects within theoretical and policy contexts. Then after indicating the sources of data, we summarise the pilot intervention and results, which have been reported in detail elsewhere (Baines et al, 2021). This chapter goes on to focus in more depth upon two aspects: a promising but ultimately unsuccessful attempt to trial a dedicated software application; and a review of relevant social media. We draw attention to some similar and different challenges of the Nieuwegein pilot. The final section reflects on lessons relating to digital ambitions, limitations and set-backs in co-creation.

Criminal justice, innovation and digital technology

Criminal justice is a particularly difficult context for co-creation, and for innovation, because the requirements of justice evoke concepts such as certainty, control, consistency and adherence to well-defined processes (Fox and Marsh, 2016). Co-creation does not sit easily with the Risk, Need and Responsivity (RNR) model dominant in criminal justice. According to its critics, RNR is based on a restricted and overly passive view of human nature and leads to standardised interventions (McNeill and Weaver, 2010). My Direction was informed by a theoretical approach in criminology known as 'desistance'. Desistance contrasts with theories that concentrate on criminological risk. It contends that individuals need to establish an alternative, coherent and pro-social identity in order to justify and maintain cessation from offending. Desistance can be summed up as meaning that an offence-free life is associated with 'viewing oneself as a different person with the capabilities and opportunities to achieve personally endorsed goals' (Ward and Maruna, 2007: 22–23). Although co-creation is quite novel in criminal justice, the theory of desistance emphasises agency, assets and relationships in ways that closely reflect its principles.

Probation is a service that faces a pressing need for innovation to address many challenges, including high reoffending rates, a changing client group, demand for effective interventions and the requirement to achieve 'more-for-less'. Innovation is not invariably conflated with digital technologies but there are high expectations in criminal justice, as in other public services, of mobile tools and apps as well as the promise of unencumbered traffic of digital data (Carr, 2017). For example, in 2019 the then UK Secretary of State for Justice (responsible for prisons and probation in England and Wales) declared the goal of 'harnessing and embracing modern technology … to help deliver the outcomes we all want to see' (Buckland, 2019). Yet efforts to incorporate digital technologies within offender services have been generally underwhelming (Carr, 2017). From the perspective of practitioners, the introduction of digital technology may seem to pose a threat to the personal relationship building they value (Phillips, 2011; Grant and McNeill, 2015).

In other public services including health and care there are many examples of resistance when workers perceive digitalisation as degrading their roles and undermining professional practice (Wastell et al, 2010; McLoughlin and Wilson, 2013; Hamblin, 2022).

Adoption of technology in probation services in the UK has been for control and monitoring rather than exploring its potential for rehabilitative functions (Nellis, 2013). More recently there has been an increase in mobile technology intended to influence behaviour within the criminal justice system (Taylor et al, 2023). Northern Ireland probation services have trialled 'Changing Lives', which claims to be the first app designed to support desistance from crime (McGreevy, 2017). A development in youth offending services in England aims to improve engagement via a smartphone app between youth justice practitioners and young people in conflict with the law (Barn and Barn, 2019). There is, however, a dearth of evidence to indicate that technological solutions are effective in producing pro-rehabilitative outcomes (Smith et al, 2019; Taylor et al, 2023).

CoSIE anticipated that taking advantage of social media would have potential to help enhance public services and engage citizens' voices (Jalonen and Helo, 2020). Commercial social media sites enable citizens to create, share and comment on issues in ways providers and public authorities cannot control (Driss et al, 2019). Members of the public can involve themselves in online communities and engage within real-time comment threads and discussion groups. As a result, there would appear to be potential for greater individual input into services normally dominated by professionals (Brandsen et al, 2018; Torfing et al, 2019). This implies prima facie alignment between social media and co-creation, although the evidence base remains quite weak (Lember et al, 2019).

Particular threats however are associated with the internet for rehabilitation service providers and users. Messages about criminality and criminals are increasingly available online and digital platforms enable members of the public to interact with them instantaneously. Greater access to information via social media can be detrimental to rehabilitation by undermining the 'right to be forgotten' (Dunsby and Howes, 2019). Although research specifically focused on social media and rehabilitation is quite limited there is evidence that people on probation can be harmed by labelling and stigmatisation via online spaces and platforms, and this can impede desistance (Rutter, 2021). Active citizen engagement in online naming and shaming in the context of criminal justice has even been called a form of digital vigilantism (Dunsby and Howes, 2019).

The policy background to this pilot was a major overhaul of the probation service in England known as *Transforming Rehabilitation* (Ministry of Justice, 2013). *Transforming Rehabilitation* involved a split between the national service, which dealt with the most serious offenders and remained in the public sector, and services for low- and medium-risk offenders. The latter were contracted out to the private sector in a reform driven by the conviction that these services would be better provided in a market context (Albertson and Fox, 2019). Part of the rationale was to bring in independent providers who would innovate (Ministry of Justice, 2013). Services that are more personalised including elements of co-creation represent one route to innovation that private providers trialled (Fox et al, 2018).

When My Direction commenced in early 2018 *Transforming Rehabilitation* appeared set to continue. The pilot partner as a private service provider was motivated at least in part by ambitions to build its reputation and become a thought leader in rehabilitation. *Transforming Rehabilitation* however faced increasingly strenuous criticism for failing to meet performance targets. Her Majesty's Chief Inspector of Probation declared it 'irredeemably flawed' (Stacey, 2019: 3). The Ministry of Justice terminated all the CRC contracts two years earlier than expected and in March 2019 announced the return of the whole service to the public sector, only five years after partial privatisation. The pilot was troubled by uncertainty about the future of the company and the service during most of its lifetime.

Data collection

The site in which the pilot and evaluation took place was the probation service for Humberside, Lincolnshire and North Yorkshire. To maximise opportunities for data collection, a researcher (the second author of this chapter) was based in the main office of the service, situated in Hull, between May 2018 and May 2019. He undertook fieldwork for a total of nine months in two phases during which he spent two to three days a week there. Each phase was followed by an intensive period of analysis. Members of the university evaluation team attended monthly pilot implementation meetings and project management meetings. These served as feedback loops allowing interim findings to be shared to inform implementation and decision-making. Data referred to in the chapter were collected by the following activities:

- Semi-structured one-to-one interviews with people on probation, professionals (front-line and senior) and volunteers. There were 48 interviews in total.
- Observation of project meetings, events and interactions.
- Desk-based reviews of project documentation (for example, minutes, marketing material, internal reports, risk assessments).
- Systematic collection, analysis and interpretation of publicly available social media posts about criminal or deviant activity – focusing on those emanating from sources local to the CRC in the pilot.

- Curated stories told by people on probation, staff and volunteers as Community Reporters (available digitally in the public domain).

The evaluation team also undertook quantitative impact evaluation making use of anonymised data sets shared by the CRC for individuals on probation who were not part of the pilot.

Pilot implementation and results

Co-creating probation services

The UK CoSIE pilot implemented a form of co-creation adapted from social care to suit the context of criminal justice, where it is essential to ensure that the sentence of the court is delivered. My Direction required front-line probation staff to work with people on probation throughout the duration of their order to co-design a support plan for their rehabilitation and undertake actions that would allow them to meet their individual and holistic needs. Most of the project's resources were dedicated to coaching for front-line probation workers and providing ongoing support. Exposure to My Direction meant a more personalised service experience, and one that necessitated a greater emphasis on community capacity building. Eighty-four people on probation and nine probation workers (known in the privatised service as case managers) were enrolled onto the pilot.

At the heart of the pilot was the 'Three Conversations Model', adapted from social care while ensuring compliance with the mandated service user journey. This was delivered to all participants. 'Three Conversations' emphasises an individual's strengths and community assets. In the probation context, case managers have three distinct and specific conversations as follows:

- The first conversation (which should take place during the first meeting) seeks to empower people to generate solutions to meet basic practical needs.
- The second conversation aims to provide help when needed and focuses on self-efficacy, wellbeing and motivation to change.
- The third conversation aims to help the person on probation to live their life with a pro-social lifestyle, focusing on achieving longer-term goals and sustained lifestyle change.

The pilot's achievements fell short in many respects of those anticipated. There was an observed difference in reoffending between My Direction participants and a cohort of other individuals supervised in the same probation office over the same time period. Of those enrolled in My Direction, 13.10 per cent reoffended within 12 months whereas slightly more (15.12 per cent) of the 'untreated' group did so. However, assignment to the pilot was not randomised and the groups were unbalanced on various characteristics such as gender, age and risk levels. Regression modelling showed that the observed small reduction in reoffending was not statistically significant. It was therefore not possible to reject the null hypothesis that My Direction had no effect on reoffending outcomes. In other words, impact evaluation did not provide evidence that participation in My Direction reduced the probability of reoffending (Baines et al, 2021).

Nevertheless, qualitative evidence from interviews and observation identified some positive examples of personalisation with individual case managers and people on probation that indicate there was positive change. Training put in place by the pilot to provide probation workers with an understanding of person-centred practice was very well received and they gave positive feedback, reporting especially that it instilled confidence. Staff explained in interviews that person-centred practice promoted dialogue with people on probation and generated mutual understanding. Some individuals on probation also noted a more flexible and responsive experience of the service (Baines et al, 2021).

While the results of this pilot overall appeared rather disappointing, it is important to remember that it was delivered in the context of a turbulent policy environment and unsettling organisational change. The pilot suffered from detrimental effects on morale, workloads and staff turnover. Attempting co-creation at all in the difficult context of criminal justice was in itself a bold innovation. My Direction demonstrated that elements of co-creation can be extended to non-voluntary service contexts despite the many challenges this entails. The evaluation offers some evidence that, despite many setbacks, the co-created, strengths-based model inspired by social care is promising as a strategy for operationalising desistance at the individual level of front-line staff and people on probation, although much more would need to be done to embed change in the system (Baines et al, 2021).

Developing a mobile app for probation

Five additional options in My Direction were intended to supplement person-centred practice and enhance co-creation in the pilot. They were implemented only in very reduced form or not at all, mainly due to the many obstacles faced by the pilot in the light of changes to the service and pressure on time and resources. Only the so-called 'enabling fund' was enacted as planned, although on a smaller scale than originally intended. This fund was modelled on direct payments in social care and involved small cash payments to people on probation to pursue individual goals that the service could not meet. In the context of probation, it was a far-reaching innovation and it encountered some resistance from front-line staff, even those who were generally supportive of the project's strengths-based approach (Baines et al, 2021). One of the unsuccessful options, on which we concentrate here, was a smartphone app.

An application (app) is a program or group of programs executed using a platform and designed for end users. Apps perform a bounded set of operations and can be customised, configured or updated by developers at any point. Typically accessed via a smartphone, mobile apps can be accessed both online and offline, although use offline may be limited. The idea of a smartphone app in probation is not totally new (McGreevy, 2017; Barn and Barn, 2019). The 'Changing Lives' app in Northern Ireland offers advice on how to overcome problems with addiction and mental health, signposts to appropriate services and has a contacts section to ring through to probation staff and other services (McGreevy, 2017). The CRC in Hull worked alongside a private company to build its app. This was not funded within the project but negotiated through personal contacts via the networks of the project manager. At the time, the company was already providing digital solutions mainly to prisons and other services in various locations around the world and its leaders were keen to extend its presence in probation.

Fundamental characteristics of the app design were intended to promote more active participation by people on probation in their rehabilitation. Featuring a user-friendly interface, it promised to facilitate communication between the person on probation and caseworker, enabling different modes of interaction outside one-to-one sessions. Users were to benefit from instant and remote access to individualised sentence plans, license/order information, local service information and rehabilitation programmes using an online platform whereby they could view and store content. The app would support the scheduling of appointments, messages, notifications and reminders, and also deliver motivational messages and encouragement at key points such as after training and learning modules were complete, or other rehabilitative activities had been undertaken. The scheduling/rescheduling of appointments would be delivered in a more efficient way, providing a flexible and efficient alternative to traditional phone calls or texts. Other advanced features were also mentioned. These included live service waiting times, instant messaging, timely notifications and prompts (for example, at stress points), plus feedback, progress reports and a record of achievement, as well as video and time stamping. It was anticipated that all this would increase the likelihood of compliance. Overall, the app aligned with desistance by offering a greater sense of control to empower individuals.

Interest in the mobile phone app was high from senior and front-line staff alike due to its potential to improve the user experience and promote greater involvement of individuals in their rehabilitation. There was no evidence at all of resistance to this form of digital technology. Indeed, the reverse was the case. As one staff member reported in an interview:

'We were really happy and excited about the application. It wasn't going to replace anything; it was instead going to be used as an add-on. We would be using it with those who have a smartphone, the app and discussions were all very exciting and it was definitely something we wished to do.'

In the early months plans to advance the app were reported enthusiastically to monthly project management meetings. Several meetings with the supplier took place and there were arrangements for a representative to attend and deliver training to the case managers on how to use the app. Workers even began to identify individuals on probation who could benefit from using it. However, doubts around data security and regulatory concerns became pressing. It was apparent that the app would require a secure platform to operate from. Accreditation from the Ministry of Justice, needed to access their data, would involve a review process that could take up to two years. These considerations could not be overcome in the lifetime of the project. The pilot team mooted a 'lite' version that would avoid or minimise the use of personal data. However, this was not pursued because such modifications would drift from the intended aims and fall far below the expectations that had been raised. In short, although ambitions were high, efforts to implement the app failed to come to fruition. Progress was impeded by the nature of data likely to be stored in it, together with its inability to sit within existing structures. The app was abandoned. This was a demoralising set-back for the pilot and a disappointment for the wider project.

The perils of social media

The CoSIE project undertook to explore possibilities of social media to enhance co-creation (Jalonen et al, 2019; Jalonen and Helo, 2020). For the UK pilot some tension was almost inevitable as the relationship between social media and criminal justice is to say the least uncomfortable. The pilot team in Hull feared adverse publicity through traditional and social media and steps were taken to mitigate this risk, such as having a reactive press release prepared in advance. As the CoSIE project unfolded and faced external review it became apparent that the UK pilot was not making the expected contribution with regard to social media, and this became perceived as a shortcoming in delivering the project. With all this in mind, we designed and implemented an additional research exercise as part of our process evaluation in order to provide context about the role of social media and the opportunities or challenges it could offer for co-creation in the specific context of probation services in the Hull area.

We undertook a systematic collection, analysis and interpretation of publicly available social media posts. Initially we hoped to use the

Luuppi tool, which had already been deployed successfully in Finland and demonstrated to the consortium, for this purpose (see Chapter 5). Technical glitches exacerbated by the pandemic and lockdown (when the university campus was closed) frustrated this. Instead, tweets and Facebook posts that emanated from local sources with criminal or deviant activity as their focal point were collected manually between the specific date frame of 1 December 2017 and 31 August 2019. To make the task manageable, analysis focused on the third full week of the month across the specified time frame.

The online Twitter platform of the local newspaper was the most active source, sharing stories displaying messages about criminality and criminals. A total of 879 tweets were recorded. Tweets (as well as a small amount of data collected from an associated Facebook page) typically included an individual's name and a police mugshot or a picture. Nearly three-fifths (57 per cent) of these tweets made use of additional imagery, most frequently attachment of an online news article which often included the name and address of individuals who had been involved in criminal behaviour. In addition to current events, tweets were shared that covered historical content and criminal behaviour. With regard to labelling and stigmatisation this is important because the personal details remain online. Perhaps surprisingly, accounts with the highest average of interaction were those which took a more rehabilitative than punitive stance to crime and deviance. Overall, however, the evidence from this analysis of social media confirmed that wider communities' direct involvement in the news process and public interactions makes for an extremely hostile environment for rehabilitation. This confirmed anecdotal assertions of fear and loathing of social media expressed by the service provider's staff and users.

My Direction was one of two pilots in CoSIE that entirely shunned social media as a tool for co-creation despite strong encouragement to consider it. The other was the very local pilot 'No Time to Waste' in Nieuwegein, the Netherlands. The setting for 'No Time to Waste' was a neighborhood beset by many social problems, including low incomes, high economic inactivity, poor housing and crime. This pilot was directed at the improvement of partnership between the inhabitants of the neighbourhood and the municipality of Nieuwegein. It focused on improvement of public services regarding waste disposal and litter in the streets, identified as pressing problems by the inhabitants. Barriers to engagement with social media were quite similar to the UK pilot. The digital divide for the marginalised community was intense. Many inhabitants lacked skills in digital media, exacerbated by often limited command of the Dutch language for residents who were recent migrants. Analysis of a Facebook page which already existed in the neighbourhood showed it did not lead to positive interaction. Inhabitants in the pilot site were distrustful of digital communication with municipality services. They also thought their community was unfairly stigmatised in social media because of the local reputation for crime and anti-social behaviour. One pilot team member in Nieuwegein reflected at the end of the project: "We learnt that what we want (in terms of using social media and other advanced technology) is again something WE (researchers or a municipality) might want, but it is not always a solution recipients of our services might need."

Storytelling was an important vehicle for co-creation in CoSIE. People were trained and supported to tell their own stories in their own ways through Community Reporting. How the telling, curation and mobilisation of stories in digital form was deployed in CoSIE is covered in detail in Chapter 7. In the Nieuwegein site Community Reporting enabled professionals to hear stories in a more open manner than the familiar consultation and tick-box approaches. Moreover, it helped to make made an emotional connection to the issue (waste) as a catalyst for change and encourage co-ownership of policy. In stark contrast to other attempts to harness digital resources, Community Reporting was also successful in My Direction. This was notable in the light of the near refusal of probation staff initially to work with Community Reporting at all. When Community Reporting was first introduced to them in their Hull office most listened politely but were unsure it offered added value when compared to more traditional tools such as feedback forms. Two of the workers were overtly hostile. One was particularly angry about what she perceived as exploiting vulnerability, especially of women on probation, and the prospect of their stories being used for 'entertainment'. Thanks to the tact and skill of the Community Reporting leader these fears were eventually allayed. After this difficult first meeting the CoSIE team realised on reflection that this initial negative perception was framed within experiences of stories online that are painfully familiar in the context of criminal justice.

Stories from people on probation, front-line workers and volunteers were part of a process of insight gathering for co-creation in My Direction. Some of the stories were mobilised in well-attended events and feedback showed they moved participants (including powerful stakeholders) quite profoundly, and stimulated them to reflect on the need for change. In summary, unlike other technological possibilities including social media, the digital content created and curated by Community Reporting was an important vehicle for co-creation in My Direction and also in the Dutch (Nieuwegein) pilot.

Conclusion

In this final section we reflect on learning from the My Direction and Nieuwegein pilots, and critically assess the hopes, successes and failures encountered by them. CoSIE achieved some notable successes in digital innovations and they are covered elsewhere in this volume. While in no way denigrating those achievements, this chapter makes a contribution to current knowledge by documenting some limitations of technology-driven innovation in public service reform. As noted by Lember et al (2019), while developments in digital technology are becoming increasingly associated with new opportunities for co-created services, claims must be treated cautiously and contextually. This chapter has examined a criminal justice context using a desistance framework (aligned to co-creation). In doing this it exposes weaknesses and unfulfilled promises associated with the co-creative potential of heavily promoted digital solutions. Commercially owned social media, in particular, appears a particularly bad fit with the world of rehabilitation despite hype about democratising/co-creative potential.

The promises of digital technology (apart from social media) resonated very positively for probation workers involved in the My Direction pilot. This applied to front-line and senior staff alike. Workers in Nieuwegein also showed no aversion to technology as such, although they were sympathetic to residents' bad experiences of municipal IT systems and decided that a face-to-face approach to information gathering was essential in the local context. With hindsight the enthusiasm of probation staff for a proposed app may look somewhat naive in the light of regulatory and governance obstacles. It is clear however that there was an appetite for the transfer of agency to people on probation via the affordances of the app. It appeared to offer a highly practical enactment of co-creation ideals. Professional resistance did not feature at all in their responses to the app. What they did resist, despite general willingness to embrace co-creation, was the direct transfer of cash to people on probation. This was partly explained by fear of being blamed for any misuse (exacerbated by panic about unfair reporting in traditional and social media). There was also an aspect of not wanting to relinquish professional control. The evaluation concluded that although front-line workers in probation were generally receptive to co-creation, the very radical innovation of the enabling fund pushed the limits from their perspective (Baines et al, 2021). The proposed app, in contrast, fit well with case managers' notions of co-creation. The app failed because insufficient attention was given to the need for a governable infrastructure.

It is very easy at policy level to overstate the potential of digital media and understate the reasons they may be unwelcome, inappropriate and unethical for some marginalised and stigmatised groups. The digital divide is an aspect of this but not the only one. It goes deeper than limits of assets and skills that, in theory at least, could be relatively straightforward to fix. Commercial social media channels and platforms in some contexts are seen as inherently harmful (a position that worldwide events since the start of the CoSIE project may tend to support). They certainly appear to have no traction for co-creation in the real world of criminal justice but rather exacerbate the labelling and public denigration of people who use services, and do this in ways that may be inimical to desistance.

Although stories conveyed through social media can be harmful, storytelling itself is an important tool in the spirit of co-creation (Durose et al, 2017). People tell stories about what matters to them and what they long for in ways that more structured methods of opinion gathering cannot communicate (Cottam, 2018). The use of Community Reporting in CoSIE involved imaginative adaptation of low-cost, everyday technologies as an ethical and governable resource that became a vital component of co-creation. This chapter notes that Community Reporting was successful in two contexts (criminal justice in the UK and a depleted, stigmatised community in the Netherlands) that were entirely hostile to commercial social media. Community Reporting with reference to other CoSIE pilots is covered in Chapter 7.

References

Albertson, K. and Fox, C. (2019) 'The marketisation of rehabilitation: some economic considerations', *Probation Journal*, 66(1): 25–42.

Baines, S., Fox, C., Harrison, J., Smith, A. and Marsh, C. (2021) 'Co-creating rehabilitation: findings from a pilot and implications for wider public service reform', *Probation Journal*, 69(4): 452–471, https://journals.sagepub.com/doi/10.1177/02645505211065683

Barn, R. and Barn, B.S. (2019) 'Youth justice in the digital age: a case study of practitioners' perspectives on the challenges and opportunities of social technology in their techno-habitat in the United Kingdom', *Youth Justice*, 19(3): 185–205.

Brandsen, T., Steen, T. and Verschuere, B. (2018) 'Co-creation and co-production in public services: urgent issues in practice and research', in Brandsen, T., Steen, T. and Verschuere, B. (eds) *Co-Production and Co-Creation: Definitions and Theoretical Perspectives*, London: Routledge, pp 3–8.

Buckland, R. (2019) Keynote speech, Modernising Criminal Justice Conference, 11 June, https://www.gov.uk/government/speeches/robert-buckland-qc-speech-modernising-criminal-justice-conference-2019

Carr, N. (2017) 'Technologies of crime, control and change', *Probation Journal*, 64(3): 187–190.

Cottam, H. (2018) *Radical Help: How We Can Remake the Relationships between Us and Revolutionise the Welfare State*, London: Virago Press.

Driss, O.B., Mellouli, S. and Trabelsi, Z. (2019) 'From citizens to government policy-makers', *Government Information Quarterly*, 36(3): 560–570.

Dunsby, R. and Howes, M. (2019) 'The NEW adventures of the digital vigilante! Facebook users' views on online naming and shaming', *Australian & New Zealand Journal of Criminology*, 52(1): 41–59.

Durose, C., Needham, C., Mangan, C. and Rees, J. (2017) 'Generating "good enough" evidence for co-production', *Evidence and Policy*, 13(1): 135–151.

Fox, C. and Marsh, C. (2016) 'Operationalising desistance through personalisation', *European Journal of Probation*, 8(3): 185–206.

Fox, C., Harrison, J., Marsh, C. and Smith, A. (2018) 'Piloting different approaches to personalised offender management in the English criminal justice system', *International Review of Sociology*, 28(1): 35–61, https://doi.org/10.1080/03906'701.2017.1422886

Grant, S. and McNeill, F. (2015) 'What matters in practice? Understanding "quality" in the routine supervision of offenders in Scotland', *The British Journal of Social Work*, 45(7): 1985–2002.

Hamblin, K.A. (2022) 'Technology in care systems: displacing, reshaping, reinstating or degrading roles?', *New Technology Work Employment*, 37(1): 41–58.

Jalonen, H. and Helo, T. (2020) 'Co-creation of public service innovation using open data and social media: rhetoric, reality, or something in between?', *International Journal of Innovation in the Digital Economy*, 11(3): 64–77.

Jalonen, H., Jäppinen, T. and Bugarszki, Z. (2019) *Co-creation of Social Innovation Policy Brief*, Co-creation of Service Innovation in Europe (CoSIE), https://docplayer.net/200121040-Co-creation-of-social-innovation.html

Lember, V., Brandsen, T. and Tonurist, P. (2019) 'The potential impacts of digital technologies on co-production and co-creation', *Public Management Review*, 21(11): 1665–1686.

McGreevy, G. (2017) '"Changing lives": using technology to promote desistance', *Probation Journal*, 64(3): 276–281.

McLoughlin, I. and Wilson, R. (2013) *Digital Government @ Work*, Oxford: Oxford University Press.

McNeill, F. and Weaver, B. (2010) *Changing Lives? Desistance Research and Offender Management*, Glasgow: The Scottish Centre for Crime and Justice Research.

Ministry of Justice (2013) *Transforming Rehabilitation: A Strategy for Reform*, London: Ministry of Justice.

Nellis, M. (2013) 'Analysing penal innovation', *International Journal of Offender Therapy and Comparative Criminology*, 57(3): 267–268.

Phillips, J. (2011) 'Target, audit and risk assessment cultures in the probation service', *European Journal of Probation*, 3(3): 108–122.

Rutter, N. (2021) 'Social media: a challenge to identity and relational desistance', *Probation Journal*, 68(2): 243–260. https://doi.org/10.1177/0264550520962207

Smith, A., Harrison, J. and Fox, C. (2019) *A Rapid Evidence Assessment on the Effectiveness of Remote Supervision and New Technologies in Managing Probation Service Users*, Manchester: HM Inspectorate of Probation.

Stacey, G. (2019) *Report of the Chief Inspector of Probation*, HM Inspectorate of Probation, https://www.justiceinspectorates.gov.uk/hmiprobation/wp-content/uploads/sites/5/2019/03/HMI-Probation-Chief-Inspectors-Report.pdf

Taylor, H., Van Rooy, D. and Bartels, L. (2023) 'Digital justice: a rapid evidence assessment of the use of mobile technology for offender behavioural change', *Probation Journal*, 70(1): 31–51, https://journals.sage pub.com/doi/full/10.1177/02645505211065694

Torfing, J., Sørensen, E. and Røiseland, A. (2019) 'Transforming the public sector into an arena for co-creation: barriers, drivers, benefits, and ways forward', *Administration & Society*, 51(5): 795–825.

Ward, T. and Maruna, S. (2007) *Rehabilitation: Beyond the Risk Paradigm*, London: Routledge.

Wastell, D., White, S., Broadhurst, K., Peckover, S. and Pithouse, A. (2010) Children's services in the iron cage of performance management: street-level bureaucracy and the spectre of Švejkism, *International Journal of Social Welfare*, 19(3): 310–320.

7

Connecting citizens and services through the power of storytelling

Hayley Trowbridge

Introduction

Stories – whether visualised, written or spoken – have long been a way of communicating experiences. Stories are a way through which we learn and pass on our learning (Copeland and Moor, 2018). Stories help us to make sense of the world and understand the different ways we experience it.

With the digital (r)evolution bringing about accessible means of creating and disseminating stories, it is therefore unsurprising that digital storytelling in particular has thrived as a tool for social transformation and the pushing of social justice agendas. Portable devices, such as smartphones and tablets, provide people with the tools needed to (relatively) simply create stories via a range of mediums, and the internet and various platforms on it enable people to share digital stories across geographies at the click of a button. Such tools and access within the citizen sphere create the scope for people to tell and share their experiences outside formal channels.

Yet the scope to tell and share your story does not always correlate to direct change, particularly when such experiences are not connected into the services and institutions that are woven into the fabric of society. This chapter explores the extent to which digital storytelling – specifically the Community Reporting methodology – can be used as a tool to connect citizens with services. Focusing on pilot services from the Co-creation of Service Innovation in Europe (CoSIE) project, the chapter examines how Community Reporting has been utilised as tool for co-creation within public services across Europe from a practitioner perspective, and details how digital storytelling can be practically applied as a tool for connecting citizens and services. The pilots examined within this chapter are:

- Co-Crea-Te (Valencia, Spain): the pilot aimed to create an entrepreneur support service suited to the needs of unemployed people in the region.
- Improving services for unemployed people (Utrecht, the Netherlands): the pilot aimed to improve public service delivery to unemployed citizens in order to increase citizen participation in the community of Houten.
- ProPoLab – co-housing of seniors (Wroclaw, Poland): the pilot aimed to work with the housing community of Popowice and wider stakeholders to improve older people's lives within the housing estate through the adoption of co-creation techniques.

Drawing on reflections from the pilots' actors, this chapter demonstrates the opportunities and challenges of working with stories as a means to develop services in a way that draws upon the existing assets of the people and communities that the services support.

Storytelling with a social agenda

Storytelling – particularly when rooted in lived experience – has recently been galvanised as a tool for progressing social agendas. As a concept it wears many hats; whether it be the advocating storytelling for social justice within anti-racism work (Bell, 2020), as an enhancer of community participation and a catalyser of action (Talmage, 2014) or as a way to explore and co-create policy agendas in diverse communities (Keresztély and Trowbridge, 2019). Such advocacy and usage of storytelling, as Copeland and Moor suggest, can enable 'authentic voice to be heard and recorded' (2018: 106).

Yet, we must not view this surge in the practice of working with stories for social change through rose-tinted glasses. As Nassam Parvin states:

> The dominant framing of digital storytelling practices as a form of empowerment is deeply problematic, especially when we consider how activities of storytelling and listening may indeed be oppressive, advancing age-old practices of extraction and colonization in new guises. Such strategies risk taking away from what is meaningful and worthwhile in experiences of storytelling and listening by tokenizing and using stories for political purposes without reaching the kinds of conversations, understandings, and commitments that is their potential. (Parvin, 2018: 530)

It is thus important to be responsible with how we approach storytelling within services and institutions, and think carefully about how we work with people and communities and the power dynamics involved in this.

Working with stories in an asset-based manner could address some of these issues. As discussed in Chapter 2, rather than assuming a deficit or problem within a person or community, asset-based approaches to community development focus on how to maximise the existing capacity that lies within people and their communities (Baron et al, 2019). These assets and capabilities can be tangible, such as skills or community buildings but can also be 'intangible resources' such as lived experience of citizens and their networks/relationships (Fox et al, 2020). This implies activating the agency within citizens and working in a way that is collaborative and 'alongside', rather than simply 'done to'.

Community Reporting is an approach to digital storytelling rooted in lived experience, and is aligned in many ways to the arenas of social justice and asset-based community development. Originating in 2007, Community Reporting has been developed by People's Voice Media as a mixed methodological approach for enhancing citizen participation in research, policy making, service development and decision-making processes (Trowbridge and Willoughby, 2020; Geelhoed et al, 2021). As depicted in Figure 7.1, Community Reporting has three distinct components – story gathering, story curation and story mobilisation – based around the Cynefin decision-making framework for complex environments (Snowden and Boone, 2007). This model supports citizens to share their own lived experiences, collate their own and their peers' collective experiences to better understand the world they inhabit and use this knowledge as a catalyst for change. It uses digital, portable technologies to support people to tell their own stories, in their own ways via largely peer-to-peer approaches. It then connects these stories with the people, groups and organisations who are in a position to use the insights within them to influence and inform research findings, service provision and policy direction.

In line with work such as Glasby (2011) and Durose et al (2013), Community Reporting purports the validity of lived experience and

Figure 7.1: Component of Community Reporting

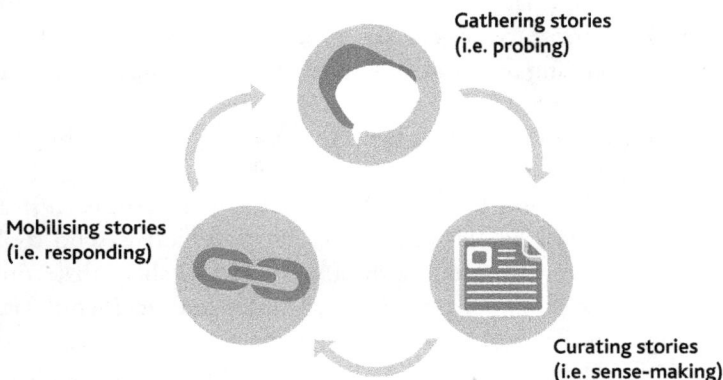

Gathering stories
(i.e. probing)

Mobilising stories
(i.e. responding)

Curating stories
(i.e. sense-making)

knowledge-based practice in these fields. When used like this, storytelling, as Durose et al argue, allows for the representation of 'different voices and experiences in an accessible way' (2013: 22). Practices such as this connect digital storytelling with social justice aims, supporting citizens and communities be a part of 'conversations' from which they are often excluded.

Through the practitioner's lens

The evidence for this chapter was largely collected via reflective interviews with key actors within the pilots (that is, public service professionals) using the Community Reporting methodology. The interviews were gathered using a 'dialogue interview' technique that supports something more akin to a conversation than a traditional interview. This format of storytelling is designed as a peer-to-peer interview and thus public service professionals working on each of the pilots 'interviewed' one another about their experiences of using Community Reporting within the service. While conventional interviews tend to have pre-determined questions, or at least a loose list of topic areas to cover, dialogue interviews only have one question – the opening one. We refer to this as a 'conversation starter' and it should be a broad, open question that enables the person being interviewed (that is, the storyteller) to start to share their lived experiences. For this particular piece of work, the conversation starter was: Can you share with me your experiences of using Community Reporting in your pilot? The person in the interviewer role (that is, the Community Reporter) who is recording the story then asks any questions within this storytelling process that naturally occur to them. In essence, the interviewer is actively listening and engaging with the storyteller, supporting them to communicate their experiences and explore their own reflections. As stated, the structure of this practice mimics our day-to-day conversations and the questions and interactions that take place within the storytelling are those that occur naturally as the story progresses. Within this technique, the storyteller is largely determining the 'agenda' of the conversation (that is, what aspects of the application of Community Reporting they choose to speak about), whereas the Community Reporter is the 'agency' facilitating the conversation (that is, providing further questions that garner deeper insights and reflections).

In order to extract the learning from the stories needed for this chapter a mixture of vertical and horizontal analysis techniques were used as part of a sense-making process. Starting with the vertical analysis, each story was individually reviewed by the public service professionals who took part and the results were documented on a story review sheet that contained a summary of the story in chronological order and an identification of the key insights and quotes within it. Following the vertical analysis and the receipt of individual review sheets, a horizontal approach was adopted by the research team in which we looked across the individual stories, grouped the insights and identified any key themes within them – as well as recognising anomalies within the collection of stories. An important point to note here is that the insights are not positioned within a predetermined criteria and instead the 'framing' of the results emerges from within the horizontal analysis. Such an approach is informed by grounded theory approaches (Glaser and Strauss, 1967; Tummers and Karsten, 2012), and thus enables hypotheses and learning to 'emerge organically rather than being imposed on the data' (Trowbridge, 2022).

The aforementioned insights from the stories were then combined with individual Strengths, Weaknesses, Opportunities and Threats (SWOT) analyses that the pilot's key and wider actors conducted with regard to the use of Community Reporting as a tool for co-creation in their pilots. The SWOTs focused on the following questions:

- Strengths: What worked well when applying Community Reporting within your pilot?
- Weaknesses: What didn't work well when applying Community Reporting within your pilot?
- Opportunities: What opportunities are there to expand how Community Reporting can be used as a tool for co-creation either within your pilot or wider public services?
- Threats: What internal (that is, within your organisation) or external (that is, wider societal context) issues act as barriers to using Community Reporting as a tool for co-creation?

Each pilot provided a written response to these questions, and further conversation-based clarification was gathered on aspects of their responses. In short, reflective practice was the central tool used to gather the evidence for this chapter.

Community Reporting and the Co-creation of Service Innovation in Europe

Within the CoSIE project, Community Reporting was applied as a tool for co-creation in three distinct, yet interlinked ways (see Figure 7.2). First, the methodology was applied as tool for insight. When applied this way, Community Reporting broadly fits into the realms of participatory research fields (Cornwall and Jewkes, 1995; Cargo and Mercer, 2008; Bergold and Thomas, 2012). It engages citizens (that is, the people accessing the public services) and wider stakeholders (that is, public service workers, policy makers, civil society actors, and so on) to be a part of a process in which people tell their stories, listen to one another's stories, collectively identify

Figure 7.2: Application of Community Reporting as a tool for co-creation

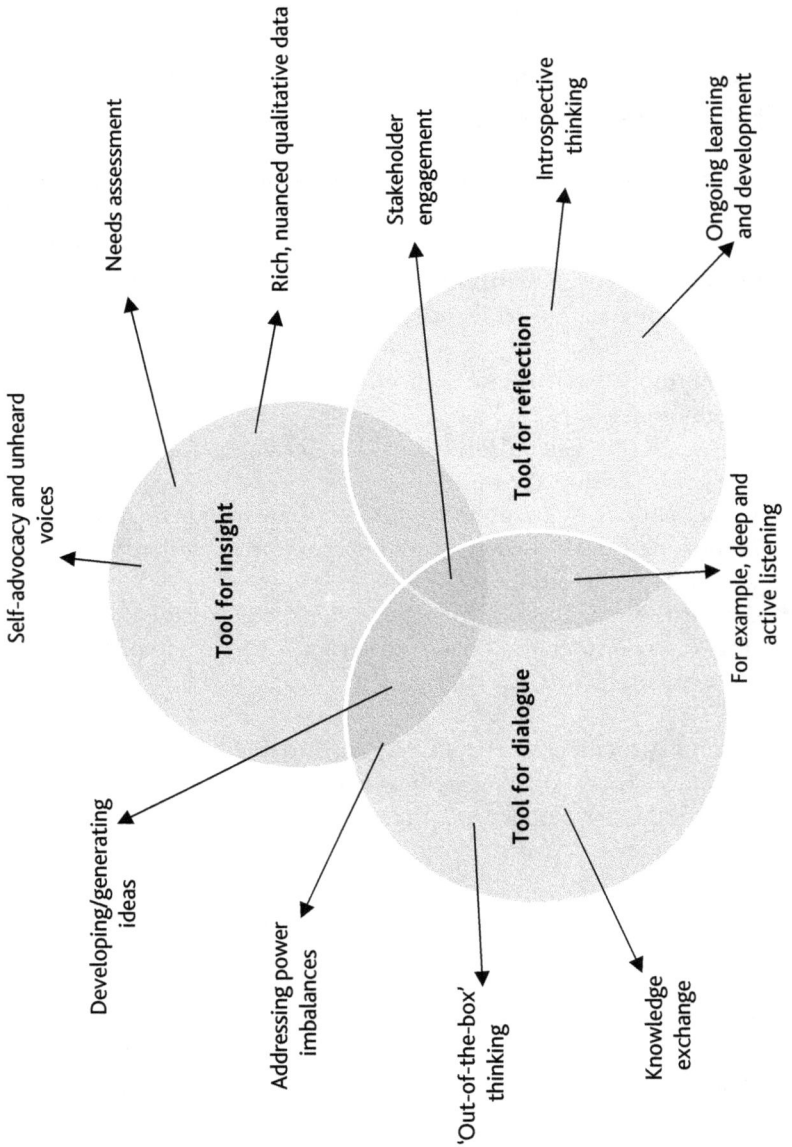

Needs assessment

Rich, nuanced qualitative data

Stakeholder engagement

Introspective thinking

Ongoing learning and development

Self-advocacy and unheard voices

Tool for insight

Tool for reflection

For example, deep and active listening

Developing/generating ideas

Tool for dialogue

Addressing power imbalances

'Out-of-the-box' thinking

Knowledge exchange

the insights in them and then deliberate the core findings that emerge from across the stories.

Another usage of Community Reporting within the CoSIE pilots was as a tool for dialogue. The approach aids dialogue by providing people with the tools to use storytelling to engage in conversations with their peers and other people beyond their peer groups in co-creation processes. Conversation of Change events are a key part of this application. These events are spaces in which people's stories are used to stimulate dialogue between different stakeholders about a topic, issue, service, and so on. Strongly influenced by Labonte and Feather's (1996) story dialogue approach, these events enable different stakeholders to work together to identify how the learning from the stories can be applied in real-world contexts. Additionally, Community Reporter stories can be used as a communication tool when addressing decision-makers so that they get real insights on the people whom their decisions affect.

Finally, Community Reporting was applied as a tool for reflection within the CoSIE pilots. This approach to digital storytelling supports people to reflect on their experiences and the experiences of others. This proactive, critical reflection provides people with the space and time to understand in greater depth how they and others experience the world, and hence supports people to identify how public (and other) services can better meet the needs of those that access them. As identified, in Cargo and Mercer's work on understanding the role of participatory research methods in achieving health outcomes and enhancing practices and processes within the sector, a key benefit of such approaches to practitioners in the field is that they provide an 'enhanced understanding of health problems, their root causes' and can support the 'development of decision-making skills' (Cargo and Mercer, 2008: 338–339).

In each of the pilot services within CoSIE, Community Reporting was applied in bespoke ways in order to meet the needs of the pilot and embed itself within the co-creation process as a whole. Within the Spanish pilot, Community Reporting was applied as a tool for insight, dialogue and reflection. The key objectives of its application were to:

- gather initial insights into the 'needs' of unemployed people in the city of Valencia;
- work with different stakeholders to generate initial ideas about how entrepreneurship can be used to support people out of employment; and
- provide a tool for people accessing the pilot's service to reflect on their own learning and development.

In the Dutch pilot 'Improving services for unemployed people' Community Reporting was applied initially as a tool for insight but was then also used to create dialogue between people at a distance from the labour market and services that sought to address unemployment. The anticipated outcomes of this work were:

- better understand why there seemed to be a skills mismatch between people seeking employment and available job opportunities; and
- generate concrete ideas for a pilot service to address this perceived skills mismatch.

Finally, in the Polish pilot, Community Reporting was used as a tool for insight and to initiate dialogue within residents of the housing estate. Specifically, the approach was used to engage older residents in the co-creation process and contributed to:

- identifying the needs of the residents; and
- how these needs can be met by the pilot.

With these contexts and ambitions in mind, the chapter goes on to examine the results of using Community Reporting as a tool for co-creation within these three pilots and explore what we learned from this practical application of storytelling and its ability to connect citizens and services.

Key learning from the pilots

A space to reflect meets challenges from existing norms: applying Community Reporting in the Co-Crea-Te pilot (Spain)

Within the Spanish pilot, Community Reporting was able to provide richer and more intricate data than other tools. At the beginning of the pilot, people experiencing unemployment, existing entrepreneurs and people working in employment support services engaged in a workshop in which they exchanged stories that focused on topics connected to the pilot, such as people's experiences of work, routes taken to get back into work or start careers, and support available for people to enter into the labour market. The core findings from these stories were that the pilot should:

- Embrace person-centred practice: "Every person is a different world so you have to focus on the needs and on what each person asks you for" and thus the pilot should see people as individuals and support them from where they currently are.
- Adopt an asset-based development approach: "Society has a long way to go to understand that everyone is able to do something" and this understanding should be embedded into the pilot.

- Promote peer support: "Motivation and a supporting environment are needed to achieve the goal" and developing alongside peers can help create this.

These ideas, which were initiated by the stories told by the group in this workshop, contributed to the pilot not being a traditional business development training programme and instead saw it develop as a more holistic service that supported unemployed people to establish their own business ventures. This involved mentoring, one-to-one support, peer-sharing skills sessions, co-management of a co-working space and a range of more flexible and ongoing support options than the usual, structured, linear entrepreneurship and business development training schemes offer.

In terms of evaluation, it was felt that the dialogue interview methodology enabled the pilot to gain insights that were not visible in their more quantitative methods that were capturing baseline data on numbers of users, firms created, and so on. As a member of the pilot team explains, Community Reporting provided an opportunity for the people accessing the service to reflect on their experiences in a concrete way: "[The people coming to Co-Crea-Te] realised that they, at that point, were made conscious about their journey by using this methodology because we asked them to think about this journey." This helped the pilot to garner otherwise unattainable qualitative information and gauge the intangible effects of the pilot on the beneficiaries, such as the pilot's positive impact on their wellbeing. For example, when telling his story, one entrepreneur became emotional and that was because "he was looking inside of himself ... an introspective look ... so suddenly he realised that his life had changed over the past few months". This level of self-awareness was achieved via only a few minutes of storytelling. Such findings have provided integral material for the pilot's policy roundtable and summative knowledge exchange event, and has created a knowledge bank for future related schemes. As one stakeholder of the pilot explains: "We share more information and learn from others' mistakes. We need to listen to other people. Citizen participation makes things work."

When using the methodology, the main challenge that the pilot encountered was that people were simply not used to this approach, as it was seen as innovative and different from more traditional approaches. Due to this, some people were initially reticent to talk about their experiences in-depth and in a loose, undirected manner; they were not used to having the opportunity to set their own agenda. One person was concerned about the visibility of the material and who would see it (that is, the Town Hall) and withdrew consent. However, most people engaged productively with the method and initial reticence was overcome by pilot leaders building a relationship of trust with the storytellers prior to recording the dialogue interviews with them. This helped to create an environment in which they were comfortable and open to sharing their experiences via a new method. Similarly, a context in which many decision-makers (that is, politicians and policy makers) value quantitative data – even if it lacks depth – is key in explaining the role of Community Reporting in this these contexts and its added value. One angle on this is to explain such approaches where narrative is valued alongside traditional quantitative data as having a role in developing better services. As one stakeholder of the pilot asserted: "Cooperation and co-creation are something essential, not just as a fashion, it is needed to reduce risk." In essence, to overcome fixed mindsets about what data is valuable and what data isn't, it is important to take decision-makers on a learning journey about how different forms of data can be used and why lived experience can deliver better results in commissioning. A possible solution for this barrier could be to include decision-makers in the Community Reporting training so that they understand the power and usefulness of this type of data in their line of work.

Changing the agenda meets scepticism to new methods: applying Community Reporting in the redesigning social services (the Netherlands)

Community Reporting enabled the Dutch pilot to gather rich, qualitative insights that had more depth to other approaches they had previously used or existing data that they held. While the pilot's existing knowledge helped them to identify that unemployment was an issue within the area, they found the storytelling approach garnered insights into the underlying problems (that is, the root causes) that jobseekers and employers were encountering. In essence, the stories gathered dug beneath the surface and the pilot was able to hear a more nuanced story from the perspectives of the people experiencing unemployment rather than the municipalities' own perceptions of the issue. As a policy advisor working on the pilot stated: "It's not rocket science. It's a basic thing that as a civil servant we tend to have an agenda – a well-meaning agenda but an agenda nonetheless. [Community Reporting] took us away from our agenda and allowed people to make their own."

The storytelling approach had a huge impact on the pilot as it took them away from their presupposed agenda and led them to conclude that "something much more profound has been shown – you need to make sure that basic needs are addressed", as well as sorting out more basic issues such as job application processes. At a Conversation of Change, these insights were juxtaposed with social media to elicit further discussion and depth and the Community Reporting approach overall enabled them to engage with people who wouldn't usually attend municipality meetings. This, however, does take time in terms of actively seeking out these people, establishing relationships of trust with citizens in advance, and working with stakeholders with connections to the target group to gather the stories. This should be factored in when using the method – it is not a quick bit of consultation or a tick-box exercise. The benefits, however, of investing this time and resource from the pilot's perspective is that the stories reach people on an emotional level that, perhaps, other forms of data fail to do. This emotional connection to the issue can be a key catalyst for change within public services and encourages co-ownership of policy.

Beyond the time and resources consumed by Community Reporting, issues with utilising the methodology that the pilot identified revolved around it being different to, and sometimes challenging of, the status quo. While the municipality and other stakeholders are curious about the approach and are willing to learn and test out more and share this knowledge with others, it was still felt that Community Reporting is quite challenging to bureaucratic thinking. This issue is hard to combat and people can see the approach as a threat, as it challenges existing power relations and supports the creation of more equitable environments within an institutionalised system that is largely top-down in nature. Furthermore, municipalities have questions about whether the method is representative and, if not, what is its value, as well as whether the cost-benefit ratio can be justified. Questions such as these are common, as long-held values such as representative sampling and traditional economic thinking are brought into question by the method. The pilot found that producing an infographic to explain the approach and why they were using it in the scheme of the pilot was an effective way of overcoming some of these apprehensions. Moreover, the 'systematic analysis' of the stories gathered was also a feature of the method that can reassure its critics.

A sense of identity meets the digital divide: applying Community Reporting in the ProPoLab pilot (Poland)

For the pilot, a key strength of Community Reporting lay in its ability to connect the older residents to a social change agenda. As the pilot recognises, the added value of the Community Reporting training was that the older people who were trained as 'Community Reporters' adopted the branding and identity of the Community Reporting movement. They felt proud to call themselves Community Reporters and really bought into their role in trying to creating a positive influence in the neighbourhood. As one of the pilot team explains:

'I believe that the biggest impact from the Community Reporting method has been in making some kind of connection between the local resident leaders and empowering them to have an influence on local activities – they can influence their surroundings, they can influence the decisions of the local authority. This name – Community

Reporter – created a social group for them and they feel more connected and proud of their new function.'

The pilot has built on this by providing them with badges and lanyards, a designated space on the pilot's website and in promoting their activities on social media. In addition, the stories gathered by the older people have been used during a roundtable with stakeholders. This level of visibility of the Community Reporting movement and the work of the Community Reporters has built confidence in the elderly in being actors for social change, as well as their motivation and commitment. Essentially, Community Reporting helped the pilot to connect the residents around a common goal and this added impetus to the co-creation activities that followed.

In addition to this, the stories gathered collected a lot of qualitative knowledge to inform the pilot with regard to the needs of older people and their vision for the neighbourhood. One of the surprising findings from this was that the older people are very happy with the estate they live on, despite some issues being raised. Culturally, it was felt by the pilot that it is typical in Poland to complain about things and other 'voice' tools and approaches (that is, focus groups, surveys, and so on) sometimes just get negative responses. However, given the agenda-less nature of the storytelling method and the fact that it does not use simple questions, it has allowed the pilot to dig deeper into people's statements and provided a mechanism through which they can open up more. Both of these factors have meant that the non-directive interview technique used in Community Reporting has garnered far more complex answers than other more traditional forms of data gathering. It supported residents of the area to talk about the assets of their area such as the green spaces and their relationships with other residents – while simultaneously allowing them to express the issues they are facing (for example, shared responsibility for cleanliness, and so on). The method enabled the pilot to reframe a conversation about the neighbourhood from one that could have been entirely rooted in deficit, to one that was much more about the existing capacities and assets in the community – both in terms of physical spaces and the inhabitants themselves.

One of the key barriers to its implementation and sustainability within the pilot was the technology skills possessed by older people. As a pilot team member explains, "because they are quite old and they don't get on well with the technology … it's really hard for them". This has meant that the pilot team had to support them in their activities and run recap sessions on filming techniques and how to upload the stories to the Community Reporter website. For a different target demographic, it may be easier for them to retain the knowledge and skills, and act more independently as Community Reporters. Currently, the older people who are trained as Community Reporters are still keen to continue working with the method and "still co-operate" with the pilot through storytelling and the dissemination of stories. In the future, they may start with this method to engage residents in change-making processes, but then switch to other more technologically simpler storytelling activities to enhance independence and sustainability. To offset the technical difficulties encountered by the older people and embed digital storytelling more widely within the system, the pilot opted for a 'training-the-trainer' approach. A workshop was held that trained other local leaders, such as non-governmental organisation professionals who work in communities connected to the city's network of Local Activity Centres, in Community Reporting techniques so that they could use the method where they are based to gather resident insight in the future. This network is in its infancy but the pilot feels that the Community Reporting approach will support them to realise their work through better identifying with the needs of their communities outside the CoSIE project. However, attendees of the workshop reflected that, for the municipality to accept the stories produced through Community Reporting into decision-making realms, there is still work to be done. As one contributor explains, "[w]e live in a mentality where decisions are made by a narrow group of people whether the community likes it or not", and despite the community knowing through their lived experience what an area needs, culturally, the working practices of the municipality do not value this type of knowledge. "I totally do not understand the lack of engagement of the local administration", was the reflection of a storyteller and why it must be in the hands of civil society actors to bring about this new way of working.

Conclusion

While the contexts and intended objectives of how Community Reporting was applied in the pilots discussed in this chapter varies, it is possible to identify some overarching learning from across the sites. The key strengths or benefits for services to engage with citizens' lived experience and use storytelling as a tool for co-creation, can be broadly summarised as being:

- Stories provide rich insights – they enable services to gather more nuanced, qualitative knowledge that is particularly of use when addressing 'wicked' social problems.
- Storytelling enables citizens to set the agenda – it provides services with the ability to see things from a citizen's perspectives and enables new ways of thinking to emerge.
- Storytelling supports trust building and relationship development – it reduces power imbalances and can lead to a different type of relationship between service and citizen, one that is more rooted in mutual support and builds on the assets already existing within communities.

- Storytelling is a key tool for learning – it enables services to actively listen to citizens and supports reflective practice, thus progressing institutions from being focused on 'voice' and into what Scudder et al (2023) describe as a more deliberative logic and institutional listening.

Yet despite such strengths, the application of digital storytelling methods within services is not without both its challenges and weaknesses. From the accounts we have worked with, such barriers can broadly be summarised as:

- Digital exclusion remains an issue for some demographics – technology know-how and access are not equal among all groups in society and thus digital storytelling can be difficult for some people to engage with due to lack of skills or resources. There are ways in which such barriers can be overcome (for example, providing access to technology, support and training), but such inclusion processes need to be actively embedded.
- It is not a quick win – building relationships of trust in communities in order to be able to gather lived experience stories takes time and working with the stories (that is, sense-making) can be time-consuming. Therefore, this type of work is an investment for the future, not an immediate goal.
- It is a new way of working – practices like Community Reporting ask institutions to think and behave differently and thus require a culture change that involves winning over the hearts and minds of those working within the system. It can take time for people to see the value of this type of work, and as it actively disrupts the status quo, resistance from those who currently hold power is not uncommon.

Based on this learning, it then seems apt to end with a set of recommendations on how practitioners can progress the agenda of storytelling within service design, improvement and evaluation. First, we would suggest that, before commencing any storytelling, practitioners should invest time in developing responsible practice. What we mean by this is to carefully think about the ethics that underpin the storytelling. Take the time to create the conditions for the storytelling and do the groundwork in the community being addressed, and thus strive to avoid the 'extraction and colonisation' prevalent in some applications of practice that Parvin (2018) has warned us about. Second, we should be realistic about the change that the stories can make. It is important that to be honest about this with communities, while a complete overhaul of a service may be the end goal, its likelihood – at least in the near future – is potentially unlikely. Therefore, managing expectations among the storytellers about the changes they are likely to see and when they are likely to be seen is paramount – keep them in the 'loop' about these developments. Such an approach will build and maintain relationships of trust for the future. Finally, we need to be bold and put trust in citizen-led agendas. Practitioners in this field need to avoid trying to control and manipulate the storytelling to fit the service's vision or agenda, as such techniques ultimately undermine what you are trying to do. The easiest way to do this is to ensure buy-in at all layers in the service. However, it is clear that sometimes buy-in can only be attained once people see the fruits of the labour and is not always possible at the start. If this way of working is new within a service, then it may be necessary to act as a shield between the pressure from the service and the storytelling, navigating and treading a new path and, ultimately, playing a role in a greater paradigm shift. An arduous task, but one that is worth the effort.

References

Baron, S., Stanley, T., Colombian, C. and Pereira, T. (2019) *Strengths-Based Approach: Practice Framework and Practice Handbook*, London: DHSC.

Bell, L.A. (2020) *Storytelling for Social Justice Connecting Narrative and the Arts in Antiracist Teaching*, New York: Routledge.

Bergold, J. and Thomas, S. (2012) 'Participatory research methods: a methodological approach in motion', *Historical Social Research / Historische Sozialforschung*, 37(4): 191–222.

Cargo, M. and Mercer, S.L. (2008) 'The value and challenges of participatory research: strengthening its practice', *Annual Review Public Health*, 29: 325–350.

Copeland, S. and Moor, A. (2018) 'Community digital storytelling for collective intelligence: towards a storytelling cycle of trust', *AI & Society*, 33(2): 101 – 111.

Cornwall, A. and Jewkes, R. (1995) 'What is participatory research?', *Social Science and Medicine*, 41(12): 1667–1676.

Durose, C., Mangan, C., Needham, C. and Rees, J. (2013) *Transforming Local Public Services through Co-Production*, Birmingham: AHRC Connected Communities/Department for Communities and Local Government/University of Birmingham.

Fox, C., Baines, S., Wilson, R., Martin, M., Prandini, R., Bassi, A., Ganugi, G., Jalonen, H. and Gründemann, R. (2020) *Where Next for Co-Creation? Emerging Lessons and New Questions from CoSIE*, Turku University of Applied Sciences.

Geelhoed, S., Trowbridge, H., Henderson, S. and Wallace-Thompson, L. (2021) 'Changing the story: an alternative approach to system change in public service innovation', *Polish Political Science Review*, 9(2): 52–70.

Glasby, J. (2011) *Evidence, Policy and Practice: Critical Perspectives in Health and Social Care*, Bristol: Policy Press.

Glaser, B.G. and Strauss, A.L. (1967) *The Discovery of Grounded Theory: Strategies for Qualitative Research*, Hawthorne: Aldine de Gruyter.

Keresztély, K. and Trowbridge, H. (2019) 'Voicitys: living with diversity in European cities', in Scott, J. (ed) *CESCI Cross-Border Review Yearbook*, Budapest: Central European Service for Cross-Border Initiatives, pp 103–128.

Labonte, R. and Feather, J. (1996) *Handbook on Using Stories in Health Promotion Practice*, Regina: Prarie Region Health Promotion Researcher Centre, University of Saskatchewan.

Parvin, N. (2018) 'Doing justice to stories: on ethics and politics of digital storytelling', *Engaging Science, Technology and Society*, 4: 515–534.

Scudder, M.F., Ercan, S.A. and McCallum, K. (2023) 'Institutional listening in deliberative democracy: towards a deliberative logic of transmission', *Politics*, 43(1): 38–53.

Snowden, D.J. and Boone, M.E. (2007) 'A leader's framework for decision making', *Harvard Business Review*, 85(11): 68–76.

Talmage, C. (2014) 'A story about storytelling: enhancement of community participation through catalytic storytelling', *Community Development*, 45(5): 525–538.

Trowbridge, H. (2022) 'Changing the world, one story at a time: a methodological approach to curating stories of lived experience', in Liguori, A., Rappoport, P. and Gachago, D. (eds) *Story Works*, Washington, DC: Smithsonian Scholarly Press.

Trowbridge, H. and Willoughby, M. (2020) 'Connecting voices, challenging perspectives and catalysing change: using storytelling as a tool for co-creation in public services across Europe', in Scott, J. (ed) *CESCI Cross-Border Review Yearbook*, Budapest: Central European Service for Cross-Border Initiatives, pp 59–72.

Tummers, L. and Karsten, N. (2012) 'Reflecting on the role of literature in qualitative public administration research: learning from grounded theory', *Administration & Society*, 44(1): 64–86.

8

Co-governance and co-management as preliminary conditions for social justice in co-creation

Riccardo Prandini and Giulia Ganugi

Introduction

Co-creation is widely conceived as a tool to achieve innovative service and create wellbeing for all, leaving no one behind (von Heimburg et al, 2021). Indeed, it seems to answer the desire to create fairer, more sustainable and socially more inclusive societies in the face of increasingly complex challenges with which public organisations struggle (Leino and Puumala, 2021; Rossi and Tuurnas, 2021). This chapter is specifically about the social justice of co-creation processes. While raising this issue and claiming the need for more analysis about it, Verschuere et al define social justice, or the democratic quality of co-creation, as the equity and inclusion of stakeholders in the process, at the same time attending to their effective participation and empowerment (Verschuere et al, 2018). Indeed, since co-creation concerns the generation of new services or the improvement of existing services through the engagement citizens who use them, it seems obvious as discussed in Chapter 2 that a just and fair process of co-creation needs to provide for the activation of the same beneficiaries, giving them the opportunities to participate and raise their voices along the whole process. Using Claassen's words, the heart of co-creation is the concept of individuals exercising agency and 'agency becomes the normative criterion for the selection of basic capabilities required for social justice [because] in a just society, each citizen is equally entitled to a set of basic capabilities' (Claassen, 2018: 1). Within a co-creation process, the opportunity to be included is a social justice precondition for activating individuals' capabilities. In the Co-creation of Service Innovation in Europe (CoSIE) project, indeed, all pilots emphasised issues of social justice for people who are marginalised and lack power (Fox et al, 2021).

Building on the work of Verschuere and colleagues about social justice dimensions of inclusion and participation, we argue that scholars and practitioners need to address the issue of social justice in co-creation much earlier in the process. While much research focuses on the co-production of the service, we emphasise the necessity to organise and manage the inclusion and participation of stakeholders – including but not only the beneficiaries – from the very outset in the processes of co-governance and co-management. Indeed, the quality of social justice achieved by the whole process of co-creation relies on:

1. the criteria of inclusion used to constitute the collective responsibility of the project; and
2. the way in which each stakeholder actually exercises their capabilities by participating in the process.

This chapter returns to the Italian CoSIE pilot introduced in Chapter 4. Our focus is the conditions of inclusion and participation in the initial phases of the co-creative process, investigating whether and how these conditions contribute to producing – besides efficiency and effectiveness – social justice in co-creation.

Reducing childhood obesity in Reggio Emilia, Italy

The Italian pilot aimed to reduce childhood obesity in Reggio Emilia through the provision of an app facilitating the relations between parents, family paediatricians and healthcare services. As discussed in Chapter 4, beneficiaries of the pilot were children (aged 3–11) diagnosed as overweight or obese, and their families. Indeed, childhood obesity is one of the most serious health challenges of the 21st century. The Italian statistics in the early 2000s showed that Reggio Emilia was the city in Emilia-Romagna with the highest rate of obesity and overweight among almost all age groups. In 2008, the concerns of the health professionals of the Primary Care Department and Reggio Emilia paediatricians triggered the first big project to address the issue: the BMInforma project (*Bambini Molto in forma* [very fit children]). It was a multisector and multilevel public health programme conducted by the Local Health Authority involving primary and secondary childhood obesity prevention interventions. The Italian CoSIE pilot built on the existing network of services initially developed in 2011, consolidating the collaboration and co-creating the new app (Prandini et al, 2021).

This chapter shows how the final version of the app was strongly influenced by the modality of the constitution of the stakeholders' collectivity and by co-governance and co-management, which included a very wide range of stakeholders and organisations. Co-governance refers to an arrangement in which the stakeholders participate in the planning and delivery of public services: it concerns mainly policy formulation of the service – its 'vision', and the actual process of decision-making. Co-management concerns primarily the interactions between organisations and refers to an arrangement in which the stakeholders decide together the rules and procedure to collaborate and produce services (Brandsen and Pestoff, 2006; Pestoff, 2012; Fox et al, 2019). In the Italian CoSIE pilot co-governance had both criticalities and strengths. Observing them through the dynamics and negotiations among diverse and various stakeholders contributes to shedding light on fundamental criteria to improve social justice and democratisation of co-creation processes.

Social justice as inclusion and participation

In the past 40 years, the public services literature has offered a variety of scholarly discussions addressing different aspects of co-creation, ranging from defining its meaning, delineating its practical aspects, and examining its growth in several policy realms. Conversely, the 'democraticity' and fairness of co-creation processes have not been analysed so deeply yet. Nonetheless, co-creation is already seen as a tool to achieve sustainable development and create wellbeing for all, leaving no one behind (von Heimburg et al, 2021). It seems to answer the desire to create fairer, more sustainable and more connected societies in the face of increasingly complex challenges with which public organisations struggle (Leino and Puumala, 2021; Rossi and Tuurnas, 2021). Despite the justice of general participatory processes being greatly observed, a critical reflection on the type of participation in and access to co-creation processes is needed. Indeed, there may be empirical differences between generic citizen participation and specific co-creation, in terms of who is in, whose voices get heard and what representativeness really means. Stakeholders are diverse and some of them have more resources – time, energy, information and networks – to participate in co-creative processes than others (Häikiö, 2010; Michels, 2011). Yet, this does not mean that those who fall outside of these processes had nothing valuable to create and share (Leino and Puumala, 2021).

According to Verschuere et al (2018), the 'democratic quality' is often conceptualised as the extent to which people from different societal groups or backgrounds are included and are capable to participate in co-creation. More specifically, it concerns concepts 'like equity, inclusion (or exclusion), (lack of) impact while participating or co-creating, and empowering participants or co-creators' (Verschuere et al, 2018: 244). Indeed, even when all stakeholders are included in the process, there might be still a risk of inequity, if the most powerful members enforce selfish decisions or impose their identity and interests (Verschuere et al, 2018). Therefore, the justice (justice-ability) of co-creation depends on the extent to which:

1. the project leads to equity and to the fair inclusion of the greatest variety of stakeholders; and
2. the project allows for real participation, empowerment and enablement of people (Verschuere et al, 2018).

For the achievement of a just co-creative process, these elements need to be clarified and activated at the very beginning of the process, when the participating stakeholders are constituted in a collective 'We' and the decisions for the governance and management are taken.

The first condition – social justice as inclusion – relies on the capacity to map the potential stakeholders, representing the social complexity of the local context (Rosanvallon, 2011) and convening 'around the table' all the representatives of people who could influence and be influenced by the service to be produced and delivered. A high level of inclusion usually signifies a clear willingness for a fair collaboration with as many people as possible. On the contrary, a low level of inclusion usually causes 'exclusivity' as a situation where one or more stakeholders are excluded without a just reason. Moreover, the stakeholders' diverse identities need to be recognised and not assimilated into the majority (Fraser, 1998), giving each actor the voice to express her own needs, desires and values and to forge their collective 'We'-identity (Preyer and Peter, 2017). The second condition – social justice as participation – regards the possibility of each stakeholder having real agency, participation, effectiveness and legitimacy in the decision-making of the co-creative process. This legitimation means also harnessing ideation from diverse communities, fostering new relationships and innovating the welfare services (Murray et al, 2010; Moulaert et al, 2013).

As discussed in Chapter 3, various 'co' elements are mentioned in the literature, typically denoting progress from weaker (less desirable) to stronger (and more desirable) levels. Participation in co-creation processes can be seen as information, consultation and decision-making. 'Information' concerns the lowest level above non-participation and although often one-way may involve initiatives of public agencies to empower citizens and to enhance their capacity to master their own lives. We use 'consultation' here as shorthand to cover a range of elements elsewhere referred to as co-implementation, co-production or co-design. This regards the voluntary work of citizens to create value for other citizens and to improve existing services through continuous adjustments, also enabling them to provide input into the design of new tasks and solutions. 'Decision-making' refers to co-governance

Table 8.1: The intersection between inclusion and participation

		Social justice as inclusion	
		Exclusivity	Inclusiveness
Social justice as participation	Information	Informed exclusivity	Informing inclusiveness
	Consultation	Consulted exclusivity	Consulting inclusiveness
	Decision-making	Decided exclusivity	Deciding inclusiveness

and co-management. This level regards the engagement of both public and private actors in a mutual dialogue aimed at designing new and better solutions and coordinating their implementation. In this case, all stakeholders participate in institutional arenas that facilitate collaborative innovation based on joint agenda-setting and problem definition, joint design and testing of new and untried solutions, and coordinated implementation.

Crossing the two conditions for social justice – inclusion and participation – the result is a combination of different possible forms of social justice, which a process of co-creation may achieve. Table 8.1 illustrates the fundamental conditions for social justice. The generation of the most socially just co-creation process lies in the intertwining of inclusiveness and decision-making types of participation. In this case, the co-creation process includes the highest number possible of stakeholders and empowers them in participating in the decision-making and the governance of the process. Here social justice is characterised as 'deciding inclusiveness'.

All other cases can achieve social justice only partially, with different levels of inclusion and participation. The worst scenario is labelled as 'informed exclusivity', where there is no adequate inclusion of stakeholders and where they are not empowered to decide. Here stakeholders are only informed as beneficiaries of the service, a 'target', or as people only entitled to know its new development.

We proceed now in the analysis of the Italian pilot case, by applying this framework and observing what actors were included in the process and what type of participation was promoted.

Research methodology for the Italian pilot

By being one of the main partners of the Italian pilot, the academic team from the University of Bologna had the possibility to follow the development of the co-creation process from the beginning. With the support of the health authority of Reggio Emilia, the academic team developed a specific research plan to collect data from families, paediatricians and health professionals. The research was carried out by collecting mainly qualitative data, using different techniques.

- Secondary material collection, including official documents (laws enacted by the regional government; rules, regulations and standards enacted by municipalities); unofficial documents (developed by the health authority); and research evaluation reports (by health units and research institutions).
- Face-to-face interviews with children and parents, using the approach of Community Reporting, as discussed in Chapter 7 (17).
- Semi-structured interviews with paediatricians (5), healthcare professionals (3) and other stakeholders participating in the consulting committee (17).
- Focus groups with parents (1) and paediatricians (1).
- Participant observation of the Consulting and Steering Committees' meetings of the pilot.

Among the material collected, the analysis conducted in this chapter focuses on specific elements to be investigated during the 'constitutional' and managerial phases of co-governance and co-management, in order to analyse what criteria of social justice have been used to include stakeholders and to manage their participation. The observed dimensions concern:

- who convenes the stakeholders;
- who is involved in the governance and on the basis of which criteria;
- how each member participates in the negotiation.

Analysis of the Italian pilot

The Italian CoSIE pilot was led and facilitated by the Epidemiology Service of the Local Health Unit (LHU), which built on the previous BMInforma project of the city of Reggio Emilia in order to systematise the existing collaboration among territorial stakeholders. The LHU aimed to co-create an app which could collect all the offered services and activities in the urban territory for the promotion of a healthy lifestyle and the prevention of obesity. The technical partners of the project were the IT company (Lepida) and the University of Bologna. The former supported the process and realised the app from a technical point of view. The latter observed and supported the process with the aim to investigate contextual conditions and evaluate the co-creation process (Bassi et al, 2021).

The territorial context as an enabler of co-creation

Concerning the political and juridical context, the projects developed in the last five years in the Reggio Emilia area are part of a regulatory-legislative process of change, which began at the regional level in the early 2000s. The Regional Law No. 29 of 23 December 2004 re-organised the structure of the Regional Health System, strengthening the role of local authorities in planning and evaluating services, including health workers in the health system's governance, and consolidating collaboration with the region and the university in the fields of social assistance, research and teaching. Moreover, the region's Social and Health Plan for the two-year period 2017–2019 includes – with greater emphasis than in previous plans – health promotion and prevention among other priority actions. The tools suggested by the Plan to work in this direction are the integration between the health and welfare systems, the participatory planning of services and their governance, the direct involvement of the third sector and the reorganisation of services on the basis of the ever-changing needs of the population.

On a local scale, every year the Local Health Authority of Reggio Emilia publishes the Performance Report in order to give feedback on the actions implemented throughout the year regarding the strategic objectives to be achieved. Comparing the reports of the last years, the section concerning the role of citizens appears for the first time in 2014, where it is coined as the importance of citizens' participation in the evaluation of health services and the relationship with voluntary associations. In spite of the step forward, such participation still refers only to the evaluation by citizens at the end of the process of implementation of the services, while there is still no mention of their involvement in the planning and creation phases of the services. In 2018, on the other hand, the Report lists new areas of action implemented in 2017: consolidation of primary care, prevention and health promotion activities, and development of technological infrastructures. In particular, with regard to promotion and prevention activities, the Report stresses the importance of individual and collective processes that improve people's empowerment and, consequently, their lifestyle and wellbeing.

Concerning the pilot focus, the consideration of obesity, and specifically childhood obesity, has been high since the early 2000s and has been growing steadily over time. In 2010, the LHU launched a programme of research and interventions aimed at preventing obesity, adopting a multilevel strategy that develops from primary prevention, in the pre-school and school phases, to secondary prevention organised through individual monitoring and advice and support to families by paediatricians (Davoli et al, 2013; Broccoli et al, 2016). The new strategy also envisages the care of obese children by multidisciplinary teams, which can devote themselves to all spheres of the child's life (nutrition, physical activity and social relationships).

Co-governance: the constitution of the Steering and Consulting Committee

When the Italian pilot started, one of the first actions taken by the Epidemiology Service of the LHU of the Reggio Emilia pilot was the stakeholders mapping to find and engage the actors who might be interested in and affected by the production of the app. In collaboration with the partner company of information technologies and the actors who had already participated in the BMI programme (the hospital paediatric unit, family paediatricians, the Food Hygiene Service, and others: Figure 8.1), the LHU itself drafted a list of internal and external stakeholders, decision-makers and beneficiaries of the pilot project. The list was based on two criteria: on the one hand, the professional qualification of stakeholders who had already participated in other projects about childhood obesity; on the other hand, the civic and political representativeness of stakeholders who might be interested in the project. However, the potential interest is evaluated only by LHU, according to its previous and deep knowledge of the city's stakeholders and their activities. The project coordinator did not open a call for interest to probe the willingness of other actors to participate in the process.

This activity sought to identify the contribution of each stakeholder to the process, the potential impact of the project on the stakeholders, and the potential strategies to engage each stakeholder. Based on this list, the coordinating group organised a meeting among all the selected internal stakeholders. During the meeting, the participants proceeded to another stakeholder analysis, eventually deciding on the formation of a 'Steering Committee' which included the expert stakeholders in the field of childhood obesity, informational development (for the technical creation of the app) and research (for the collection of data and the evaluation of the process).

The remaining stakeholders were included in a wider 'Consulting Committee', with the aim to represent the perspective of the actors who dealt with obesity in the city of Reggio Emilia and to provide input into the design of the app. The title 'consulting' recalls indeed the second form of participation in co-creation processes, which is precisely consultation. The Consulting Committee was composed of a high variety of stakeholders belonging to different sectors: mainly public sector organisations (for example, the city of Reggio Emilia's mobility office, the alderman for personal services, health, associations and equal opportunities of towns within the province, dieticians of the local public services, and teachers from the province) and third sector organisations (for example, sports associations). Some actors represented food industries and food distribution companies, making up the private sector contribution. Some of the LHU-affiliated members were the information technology service, the primary care department, the sports medicine sector, and the health promotion sector. This rich composition allowed the actual involvement of sectors fundamental to the children's wellbeing, such as education, municipal administrations, transport, sports associations, and food production/distribution industries, which usually are not involved in the design and production of health and social services (Figure 8.1; Rossi et al, 2020). The group met twice per year. Besides collecting advice from each participant, the meetings aimed to create

Figure 8.1: Evolution of the actors and stakeholders' map

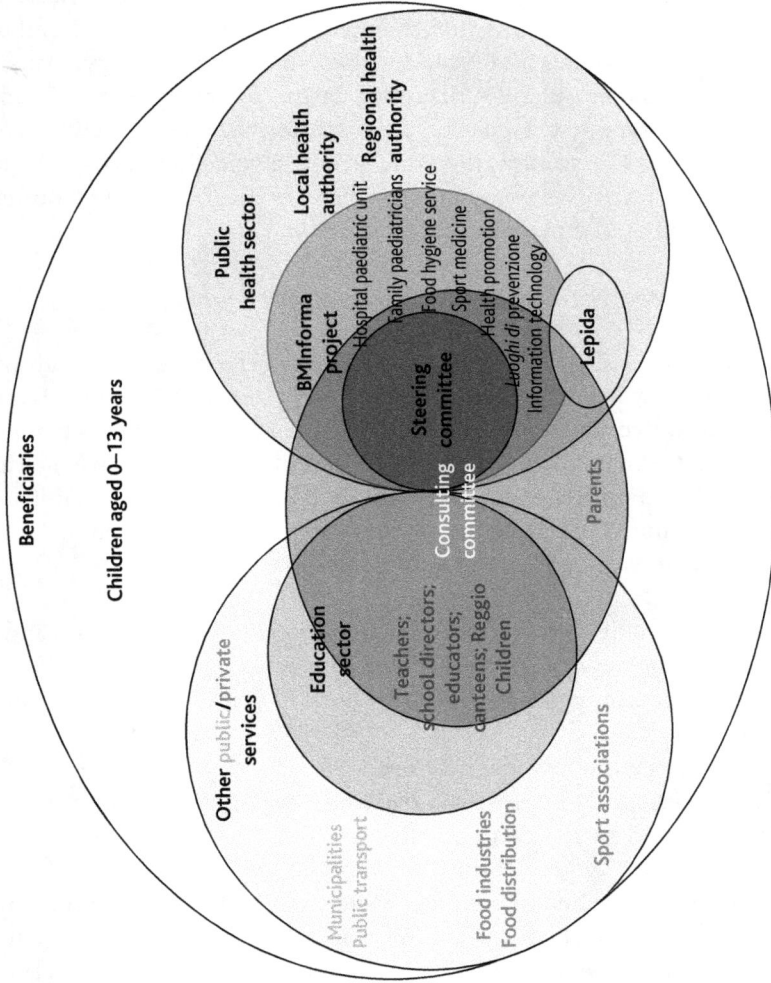

Beneficiaries

Children aged 0–13 years

Public health sector

Local health authority

Regional health authority

BMInforma project

Hospital paediatric unit

Family paediatricians

Food hygiene service

Sport medicine

Health promotion

Luoghi di prevenzione

Information technology

Steering committee

Lepida

Consulting committee

Parents

Other public/private services

Education sector

Teachers; school directors; educators; canteens; Reggio Children

Municipalities

Public transport

Food industries

Food distribution

Sport associations

Source: Rossi et al (2020)

a network that shared experiences and suggestions about the prevention and treatment of obesity, while also supporting each other's activities or projects.

Although the mapping activity identified beneficiaries' families as one of the main stakeholders of the project, the steering actors did not find any users' association or group of parents with childhood obesity concerns to involve in the Consulting Committee and in the co-governance process. All the parents' organisations active in the city of Reggio Emilia were focused on other problems (for example, divorces or disabled children). Therefore, the families have been involved in a 'compensatory' manner in the need assessment phase – described in the following section – and in the app prototype test. However, they did not have any representatives in the Consulting Committee, therefore lacking a voice in the co-governance process. The result was an asymmetry between the Consulting Committee and the families, the main beneficiaries of the app.

Co-management of the service by the constituted groups

After forming the Consulting Committee, the Steering Committee developed the needs assessment phase with the beneficiaries' families. This step was conducted in collaboration with the University of Bologna, through different activities, which included interviews with paediatricians and healthcare professionals, focus groups with paediatricians and parents, and Community Reporting interviews with parents and children. This step is aimed at answering the following questions:

- Are the initiatives and services on childhood obesity prevention and care meeting the needs of parents and children?
- Are all the components of the network linked and do they share the same objectives?
- How can we improve the network?
- Can an app really improve the network?
- What should an app do to be effective?

The materials collected in this phase were organised into main topics by the social science researchers of the University of Bologna and by the curators of People's Voice Media, in order to grasp the needs, desires and claims of families and professionals.

Figure 8.2 denotes the co-creation process which led to the design and production of the app. The dotted rectangles represent the methodologies used, the rectangles filled with diagonal lines are the actors involved, and the arrows show the influences that each phase and actor had on the process. Afterwards, the members of the Consulting Committee were asked to analyse the collected materials. Based on this material, a plenary session of

Figure 8.2: Co-creation process leading to the design and production of the app

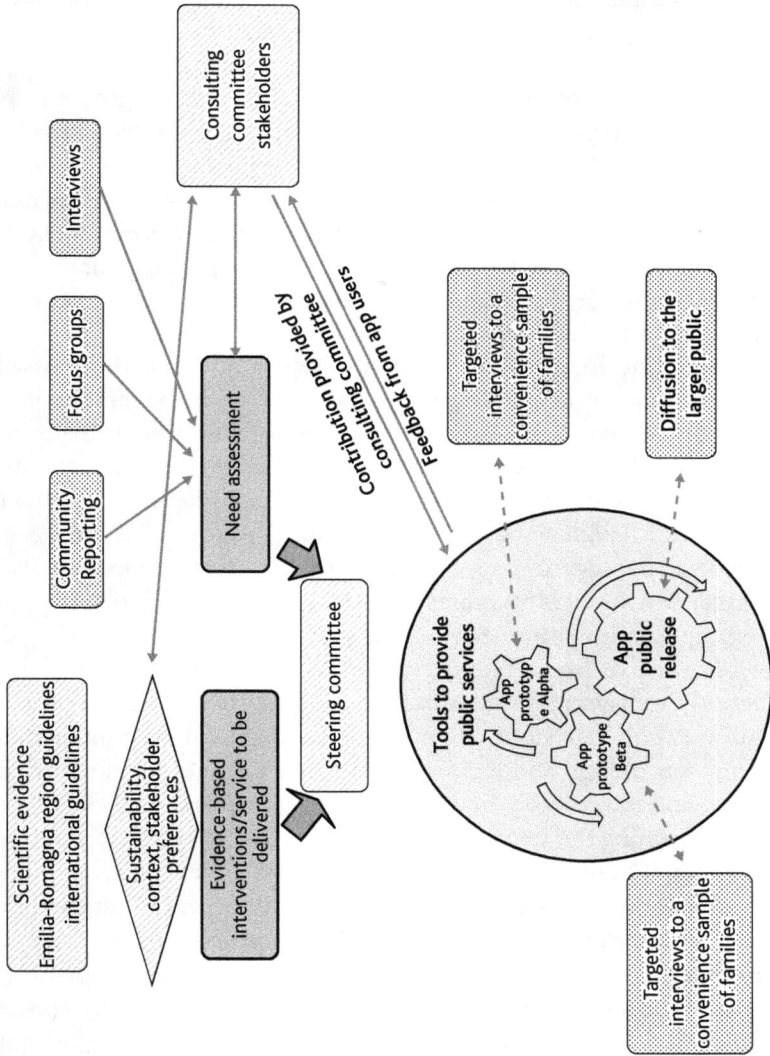

Source: Rossi et al (2020)

the Consulting Committee led to a set of unstructured ideas for the mobile app (Figure 8.2). This set was further developed in a second session by summarising the materials and the ideas in three main issues:

1. identifying all topics related to family wellbeing;
2. grouping topics into overall areas that should be covered by the app; and
3. transforming needs into content within the app.

The Consulting Committee was then reorganised into subgroups to better deal with similar topics and technical issues. Working in smaller groups helped foster greater participation of each stakeholder, because they could work more closely, communicating and showing up reciprocally individual interests and objectives. Since the work done by each subgroup was transformed into a section of the app, all stakeholders had the possibility to contribute actively to the final product, for example, by reporting their indirect experiences with families and children.

However, the interaction among the stakeholders of the Consulting Committee was not always easy during the co-management process. Within the plenary sessions, the proactive participation was limited to those stakeholders whose activities and services were more affected by the development of the app (for example, paediatricians, dieticians and the Food and Nutrition Hygiene Service) and to those who were already engaged and involved in previous projects of the LHU about childhood obesity. The stakeholders who were less directly involved in children's obesity services (for example, cultural and sports associations and school teachers) and that were not used to participating in co-creative processes, did not find the proper way to have a say and remained more isolated from the core of the committee. This behaviour might have been caused by their different levels of competence: high and legitimised by their institutional position in the first case; and lower, more informal, in the second case.

Before reaching the Beta version of the app, the Steering Committee had to take a number of important decisions about the preferences and interests previously elaborated by the Consulting Committee and about the different requests advanced by the families during the need assessment phase. To do so, the Steering Committee evaluated the coherence and the priority of each content of the app, filtering them according to criteria strictly concerned with technical and practical feasibility. One example of a technical filter was given by the language of the future app: it was originally planned to be in Italian and even if this issue raised concerns in the Consulting Committee, the technical limits imposed by the Steering Committee did not allow the translation of the content into other languages. Obviously, this decision will make it very difficult for all foreign parents not speaking Italian to use the app. Another example is given by the suggestion to include, as the families have asked for, a chat between the family and the paediatricians. Despite the initial suggestion of the Consulting Committee, the Steering Committee opted out, fearing a huge work overload for paediatricians.

Co-creation as a way to implement social justice: strength and weaknesses of a pilot project

The chapter describes the constitution of the stakeholders' group, a collective actor who has to co-govern and co-manage an app aimed to reduce childhood obesity. We highlighted how the inclusion (or exclusion) of different stakeholders and the way in which they were allowed to participate in the management were fundamental to developing the co-production process as social justice.

We clarified that social justice in co-creation concerns two dimensions: the inclusion of the highest variety of stakeholders, who might be interested and affected by the new service; and the ways they can participate in the decision-making. Inclusion reveals the willingness and capacity to reflect social complexity, by gathering different stakeholders and by trying to sustain the formation of a collective identity: a 'We' able to orchestrate the different and sometimes conflicting social 'voices'. Participation, on the other hand, implies the capacity to empower all the stakeholders and to give them a voice in institutional arenas for collaborative innovation. The more the process is fair, the more it includes diverse stakeholders affected by the co-creation. The more the process is just, the more it sets the conditions for the full participation of stakeholders in the decision-making.

The combination of these two dimensions results in different forms of social justice, ranging from the lowest labelled as 'informed exclusivity' to the highest as 'deciding inclusiveness'. The Italian pilot achieved 'high inclusiveness' by involving and engaging a rich composition of stakeholders from different societal sectors and with different previous engagements in the design and production of health and social services. Indeed, the variety of stakeholders summoned up for the Consulting Committee is one of the most important strengths (and results) of this pilot case (Ganugi and Russo, 2021). In terms of inclusion, however, the issue was the absence of parents and family associations in this group. Since they lack representative organisations for childhood obesity, the Steering Committee had a lot of difficulties in reaching them. Finally, the families have been included in a 'compensatory' way, involving them only during the need assessment activities and the prototype test.

Regarding the stakeholders' participation, the Steering Committee played a strong and determined role. In fact, the project was already presented to the stakeholders of the Consulting Committee in a detailed and ready-made way. The Consulting Committee members were asked to participate in two plenary meetings and in other subgroup meetings, to read the material collected by the need assessment and to send feedback and ideas. However, even if all members have been heard and took part in the design of the app, eventually the Steering Committee filtered all suggested contents primarily on the basis of technical and normative criteria. Thus, the Consulting Committee has seen its decision-making role (the 'decision-making' type of participation) greatly weakened and watered, at least if compared to what was actually possible. Its role was limited basically to consultation and advice ('consultation' type of participation). Furthermore, a relevant part of the stakeholders involved in the Consulting Committee – namely the third sector organisations, which are not experts in health services for childhood obesity but simply working with activities that could prevent the obesity conditions such as sports and cultural activities – was given little space to be heard, because they were not recognised as fully competent actors if compared with other more institutionalised actors. As already specified, the 'compensatory' and weak inclusion of families caused an asymmetry in terms of participation too. Due to all these elements, we can identify the Italian pilot case with a form of social justice as 'consulting inclusiveness', where a great variety of stakeholders were included as consultants, meaning without full participation and empowerment in the decision-making.

In order to have 'decision-making inclusiveness', which represents the highest possible form of social justice in co-creation processes, the Italian pilot should have conceived a way to represent the families of obese children in the Consulting Committee. Furthermore, their representatives should have participated in the meetings with the same role as the other stakeholders and without any asymmetry. The combination of high inclusiveness and appropriate participation modes would then enable stakeholders to act in such a way to enhance, improve and empower their potential of 'social agency' to the highest degree possible. The evidence from this case underlines also the correlation between having a socially recognised and instituted representative organisation and the possibility to be included in co-creation processes. Those stakeholders, people and social groups – often the more marginalised – who are not represented by any formal organisations and who were not previously in contact with institutions risk not being really included in co-creation processes. Therefore, when designing a co-creation process it is fundamental to reflect on the inclusion of each represented and not represented stakeholder and, consequently, on the modality of their participation. Eventually, to improve the social justice of the process, the Italian pilot should have had fewer technical restrictions to produce the app. This means, on the one hand, having more economical and professional resources, and on the other hand, beginning the process with a more 'drafted' project (instead of one already well defined) to be designed definitely by the group of stakeholders. The necessity to overcome these two issues – including who is not represented and loosening the informative starting point of the project – is summed up by the need to develop more constitutional imagination.

Despite this lens of analysis only being applied to a single case study, the framework composed of the dimensions of social justice as inclusion and participation can be applied to all processes of co-creation. Further analysis could also take into consideration the following phases of co-creation, investigating not only the type of social justice achievable in co-governance and co-management, but also in the phase of co-production of new services.

References

Bassi, A., Ganugi, G. and Prandini, R. (2021) 'Co-design and co-production of public service: the prevention of childhood obesity in Reggio Emilia – Italy', *Polish Political Science Review*, 9(2): 71–88.

Brandsen, T. and Pestoff, V. (2006) 'Co-production, the third sector and the delivery of public services: an introduction', *Public Management Review*, 8(4): 493–501.

Broccoli, S., Davoli, A.M., Bonvicini, L., Fabbri, A., Ferrari, E., Montagna, G., et al (2016) 'Motivational interviewing to treat overweight children: 24-month follow-up of a randomized controlled trial', *Pediatrics*, 137(1): e20151979.

Claassen, R. (2018) *Capabilities in a Just Society*, Cambridge: Cambridge University Press.

Davoli, A.M., Broccoli, S., Bonvicini, L., Fabbri, A., Ferrari, E., D'Angelo, S., et al (2013) 'Pediatrician-led motivational interviewing to treat overweight children: an RCT', *Pediatrics*, 132(5): 1236–1246.

Fox, C., Jalonen, H., Baines, S., Bassi, A., Marsh, C., Moretti, V. and Willoughby, M. (2019) *Co-creation of Public Service Innovation: Something Old, Something New, Something Borrowed, Something Tech*, Report, Turku: Turku University of Applied Sciences.

Fox, C., Baines, S., Wilson, R., Jalonen, H., Narbutaité Aflaki, I., Prandini, R., Bassi, A., Ganugi, G. and Aramo-Immonen, H. (2021) *A New Agenda for Co-Creating Public Services*, Turku: Turku University of Applied Sciences.

Fraser, N. (1998) *Social justice in the age of identity politics: Redistribution, recognition, participation*, WZB Discussion Paper, No. FS I 98-108, Wissenschaftszentrum Berlin für Sozialforschung (WZB), Berlin.

Ganugi, G. and Russo, G. (2021) 'La filiera del cibo e del movimento: politiche urbane e salute pubblica nella città di Reggio Emilia' [The food and movement supply chain: policies urban and public health in the city of Reggio Emilia], in Prandini, R., Maestri, G. and Bassi, A. (eds) *Cibo, stili di vita, salute. Un'indagine empirica nel territorio della ASL di Reggio-Emilia* [Food, lifestyle, health. An empirical investigation in Reggio-Emilia], Milan: FrancoAngeli, pp 77–103.

Häikiö, L. (2010) 'The diversity of citizenship and democracy in local public management reform', *Public Management Review*, 12(3): 363–384.

Leino, H. and Puumala, E. (2021) 'What can co-creation do for the citizens? Applying co-creation for the promotion of participation in cities', *EPC: Politics and Space*, 39(4): 781–799.

Michels, A. (2011) 'Innovations in democratic governance: how does citizen participation contribute to a better democracy?', *International Review of Administrative Sciences*, 77(2): 275–293.

Moulaert, F., MacCallum, D., Mehmood, A. and Hamdouch, A. (2013) *The International Handbook on Social Innovation: Collective Action, Social Learning and Transdisciplinary Research*, Cheltenham: EEP.

Murray, R., Caulier-Grice, J. and Mulgan, G. (2010) *The Open Book of Social Innovation*, London: NESTA.

Pestoff, V. (2012) 'Co-production and third sector social services in Europe: some crucial conceptual issues', in Pestoff, V., Brandsen, T. and Verschuere, B. (eds) *New Public Governance, the Third Sector, and Co-Production*, London: Routledge, pp 11–33.

Prandini, R., Maestri, G. and Bassi, A. (eds) (2021) *Cibo, stili di vita, salute Un'indagine empirica nel territorio della ASL di Reggio-Emilia*, Milan: FrancoAngeli.

Preyer, G. and Peter, G. (2017) *Social Ontology and Collective Intentionality: Critical Essays on the Philosophy of Raimo Tuomela with His Responses*, Cham: Springer.

Rosanvallon, P. (2011) *Democratic Legitimacy: Impartiality, Reflexivity, Proximity*, Princeton: Princeton University Press.

Rossi, P. and Tuurnas, S. (2021) 'Conflicts fostering understanding of value co-creation and service systems transformation in complex public service systems', *Public Management Review*, 23(2): 254–275.

Rossi, P.G., Ferrari, F., Amarri, S., Bassi, A., Bonvicini, L., Dall'Aglio, L., et al (2020) 'Describing the process and tools adopted to co-create a smartphone app for obesity prevention in childhood: mixed method study', *JMIR Mhealth Uhealth*, 8(6): e16165.

Verschuere, B., Vanleene, D. and Steen, T. (2018) 'Democratic co-production: concepts and determinants', in Brandsen, T., Steen, T. and Verscheure, B. (eds) *Co-Production and Cocreation: Engaging Citizens in Public Services*, London: Routledge, pp 243–251.

Von Heimburg, D., Ness, O. and Storch, J. (2021) 'Co-creation of public values: citizenship, social justice, and well-being', in Thomassen, A.O. and Borup Jensen, J. (eds) *Processual Perspectives on the Co-Production Turn in Public Sector Organizations*, Hershey: IGI Globlal, pp 20–41.

9

Evaluation and the evidence base for co-creation

Chris Fox, Andrea Bassi and Sue Baines

Introduction

The evidence base for the impact and outcomes of co-creation is surprisingly weak. After many years of research and evaluation there is a dearth of robust, widely accepted evidence. The reasons are various. They include the interconnectedness and complexity of services, making it difficult to specify and agree measurable outcomes to evaluate. Another related factor is that objectives of co-creation may not be clearly formulated. There are also different views of what counts as convincing evidence. The relational dimension of services tends to favour context-specific, experiential forms of evidence which perfectly fit co-creation as understood by many practitioners and advocates but don't meet the demands of governments and public agencies for validated measures and clear outcome indicators.

This chapter summarises the evidence base for the impact of co-creation and related aspects of social policy such as asset-based working and personalisation. There follows an overview of the evaluations undertaken in Co-creation of Service Innovation in Europe (CoSIE) pilots (which form the basis of the empirical evidence reported in Chapters 3, 4, 5, 6 and 8). University-based partners in each participating country evaluated the pilots, working closely with the local partners. Pilot evaluations were locally responsive and intended to be flexible while following broad guidelines and common reporting elements. We recognise that evaluation across the project faced challenges and limitations. There were many partners and stakeholders with varied assumptions about what counts as good information and reliable evidence. Inspired by learning from CoSIE but going beyond what the project was able to achieve in its lifetime, we proffer a new strategy for evaluation of co-creative interventions in future.

The current evidence base for co-creation

Given that co-creation in public services can trace its modern origins back to work by Ostrom and colleagues in the late 1970s and early 1980s (Ostrom and Ostrom, 1977; Parks et al, 1981; Ostrom, 1996) it might be imagined that by now there would be a strong evidence-base underpinning cocreation and the closely related concept of co-production. However, this is not the case. To date, our knowledge about whether and how co-creation and co-production contribute to outcomes is very limited. Voorberg et al (2015) identify over a hundred empirical studies of co-creation and co-production between public organisations and citizens (or their representatives) but only 14 papers evaluated the outcome of co-production in terms of an increase (or decrease) in service effectiveness, leading Voorberg et al (2015: 16) to conclude that: '[G]iven the limited number records that reported on the outcomes of co-creation/co-production, we cannot definitely conclude whether co-creation/co-production can be considered as beneficial.' Voorberg et al (2015) are able to say more about co-creation and co-production processes and identify eight factors which affect whether the objectives of co-creation and co-production between public organisations and citizens (or their representatives) are achieved, and they separate these according to whether they operate on the organisational or citizen side of co-creation. However, on the organisational side these four factors are fairly abstract, for example, an open attitude towards citizen participation or a risk-averse administrative culture. They do not pinpoint specific practices that support effective co-creation. The four factors identified on the citizen side are each supported by only a small number of studies (n ranges from two to ten).

Part of the challenge here is that qualitative case studies still dominate the evidence base for co-creation (Durose et al, 2017; Brandsen et al, 2018). Durose et al (2017) note that many evaluations identified in evidence reviews are overly reliant on single case studies. This, together with inconsistencies in how the terms co-production and co-creation are used in different studies make comparative and meta-analytical work difficult, meaning that it is hard to identify specific practice that is widely recognised as effective.

Another challenge is finding evaluation strategies that can address the complexity around co-creation in public services. Durose et al (2017) argue that co-production has a relational dimension which does not easily fit an evaluation agenda dominated by narrowly framed quantitative impact evaluations favoured in UK (and US) government policy making. One manifestation of complexity is the difficulty of defining outcomes for co-created and co-produced initiatives that are explicit and therefore susceptible to evaluation. For example, in a recent study Allen et al (2019) note the tension within health and social care between co-produced research and producing evidence of quantifiable outcomes using validated outcome measures. Thus, clear cause-effect relationships between co-production activities and their outcomes are difficult to define (Brix et al, 2020) and an important role for evaluators working in a complex system is to find leverage points in the system at which a small shift in one factor can produce widespread changes.

Another factor contributing to the challenge is that the dominant theory within which co-creation is often conceptualised, New Public Governance, is not normative. Brix et al (2020) argue that New Public Governance assumes that co-production leads to beneficial outcomes, but Osborne (2010) argues that New Public Governance is not intended to be a new paradigm of public service delivery nor is it intended to be normative. Citing Engen et al (2020), Osborne et al note that 'there is no guarantee that user interaction with public services will always create value for them. Poorly designed or delivered public services may actually have a deleterious impact on service users and detract from their lives (value destruction)' (Osborne et al, 2021: 645). Recent reviews and studies of the evidence base for co-creation and co-production in public services support this proposition and the so-called 'dark side of co-creation' has been thoroughly documented (Jalonen et al, 2020; Cluley et al, 2021).

The challenge of building an evidence base is shared by similar areas of social policy. As argued elsewhere in this book (see Chapter 2), co-creation has a close relationship with strengths-based work. In a recently published systematic review of the evidence for different strengths-based approaches in adult social work, Price et al (2020) concluded that there is a lack of good quality research evidence evaluating the effectiveness or implementation of strengths-based approaches.

Co-creation can also be understood as part of a broader set of strategies and approaches to the 'personalisation' of public services, particularly what Leadbetter (2004) refers to as 'deep' personalisation. Pearson et al (2014) note that early advocacy for personalisation by Leadbetter (2004) drew on personal narratives rather than research.

Another way to view co-creation is as a form of social innovation. In a review of evaluation practices in social innovation, Milley et al (2018) found that most evaluations had developmental purposes, emphasised collaborative approaches and used multiple methods. Prominent drivers were a complexity perspective, a learning-oriented focus and the need for responsiveness.

Evaluation in Co-creation of Service Innovation in Europe

The CoSIE project put strong emphasis on evaluation. Evaluation is distinguished by the importance of establishing value and making reasoned judgements about programmes, interventions and policies (Fox et al, 2016). It was built into the CoSIE project for two reasons. First, it was a way to support learning and reflection in a timely way within the pilots during the lifetime of the project. This is known as 'formative' evaluation. Second, 'summative' evaluation was intended to ensure that the implementation and impact of the pilots were fully documented and evidenced with regard to what worked, why and for whom.

An evaluation research team in each participating country was tasked with undertaking evaluations of their local pilot. These evaluations employed a mixed-method multidimensional approach combining theory of change with aspects of the action research tradition. Theory of change is very common in evaluations whatever the paradigm in which they are situated. It involves surfacing assumptions from many participants and stakeholders about how change should be enabled. Action research narrows the traditional gap between theory and practice. There are many variations, but a key feature is the active and intentional involvement of researchers intervening in the organisation or group studied, and working with members of it on matters of genuine concern to them (Huxham, 2003). Action research thus runs counter to objectivist concepts of the researcher as impartial bystander (Mackay and Marshall, 2001).

CoSIE pilot evaluations did not adhere to a single standard methodology or rigid protocol, but all contained four core elements:

- *Background, needs and context* to report what problematic conditions existed for whom, who had a stake in the problem, and what could be changed.
- *Theory of change* to articulate the desired outcomes, identify aspects that might prevent them, and visualise the actions needed to mitigate barriers. Each pilot worked closely with stakeholders to develop its own theory of change.
- *Process evaluation* to answer 'how' and 'what is going on' questions. Process evaluation (sometimes called implementation evaluation) concerns experiences and interactions provided by a programme, project or intervention. It verifies if it was implemented as intended and also uncovers unintended delivery issues.
- *Impact evaluation* to answer the questions 'What were the results?' and 'What difference was made?'

Each evaluation team carried out most or all the following forms of data collection:

- individual and small group interviews with professional staff and managers, citizens and stakeholders;
- participant and/or non-participant observation;

- focus groups or participatory workshops;
- document analysis;
- analysis of administrative data;
- small-scale surveys.

Running alongside and in close cooperation with these evaluation activities was Community Reporting, discussed in detail in Chapter 7. Community Reporting complemented more traditional forms of evaluation research data. It has much in common with peer research, in which people who are intended targets of an intervention receive training and support to gather and review evaluation evidence (Devotta et al, 2016).

The evaluation data were mainly although not exclusively qualitative. Only one CoSIE pilot team ('My Direction' in the UK) chose to deliver a quantitative quasi-experimental counterfactual evaluation design (see Chapter 6). The conditions that made this possible within the project timeframe were the short length of the pilot intervention, a tightly scoped pilot within an existing service, and availability of reliable data on an equivalent 'untreated' group. This combination of conditions did not exist in other pilots. In Italy, an epidemiological study with full randomised control commenced in autumn 2021. The effectiveness of the BeBa app (see Chapter 4) in triggering a lasting change in lifestyles is under assessment in a study with two groups, placebo and control, of 200 families with children between the ages of three and 11. The timescale for this 'gold standard' evidence extends beyond the life of the CoSIE project but is an important part of its legacy.

The evaluation strategy in CoSIE entailed the adoption of a flexible role by the research teams. The academic partners had to move back and forth form an 'inside/internal' to an 'outside/external' observation standpoint. This has dangers and biases but, when engaged in with due reflection, can enable researchers to develop a rich, comprehensive understanding of the dynamics of change (Badham and Sense, 2006). It demands a very high level of reflexivity among the partners involved.

In addition to evaluation reports, all academic partners undertook an exercise that could be defined as self-evaluation or reflexive inquiry on the extent of co-creation and the engagement of different kinds of stakeholders in each pilot. To do this they completed a 'co-creation matrix' concerning different phases and actors of the co-creation process. The goal was to get an estimation of the degree of co-creation using a common framework (a five-point scale) that would allow comparisons across the pilots. They also supplied free text explanations for their scores.

CoSIE involved many interlocutors, including partners, stakeholders, advisors and external monitors. Often, they held deep-seated assumptions about what constitutes good evaluation evidence. For people working on the front line as professionals or advocates, accounts of lived experience (stories) as demonstrated in Chapter 7 are uniquely authentic and map closely onto their understanding of co-creation. Public authorities, in contrast, tend to favour measurable, comparable indicators. In the midst of the project, one of the authors blogged that '[I]t can feel like the project faces a cacophony of demands and assertions about information and evidence from within and without' (Baines, 2021).

A strategy for evaluating co-creation

Durose et al (2017) advance a 'good enough' strategy for evaluating co-production. The first step in this approach is to articulate a theory of change for the programme or project being evaluated. A second step is to 'explicitly include the insights of people working within public services as a form of knowledge-based practice drawn from proximity and familiarity, rather than leaving this as an implicit part of evaluation which can be dismissed as excessively normative' (Durose et al, 2017: 138). They go on to cite a range of 'good enough' methodologies which community organisations and small-scale service providers experimenting with co-production can use to assess its potential contribution, including appreciative inquiry, peer-to-peer learning and data sharing. Durose et al (2017) argue that storytelling is particularly important in co- production, not only in evidencing the significance of its relational dynamics but also in representing different voices and experiences in an accessible way. They argue that storytelling offers a way to draw on the insights of the people working in co-productive ways, rather than assuming that they are too 'close' to the case study to be able to offer valid insights.

We agree with all of these points and, in particular, the importance of people with lived experience of services 'co-evaluating' them as 'co-creators and collaborators' (Paskaleva and Cooper, 2018: 6). However, we disagree with Durose et al that a 'good enough' approach is sufficient. Durose et al are right to point to the limitations of 'traditional' counterfactual impact evaluations in evaluating co-creation, but they pay insufficient attention to the wider range of impact evaluation designs that can answer questions about the impact of a programme or project, but that do not rely on large cohorts and counterfactuals and are better suited to addressing complexity.

To explain the value of these different evaluation strategies it is useful to start with an understanding of the different perspectives of evaluators regarding the problem of causal inference (Fox et al, 2022). These perspectives determine the approaches that researchers use, the methods they advocate and why. Causal inference considers the assumptions, study designs and estimation strategies that allow researchers to draw causal conclusions based on data (Hill and Stuart, 2015). Our starting point is to recognise that there is a fundamental distinction between two types of question that social scientists ask when they use the tools and techniques of social science in evaluation (Fox et al, 2022). First, social scientists may ask: What are the effects of a causal factor (that is, an intervention or treatment)? Second, and in contrast, they may ask: What are the causal factors that give rise to an effect? These questions are what Dawid (2007) calls 'effects of causes' and 'causes of effects' type questions.

The limitations of 'traditional' counterfactual impact evaluations

Evaluations that ask 'effects of causes' questions use designs that involve the concept of manipulation (Shadish et al, 2002); that is, some causal factor, treatment or intervention is manipulated – it is introduced, scaled up, scaled down or ended. Moreover, evaluators either have some knowledge of how the causal factor is manipulated or can intervene directly in its manipulation, as is the case in a randomised design (Fox et al, 2022). A randomised controlled trial (RCT) is designed to help the evaluator estimate the effects of a particular causal factor – the specified intervention. Due to the nature of an RCT, other factors that might influence the outcome are distributed equally over two groups – an intervention and a control group. Only the intervention group receives the intervention; the control group does not. At the point at which the two groups are created, through randomisation, they are statistically equivalent to one another. Any average difference in a prespecified outcome(s) that we subsequently observe between the two groups can be attributed to the intervention and not other causes, subject to standard statistical thresholds for sampling uncertainty. This is a classic 'effects of causes' type approach. The other factors that influence the outcome are treated as exogenous or given. Their effects are not removed or, as some critics have claimed, bracketed out. Instead, the research design holds other causal factors in balance across the two groups, enabling attention to be focused on the causal factor that can be manipulated by the evaluator – that is, the intervention itself (Fox et al, 2022).

Often manipulation through randomisation is not possible, but we may be able to intervene in some other way to determine who is exposed to the intervention (based on an explicit rule, for example) or collect enough information about how choices are made to model exposure. In both these situations, we use statistical techniques to adjust our analysis to try to improve our estimates of the potential outcomes. The UK CoSIE pilot evaluation did this using a 'non-equivalent comparison group design' (Shadish et al, 2002). These approaches are known as quasi-experimental, in that they attempt to mimic an experiment by using some other form of manipulation and/or statistical techniques to adjust the analysis to take account of likely biases (Fox et al, 2022).

However, experimental and quasi-experimental approaches have their limitations. The simplification of the causal problem may gloss over important relationships between causal factors that act together to produce outcomes. While the influence of all causal factors that affect an outcome is not 'removed' from estimates obtained from, for example, a randomised experiment, they are not specifically accounted for (Fox et al, 2022). The fundamental issue here is whether these evaluation designs are sufficient to account for complexity of many instances of co-creation. Not only is co-creation strongly relational, but it takes place in complex public service systems. Different stakeholders might have different motivations and pursue different, or even changing, outcomes. These interactions are likely to give rise to emergent properties and the relationship and interactions of the differing parts of the complex system that is developed are likely to be dynamic and, potentially, non-linear, leading to the possibility that small changes might have disproportionate outcomes and vice versa.

Impact evaluation with small cohorts

These challenges suggest that an 'effects of causes' evaluation question may not always be most appropriate for evaluating co-creation programmes and projects. It may be more appropriate to ask the question: 'What are the causal factors that give rise to an effect?' This is what Dawid (2007) calls a 'causes of effects' question, in contrast to the 'effects of causes' type questions asked in traditional, counterfactual impact evaluations. A more appropriate approach to designing an impact evaluation to answer this type of question will be to adopt a case-based (sometimes called a small 'n') approach to the impact evaluation.

Key to all small-n approaches is the idea of analysing one or a small number of cases to derive causal statements about the impact of an intervention. These relatively recent methodologies and designs for impact evaluation can be distinguished from traditional understandings of 'case studies' (Stern et al, 2012). The tradition in evaluation of naturalistic, constructivist and interpretive case studies that generally focus on the unique characteristics of a single case might contribute to richer understanding of causation but cannot themselves support causal analysis (Stern et al, 2012). By contrast, these approaches that use small numbers of cases are designed to generalise beyond a single case but distinguish 'generalising' from 'universalising' (Byrne, 2009: 1).

A key distinction between case-based approaches and experimental designs is the rejection of analysis based on variables (Byrne, 2009). Case-based approaches reject the 'disembodied variable' (Byrne, 2009: 4). The case is a complex entity in which multiple causes interact: 'It is how these causes interact as a set that allows an understanding of cases. ... This view does not ignore individual causes of variables but examines them as "configurations" or "sets" in their context' (Stern et al, 2012: 31). Perhaps the best known approach in this broad tradition is Realist Evaluation (Pawson and Tilley, 1997). Other better known ones include Qualitative Comparative Analysis (Rihoux and Ragin, 2009), Process Tracing (Bennett and Checkel, 2015), Contribution Analysis (Mayne, 2008) and General Elimination Theory (Scriven, 2008). Many of the approaches to impact evaluation associated with uncovering 'causes of effects' involve specifying mid-level theory or a theory of change together with alternative causal hypotheses. Causation is established beyond reasonable doubt by collecting evidence to validate, invalidate or revise hypothesised explanations (White and Phillips, 2012).

Small-n, case-based methodologies are varied but Befani and Stedman-Bryce (2017) suggest that case-based methods can be broadly typologised as either between case comparisons (such as qualitative comparative analysis) or within case analysis (for example, process tracing). Generally, quantitative and qualitative data is used and a sharp distinction between quantitative and qualitative methods is rejected (Stern et al, 2012).

Within what might broadly be classified as 'causes of effects' approaches to impact evaluation, Stern et al (2012) make a broad distinction between approaches based on the concept of generative causation and those based on multiple causalities. The generative conception of causation 'sees the matter of causation "internally". Cause describes the *transformative potential* of phenomena' (Pawson and Tilley, 1997: 293; original emphasis). Generative causation depends on identifying the 'mechanisms' that explain effects. This is the inferential basis for 'realist' approaches to impact evaluation (Stern et al, 2012), but is also important in approaches such as Process Tracing and the General Elimination Method where identifying and tracing mechanisms is also a central task of the evaluation design. In small-n methodologies, when multiple causes are recognised, the focus tends to switch to understanding the *contribution* of an intervention to an observed outcome. The notion of a 'contributory' cause recognises that effects are produced by several causes at the same time, none of which may be necessary nor sufficient for impact. This, in turn, leads to several impact questions that go beyond attribution to develop an understanding of *how* an intervention contributes to an observed effect:

If a causal 'package', i.e. the intervention plus other factors, is the concept most likely to be relevant in the impact evaluation of complex ... projects, this focuses attention on the role of the intervention in that package. Was it a necessary ground-preparing cause, a necessary triggering cause or something that did not make any difference and a similar effect would have occurred without the intervention? (Stern et al, 2012: 40)

What might an evaluation strategy for co-creation look like?

Many of the small-n approaches to impact evaluation start with theory of change and, like Durose et al (2017), we argue that this is a useful starting point. All the CoSIE pilot evaluations featured theory of change. The theory of change is fundamentally participatory in its process of development; it includes a variety of stakeholders and, therefore, perceptions. The process of developing a theory of change should be based on a range of rigorous evidence, including local knowledge and experience, past programming material and social science theory, all of which are brought together in an iterative process (Stein and Valters, 2012). First articulated as an evaluation tool, the theory of change developed into an approach to programme planning as well as a tool for evaluation (Fox et al, 2016) and as such is well-suited to support organisations in which co-creation is deeply embedded and which will, in turn, be learning organisations (see Chapter 2 in this volume).

It would be perverse if evaluations of co-creation and co-production were not themselves co-produced. Many small-n impact evaluation methodologies would naturally include lived experience alongside more traditional types of research data. Some, such as Most Significant Change (Davies and Dart, 2005), are built on lived experience, with people who access services supported to tell stories of significant change.

The choice of a specific methodology will depend in part on the particular evaluation question to be answered and on the nature of the programme or project being evaluated. Befani (2020) has developed a guide for selecting between different impact evaluation methodologies, including small-n designs. It is common to combine different small-n methodologies. For example, Befani and Mayne (2014) have noted that Contribution Analysis and Process Tracing are similar, both seeking to make causal inferences using non-counterfactual approaches, based on causal mechanisms and theories of change. Another example of combining methodologies would be where agent-based modelling is used to check the plausibility of inferences about mechanisms derived from Process Tracing (Bennett and Checkel, 2015).

However, the complexity of co-created approaches should not rule out the possibility of also undertaking evaluation using traditional, counterfactual impact evaluation. These are likely to come later in the life-cycle of an innovation when mid-level theory is clarified, the approach has become more settled, context is understood and investment in taking an approach to scale requires a focus on outcomes. One of two broad strategies might be appropriate. One strategy is to undertake what are variously termed mixed-method or realist randomised controlled trials or RCT+ designs (Morris et al, 2020). A related approach is to implement randomised designs that combine randomisation with mixed-method implementation process evaluation (Morris et al, 2020). While in the past such mixing of methodologies might have fallen foul of the so-called 'paradigm wars' increasingly researchers argue there is no essential link between method and paradigm. Some adopt 'pragmatism' as a philosophical perspective to underpin their research, others operate in the 'realist' tradition (Morris et al, 2020).

Evaluation lessons from Co-creation of Service Innovation in Europe

Given the size and complexity of the CoSIE project and diversity of the pilots it is hardly surprising that there were many, sometimes incompatible, views on what counted as appropriate evidence for evaluation. This is reflective of the wider co-creation field. In particular, in CoSIE there were ongoing tensions between a preference for contextual evidence drawn from lived experience and measurement of impacts perceived as more 'objective'. Although this touches upon the academic 'paradigm wars' previously mentioned it goes much deeper. It recognises that fundamentally different 'worldviews' coexist in multi-agency, cross-sector public service environments (Baines et al, 2023). These tensions were repeatedly played out within CoSIE, as illustrated in the following examples.

Members of the Netherlands CoSIE team participated in a conference entitled *Knowledge Network for Narrative Accountability*, which brought together 80 policy makers, social professionals, researchers and also storytelling specialists. Participants including professionals and civil servants were receptive to the value of working with stories of lived experience. It was also noted during the event however that public administrations and most organisations work with pre-defined plans and targets, and that working with stories does not easily fit the budgetary lines and organisational structure of local administrations (Geelhoed, 2020).

When the project faced external review, it was criticised for lack of a single, standardised evaluation framework across all the pilots. The pilot leaders, partly as a response to this feedback, introduced the self-evaluation exercise using common questions and indicative scores, as mentioned previously. The matrix was presented to the partners in a draft version during a consortium meeting. This elicited debate mainly among the academic partners on the rationale behind the score assignment. Some argued that the scores were overly 'subjective', depending on the judgement of the researchers. A lively discussion ensued about the difference between 'subjective' and 'objective' knowledge in social sciences. The research instrument was refined and improved following this exchange. The exercise produced valuable data not only in the form of scores (which enabled useful categorisation and comparison across the pilots) but also critical self-reflections on the reasoning behind the scores.

In the Italian pilot one of the partners was a local health authority and multiple stakeholders including non-profit organisations, local businesses and various public services such as transport were actively engaged (see

Chapter 8). Only the health authority demanded 'scientific' evidence of efficacy. A completely unexpected and positive outcome was the opening up of debate centred on evidence-based content typical of health protocols to stakeholders unfamiliar with it.

A key lesson from CoSIE is the importance in such complex, multifaceted public service environments of being open to many forms of evaluation evidence, and the positive benefits from entering into constructive dialogue about them. It is comfortable but ineffective to rely only on forms of evidence that meet the preferences of some groups but fail to respond to the interests and concerns of others (Baines et al, 2023).

As with other evaluations concerned with social innovations, the CoSIE pilot evaluations were done collaboratively with emphasis on development, learning and responsiveness to local contexts (Milley et al, 2018). They deployed a range of methodologies that could be considered 'good enough' in accordance with the principles elaborated by Durose et al (2017). They provided a wealth of powerful evidence about implementation of co-creation and some insights into the impact of individual pilots, much of it reported in this volume. With hindsight, we reflect that the wide range of recently developed impact evaluation designs could have been reviewed and assessed as part of the project plan, and potentially deployed across the pilots. We recommended such a strategy for future projects.

References

Allen, K., Needham, C., Hall, K. and Tanner, D. (2019) 'Participatory research meets validated outcome measures: tensions in the coproduction of social care evaluation', *Social Policy and Administration*, 53(2): 311–325.

Badham, R. and Sense, A. (2006) 'Spiralling up or spinning out: a guide for reflecting on action research practice', *International Journal of Social Research Methodology*, 9(5): 367–377.

Baines, S. (2021) *Making Sense of Information and Evidence for Co-creation*, https://cosie.turkuamk.fi/arkisto/general/making-sense-of-information-and-evidence-for-co-creation/index.html

Baines, S., Bull, M., Antcliff, V. and Martin, L. (2023) 'Good stories get lost in bureaucracy! Cultural biases and information for co-production', *Public Money & Management*, 43(2): 136–146.

Befani, B. (2020) *Choosing Appropriate Evaluation Methods: A Tool for Assessment and Selection*, London: CECAN.

Befani, B. and Mayne, J. (2014) 'Process tracing and contribution analysis: a combined approach to generative causal inference for impact evaluation', *IDS Bulletin*, 45(6): 17–36.

Befani, B. and Stedman-Bryce, G. (2017) 'Process tracing and Bayesian updating for impact evaluation', *Evaluation*, 23(1): 42–60. https://doi.org/10.1177/1356389016654584

Bennett, A. and Checkel, J. (eds) (2015) *Process Tracing: From Metaphor to Analytic Tool*, Cambridge: Cambridge University Press.

Brandsen, T., Steen, T. and Vershuere, B. (2018) 'Co-creation and co-production in public services: urgent issues in practice and research', in Brandsen, T., Steen, T. and Vershuere, B. (eds) *Co-Creation and Co-Production: Engaging Citizens in Public Services*, Oxford: Routledge, pp 1–6.

Brix, J., Krogstrup, H.K. and Mortensen, N.M. (2020) 'Evaluating the outcomes of co-production in local government', *Local Government Studies*, 46(2): 169–185.

Byrne, D. (2009) 'Case-based methods: why we need them; what they are; how to do them', in Byrne, D. and Ragin, C. (eds) *The SAGE Handbook of Case-Based Methods*, London: SAGE, pp 1–10.

Cluley, V., Parker, S. and Radnor, Z. (2021) 'New development: expanding public service value to include dis/value', *Public Money & Management*, 41(8): 656–659.

Davies, R. and Dart, J. (2005) *The 'Most Significant Change' (MSC) Technique: A Guide to Its Use*, https://www.researchgate.net/publication/ 275409002_The_'Most_Significant_Change'_MSC_ Technique_A_ Guide_to_Its_Use

Dawid, A.P. (2007) 'Counterfactuals, hypotheticals and potential responses: a philosophical examination of statistical causality', in Russo, F. and Williamson, J. (eds) *Causality and Probability in the Sciences*, London: College Publications, pp 503–532.

Devotta, K., Woodhall-Melnik, J., Pedersen, C., Wendaferew, A., Dowbor, T.P., Guilcher, S.J., Hamilton-Wright, S., Ferentzy, P., Hwang, S.W. and Matheson, F.I. (2016) 'Enriching qualitative research by engaging peer interviewers: a case study', *Qualitative Research*, 16(6): 661–680.

Durose, C., Needham, C., Mangan, C. and Rees, J. (2017) 'Generating "good enough" evidence for co-production', *Evidence & Policy*, 13(1): 135–151.

Engen, M., Fransson, M., Quist, J. and Skålén, P. (2020) 'Continuing the development of the public service logic: a study of value co-destruction in public services', *Public Management Review*, 23(6): 886–905.

Fox, C., Grimm, R. and Caldeira, R. (2016) *An Introduction to Evaluation*, London: SAGE.

Fox, C., Gellen, S., Morris, S., Ozan, J. and Crockford, J. (2022) *Impact Evaluation with Small Cohorts: Methodology Guidance. Transforming Access and Student Outcomes in Higher Education*, London: TASO.

Geelhoed, S. (2020) *The Impact of Stories: How to Translate Stories of Lived Experience to the Policy Cycle?* https://cosie.turkuamk.fi/arkisto/general/ the-impact-of-stories/index.html

Hill, J. and Stuart, E.A. (2015) 'Causal inference: overview', in Smelser, N.J. and Baltes, P.B. (eds) *International Encyclopedia of the Social & Behavioral Sciences*, Amsterdam: Elsevier, pp 255–260.

Huxham, C. (2003) 'Action research as a methodology for theory development', *Policy & Politics*, 31(2): 239–248.

Jalonen, H., Puustinen, A. and Raisio, H. (2020) 'The hidden side of co-creation in complex multistakeholder environment: when self-organization fails and emergence overtakes', in Lehtimäki, H., Uusikylä, P. and Smedlund, A. (eds) *Society as an Interaction Space: A Systemic Approach*, Cham: Springer, pp 3–22.

Leadbetter, C. (2004) *Personalisation through Participation: A New Script for Public Services*, London: Demos.

Mackay, J. and Marshall, P. (2001) 'The dual imperatives of action research', *Information Technology & People*, 14(1): 46–59.

Mayne, J. (2008) *Contribution Analysis: An Approach to Exploring Cause and Effect*, Brief 16, Institutional Learning and Change (ILAC) Initiative.

Milley, P., Szijarto, B., Svensson, K. and Cousins, J.B. (2018) 'The evaluation of social innovation: a review and integration of the current empirical knowledge base', *Evaluation*, 24(2): 237–258.

Morris, S., Smith, A. and Fox, C. (2020) 'Time to reset the clock on the design of impact evaluations in criminology: the case for multi-methodology designs', *British Journal of Community Justice*, 16(3): 1–18.

Osborne, S.P. (2010) 'Introduction: the (new) public governance: a suitable case for treatment', in Osborne, S.P. (ed) *The New Public Governance? Emerging Perspectives on the Theory and Practice of Public Governance*, Oxford: Routledge, pp 1–11.

Osborne, S.P., Nasi, G. and Powell, M. (2021) 'Beyond co-production: value creation and public services', *Public Administration*, 99: 641–657, https://doi.org/10.1111/padm.12718

Ostrom, E. (1996) 'Crossing the great divide: coproduction, synergy, and development', *World Development*, 24(6): 1073–1087.

Ostrom, V. and Ostrom, E. (1977) 'Public goods and public choices', in Savas, E.S. (ed) *Alternatives for Delivering Public Services: Toward Improved Performance*, Boulder: Westview Press, pp 7–49.

Parks, R.B., Baker, P.C., Kiser, L., Oakerson, R., Ostrom, E., Ostrom, V., Percy, S.L., Vandivort, M.B., Whitaker, G.P. and Wilson, R. (1981) 'Consumers as coproducers of public services: some economic and institutional considerations', *Policy Studies Journal*, 9: 1001–1011. https://doi.org/10.1111/j.1541–0072.1981.tb01208.x

Paskaleva, K. and Cooper, I. (2018) 'Open innovation and the evaluation of internet-enabled public services in smart cities', *Technovation*, 78: 4–14.

Pawson, R. and Tilley, N. (1997) 'What works in evaluation research?', *The British Journal of Criminology*, 34(3): 291–306.

Pearson, C., Hunter, S. and Ridley, J. (2014) *Self-Directed Support: Personalisation, Choice and Control*, Edinburgh: Dunedin Academic Press.

Price, A., Ahuja, L., Bramwell, C., Briscoe, S., Shaw, L. and Nunns, M. (2020) *Research Evidence on Different Strengths-Based Approaches within Adult Social Work: A Systematic Review*, Southampton: NIHR Health Services and Delivery Research Topic Report.

Rihoux, B. and Ragin, C. (eds) (2009) *Configurational Comparative Methods: Qualitative Comparative Analysis (QCA) and Related Techniques*, London: SAGE.

Scriven, M. (2008) 'A summative evaluation of RCT methodology: & an alternative approach to causal research', *Journal of MultiDisciplinary Evaluation*, 5(9): 11–24.

Shadish, W.R., Cook, T.D. and Campbell, D.T. (2002) *Experimental and Quasi-Experimental Designs for Generalized Causal Inference*, New York: Houghton Mifflin and Company.

Stein, D. and Valters, C. (2012) *Understanding Theory of Change in International Development*, London: Justice and Security Research Programme, London School of Economics.

Stern, E., Stame, N., Mayne, J., Forss, J., Davies, R. and Befani, B. (2012) *Broadening the Range of Designs and Methods for Impact Evaluations*, DFID Working Paper 38, London: Department for International Development.

Voorberg, W., Bekkers, V. and Tummers, L. (2015) 'A systematic review of co-creation and co-production: embarking on the social innovation journey', *Public Management Review*, 17(9): 1333–1357.

White, H. and Phillips, D. (2012) *Addressing Attribution of Cause and Effect in Small n Impact Evaluations: Towards an Integrated Framework*, Working Paper 15, International Initiative for Impact Evaluation.

10

Living Labs for innovating relationships: the CoSMoS tool

David Jamieson, Mike Martin, Rob Wilson,
Florian Sipos, Judit Csoba and Alex Sakellariou

Introduction

Living Labs have emerged across Europe to foster experimentation and testing of new solutions in public administration (Dekker et al, 2020). There are many variations, but core features include real-life settings and cooperation between multiple stakeholders (Dekker et al, 2020). The Living Lab in Newcastle (led by authors Wilson, Martin and Jamieson) is an approach to innovating relationships between stakeholders in multi-agency, cross-sector collaboration contexts. It does this through the representation of projects and programmes using a range of visualization and modelling techniques supported by a suite of open source and creative commons tools. The Co-creation of Service Innovation in Europe (CoSIE) project applied Living Labs to support pilots with meeting their goals of service innovation and co-creation through the innovation of relationships.

As the project progressed, the Living Labs approach in CoSIE evolved in response to practical challenges of working with multiple stakeholders across diverse sociopolitical, linguistic and technical contexts, as well as variations in levels of maturity (Jamieson and Martin, 2022). Constraints caused by the COVID-19 pandemic also put a halt to face-to-face interactions as originally envisaged. The evolved approach was to build an interactive digital platform which included both a representation of models created within the CoSIE project and others borrowed from outside the project. These were deployed along with tools to allow for the curation of evidence – websites, images and files, social media, and open data sources – which can be used to inform wider discussions. The platform – CoSMoS – was designed so that stakeholders could be engaged either offline, individually, within a workshop or in a real-time or asynchronous environment (Martin et al, 2019; Jamieson et al, 2020a; 2020b). The outputs can be shared with a range of involved stakeholders, and then compared and used to enhance discussions regarding aspects of service and social innovation (Jamieson and Martin, 2022). This provided a set of templated models which produced – and produces – a map of the roles and relationships and a representation of the local service development and/or delivery processes (Jamieson and Martin, 2022).

In this chapter we present an initial generic co-creation model followed by a series of four analytic models, each of which links to the practical challenges associated with co-creation. Then we illustrate how the models were adopted and used in practice in two contrasting CoSIE sites, in Greece and Hungary. We conclude with reflections on how the CoSMoS tool supports both practitioners and participants in realising and communicating co-creation within their own environments as part of reflective, emergent and evaluative engagements.

Living Labs in the context of the Co-creation of Service Innovation in Europe project

'Living Labs' is an elastic concept and has a broad appeal to a range of disciplines including those working in service and social innovation projects involving co-creation with users (Schumacher and Feurstein, 2007). From this, it is easy to see how open innovation and participation have come to be closely related with the Living Lab concept (Leminen, 2013; Schuurman and Tonurist, 2016). Hakkareinen and Hyysalo (2016) contest the idea that Living Labs will automatically lead to more (and better) collaboration and propose ways the daily challenges in Living Lab practices are overcome. They suggest that the activities taking place in Living Labs among their stakeholders and intermediaries are not fixed but evolve, and roles of stakeholders are also malleable and change over time. A recent literature review of Living Labs concludes that there is much work to do in the relationship of 'living labs' to the challenges of innovation and partnership with users, recommending a shift to a more co-creative stance (Hamed et al, 2020). Another recent paper talks about the difficulties that Living Lab produced innovations have moving from the niche to the mainstream (Greve et al, 2021). Indeed, after many years of enthusiasm for service and social innovations (Mulgan et al, 2007; European Commission, 2013), experiments in service transformation have demonstrated that the innovation of services is much more difficult in practice (Brandsen et al, 2016). Even successful projects or demonstrators have often failed to be sustainable or to scale beyond the environment where they were initially designed and/or implemented (Brandsen et al, 2016; 2018; Meijer and Thaens, 2020). Despite these challenges, the deployment of 'Living Labs' as an overarching methodology has been expanding in public service contexts (Schuurman and Tonurist, 2016; Gascó-Hernández, 2017; Dekker et al, 2020).

One of the objectives of the CoSIE project was the application of Living Labs approaches in the context of relational public services and welfare to support local activities with addressing the challenges of social innovation and co-creation. Work in these areas by the authors of this chapter and others indicates that key to carrying out such activities in a scalable and sustainable fashion is using theoretical models to create reflective, collaborative stakeholder engagement through the innovation of relationships (McLoughlin and Wilson, 2013; Wilson et al, 2013; Jamieson and Martin, 2022). The real-time provision of interactive representations through modelling can take several forms. These include online meetings using common tools such as Zoom augmented with Miro boards as well as more traditional face-to-face deliberations using tools such as Rich Picture methods, sticky notes and whiteboards. We characterize the Living Lab approach promoted and adopted in CoSIE as one of mutual sense-making, design and learning supported by the co-construction and discussion of models as 'boundary objects' (Bowker and Star, 1999). Boundary objects enable dialogue across organizational and professional divides. They can take many forms (for example pictures, artefacts, stories); the important thing about them is that they are meaningful across various communities yet can accommodate dissent between them (Bowker and Star, 1999). The result is that evolving, co-created models act as 'mirrors' and 'windows' between stakeholders to promote more focused and mutually informed debates (Hesselgreaves et al, 2021).

Developing and applying the CoSMoS tool in the Co-creation of Service Innovation in Europe social innovation pilots

Starting up: developing an initial model through co-creation

To enable and promote sense-making and reflection about how reallocations and participations were being undertaken across each pilot, we required each pilot team, as part of their collaborative work allocation, to co-create shared models of – and with – the local actors, organisations and conversations. The intention was for each pilot to model the processes and occasions in which they have undertaken their local developments including their service definitions and deployment processes. These models were used in local Living Lab engagement sessions in each of the pilots, to stimulate reflection and deliberation.

The intervention of Living Labs in the model-making process itself was somewhat conducted at arm's length. This was due to the usual resource constraints and to the fact that all the actors were pressing ahead with their local developments. Many, but not all, of the pilots adopted the aspects of the representational style which was introduced in initial models. In particular, the approach in the work involved making organizational relationships explicit in ways that supported their abstraction and the recomposition of roles and responsibilities. This allowed for an initial generic service co-creation model to be developed (Figure 10.1) which enabled a lens through which each project could be viewed and explained. This generic model was later incorporated into a new online Living Lab platform which is also described in detail in what follows.

As we can see in Figure 10.1, the service objectives and contexts of the CoSIE pilots are varied. We discovered, however, that all can be characterized in terms of aspects of needs and opportunities associated with some combination of:

- a target demographic or socioeconomic grouping;
- place or locale, ranging from a residential estate to a town or entire region;
- a set of specific legislative or policy initiatives or responses.

In each of the pilots there has been, or continues to be, contexts and occasions where deliberations take place about the identification of needs and opportunities for service innovation. The design of which is a response in the shape of a service or set of services which has been or is being initiated by particular actors. In the different pilots we see examples of this initiation at all the different levels of the administrative system: bottom up (micro), middle out (meso) and top down (macro). They operate on a spectrum which varies from consultation about policies and designs that have already been decided above to participative explorations of needs and opportunities with many variations between.

Such deliberations result in (or confirm) identifications and definitions of the intended beneficiaries, of the intended benefits or service outcomes and an identification of the combinations of agents who will provide the service. Services imply the use and consumption of resources and facilities and the source of these in the CoSIE pilots is a public administration who is usually the sponsor and the commissioner of the service.

Finally, it is a feature of all the CoSIE pilots that there are individuals who were the initiators, facilitators, enablers and nurturers of the service co-creation processes and the instigators of the moral reordering that this implies. These are not necessarily the initiators, but, like them, can belong to any level within the local system or be external to it. The relationships between all of these elements take the form of participations and conversations which may be direct contacts and deliberative occasions but also may take the form of communications by other media and mechanisms. In particular, the link

Figure 10.1: Generic service co-creation model

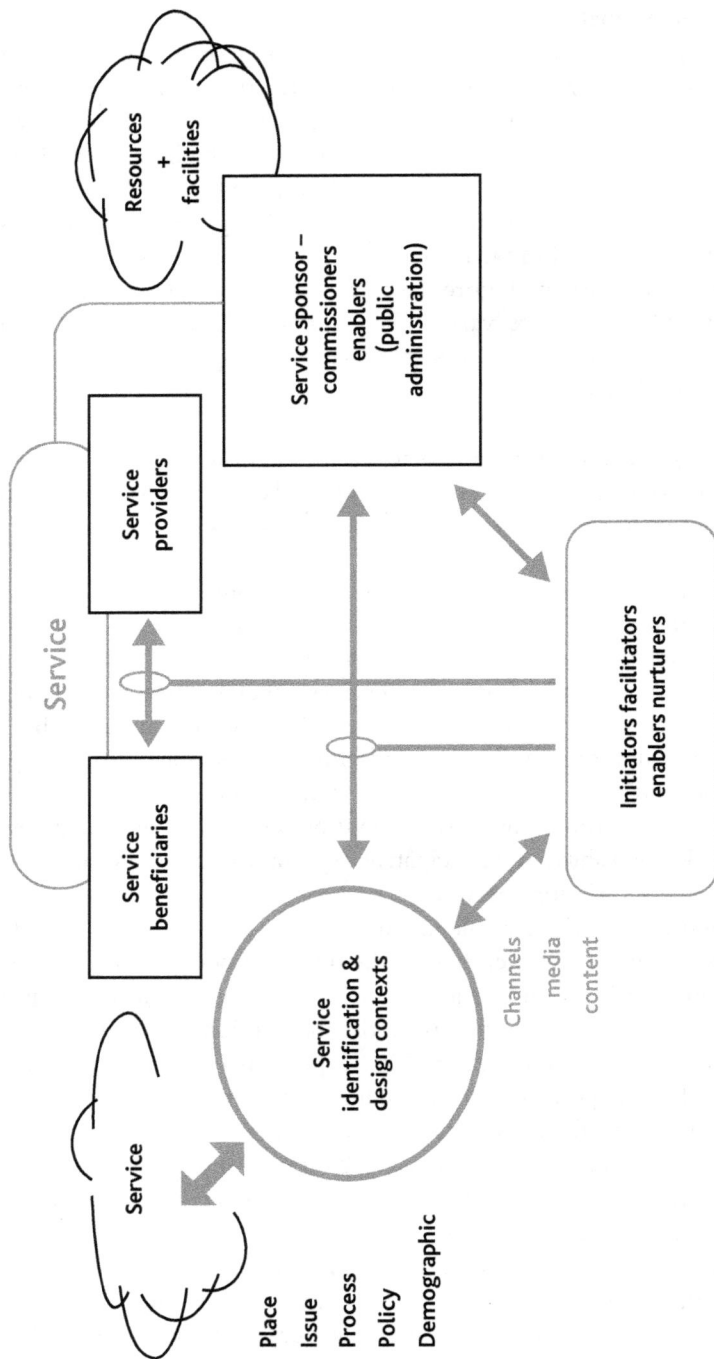

between the service context and the service creation occasions often takes the form of advertising and publicity as well as social occasions.

We now present models that represent the set of core concepts and factors that have emerged from the observation of, and interactions with, the pilots from this perspective. We will complete this section with an outline of the theory of the architectural discourse of sociotechnical systems which underpins the modelling methods and frameworks we are using.

Next steps: developing the Living Lab models

The initial models which were developed through co-creation workshops with the local pilots were a combination of developments in response to the experience of the Living Lab team. Our starting premise was that each model might help to draw out the similarities and differences across the co-creation processes, social innovations and developments of the project.

Four analytic models were developed through this process, the penultimate of which comprises three smaller probe models for the direct analysis of the conversational maps. The models are as follows:

- intervention theory and concept of human wellbeing;
- governance and moral ordering;
- analysis of innovation conversations;
- a platform for the co-creation process.

In making use of these models, we were formulating a series of questions to be addressed in a context where the pilot models and the analytic models were presented side by side. The purpose of this approach is to generate emergent conversations to innovate the relationships between stakeholders: it is therefore the process, rather than the product, of an finalized model, that represents the value.

Identifying the intention of the social innovation pilot

Our first model is an initial attempt to create a representation of the multidimensional complexity of human wellbeing because this is the 'space' in which the social innovations and co-creation processes of CoSIE pilots are taking place (Figure 10.2).

The model presents three perspectives – or projections – of wellbeing:

- A structural one which distinguishes between the internal and the environmental and between the different sorts or areas of wellbeing.
- The range of intentions or purposes of an intervention or service where a care plan may consist of a number of these at the same time or in sequence.
- A process and learning perspective.

Figure 10.2: Intervention theory and the concept of human wellbeing

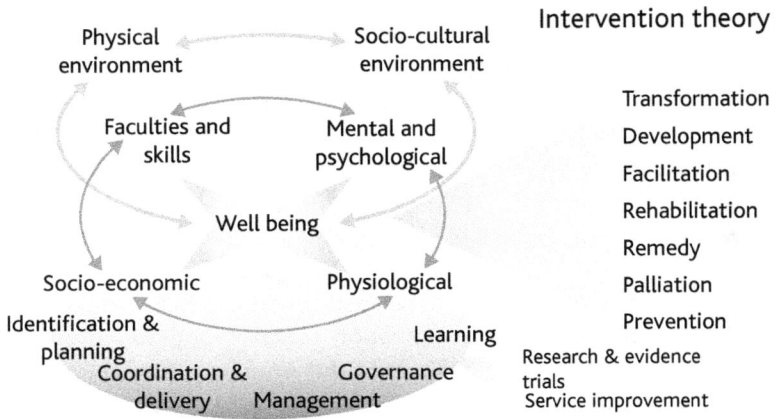

Intervention theory

Physical environment ⟷ Socio-cultural environment

Faculties and skills — Mental and psychological

Well being

Socio-economic — Physiological

Identification & planning

Coordination & delivery

Learning

Governance

Management

Transformation
Development
Facilitation
Rehabilitation
Remedy
Palliation
Prevention
Research & evidence trials
Service improvement

Based on our analysis of the local contexts, four major sub-domains or perspectives of human wellbeing were identified. These are:

• physiological wellbeing;
• mental and psychological wellbeing;
• wellbeing associated with faculties and capabilities; and
• socioeconomic wellbeing.

Each of these contain many facets which interact with each other and there are strong couplings between the four domains. These interdependencies can create catastrophic cascades of positive feedback, self-maintaining loops and deadlocks as well as sustainable coping and development. All of these are affected by, and interact with, external elements of the physical environment and the sociocultural environment which also interact in complex ways.

In most of the CoSIE contexts, what is being addressed is a complex combination of multiple challenges of the organisational, practice and client contexts. In these complex situations, remedy and rehabilitation are not the only concerns; we must also consider the wider need for palliative and the habilitative or facilitative components in a complex care response. The former approaches make symptoms bearable, without addressing their cause, while the latter bring the capacities of the service user/client up to the expected or required level to achieve and maintain some level of stability or coping.

The wellbeing service elements we have considered so far have all been concerned with addressing some failure or lack; this does not exhaust the spectrum of care responses. We must also consider developmental and transformational aspects of care, which are concerned with realising and maximising potential or creating completely new possibilities and potentials. Note that we are characterising this spectrum of interventions in terms of intentionalities what *they are trying to achieve, rather than how, and on what, they operate.*

We can complete our representation of the scope of human wellbeing by including the process-oriented perspective, which is characterised by the operational logics of identifying needs, planning, coordination and delivery, management, governance and learning, all of which operate at the level of the individual case, whether this is episodic or continuing, and also at the level of the population in service provisioning. To complete our projections of wellbeing service processes we must also include research and development, trailing and the service improvement processes of a 'Learning Care System' or 'Learning Wellbeing System' in which development and innovation take place.

The questions this model begins to raise both at the general project level and individual pilot level are:

- Which aspects of human wellbeing and of the environment are relevant to your service? Are some more significant than others?
- What are the intentionalities of your service?
- What aspects of the service life-cycle are important regarding your innovation and change?

Model of governance and moral ordering

The selection and implementation of social innovations implies moral judgements or stances on the part of those enacting the activity. Also, it does not presuppose that these 'moral ordering' processes are straightforward or uncontended (either implicitly or explicitly) or that all stakeholders have good intentions. Our initial 'moral ordering' model distinguishes between the contexts and occasions (or stages in a life-cycle of a social innovation) when different types of conversations, which are conventionally associated with the vertical or hierarchical structure of an organisation, take place (see Figure 10.3). These include:

- When the *ethos* of a social innovation is defined/reflected on and the pilot activity initiated/reviewed. (The discussion about values, principles and objectives of a pilot.)
- The *management* which plans, monitors and reports and the process of doing of the pilot activity of delivery and the experiences of stakeholders in relation to the new innovative process. (Discussion about planning, measuring, accounting, evaluating a pilot.)

Figure 10.3: Governance and moral ordering model

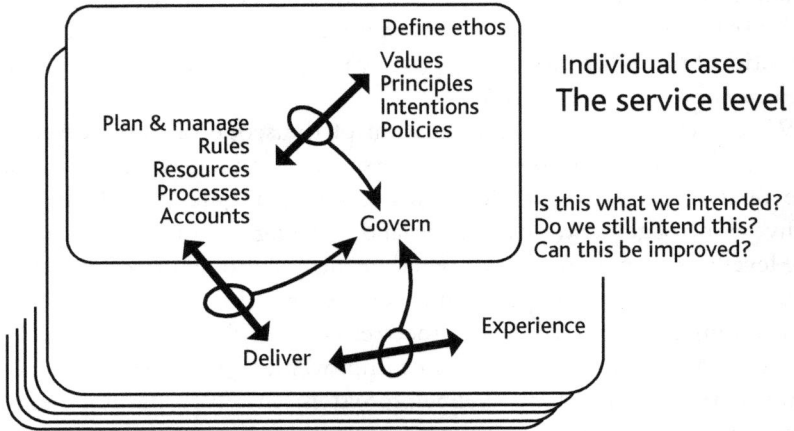

- Discussions about *feelings and experiences* of a social innovation from the perspective of the pilot activity but also the context of social innovation.

Our model then positions the *governing* process as the contexts and occasions when three key questions about the relationships between these processes are examined and evaluated. The questions this model begins to raise both at the general project level and individual pilot level are:

- Identifying the different occasions (times and places) where the following activities/conversations/reflections took/take place.
- In terms of the co-creation processes questions of who was/is involved, how were/are they recorded, what happens to the learning and how does it lead to changes or improvements?
- The presence of documentation that represent the ethos and principles of the social innovation and/or the pilot and indicators that these changed over time. Ability of stakeholders to articulate their relationship to and identify the owners, editor, publisher of these documents or texts.

Innovation conversation analysis model

All of the contexts require a sequence of organisational structures and processes which span policy making, the configuration and management of service resources and front-line delivery. Further, in some contexts there may be tensions and even conflicts of interest and value along this chain. One dimension of understanding co-creation processes should be concerned with how power and participation are distributed. The questions here to be addressed concern the identification the micro, meso (may be multiple) and macro levels in the conversational model and the examination of participation within and between them among all the actors in the pilots.

In the engagements with the local places and the evaluation elements of the project we observed both elements of locally developed, imported and blended intervention theory models which had been published and used in other contexts being appropriated, adapted and adopted. We also observed discussions about the attitudes adopted by actors at different phases of the creation and delivery of the pilot. In some cases, meso–actors were attempting third order interventions on micro-level actors who initially positioned themselves as victims and adopted a stand at the right-hand end of the attitude spectrum. Sometimes this configuration is observed in the relationship between the macro and meso levels. These last three models represent probes to assist in establishing an account through the development of reflexivity of the context of social innovation in a local area when applied to the specific conversational maps (intervention theory and moral ordering).

The model presented in Figure 10.4 emerged from an analysis of the CoSIE contexts and is an attempt, on the one hand, to identify the core internal elements that are common to all the various approaches of the pilots and, on the other, to make certain key external elements and factors – which are relevant to any service environment – explicit if it is to be sustainable. It represents an attempt to present and interrelate a number of terms and categories to provide the basis for a common language and framing of the CoSIE place-based activities.

Co-creation of service model

Our final model, the 'co-creation of service model' presented in Figure 10.5, denotes a set of structural relationships and occasions. Each pilot can populate some or all of these processes with the identities of actual participants. For example, as we have seen, in some cases, policy has represented an external input to which the pilot has had to respond, whereas in others, policy was generated internally.

The service life-cycle processes are distributed over, and supported by, a service definition and development platform and a service delivery platform. These correspond to the support of the processes identified and interrelated in detail in Figure 10.5. For example, in the Estonian context, the social hackathon (see Chapter 3) represented such a definition and development platform. The nature of the delivery platform for any service or service set defined in a hackathon is one of the outputs of the co-creation process. In the case of Spain, the business development support facility has been both service definition and development as well as the delivery platform.

Figure 10.4: Innovation conversation analysis model

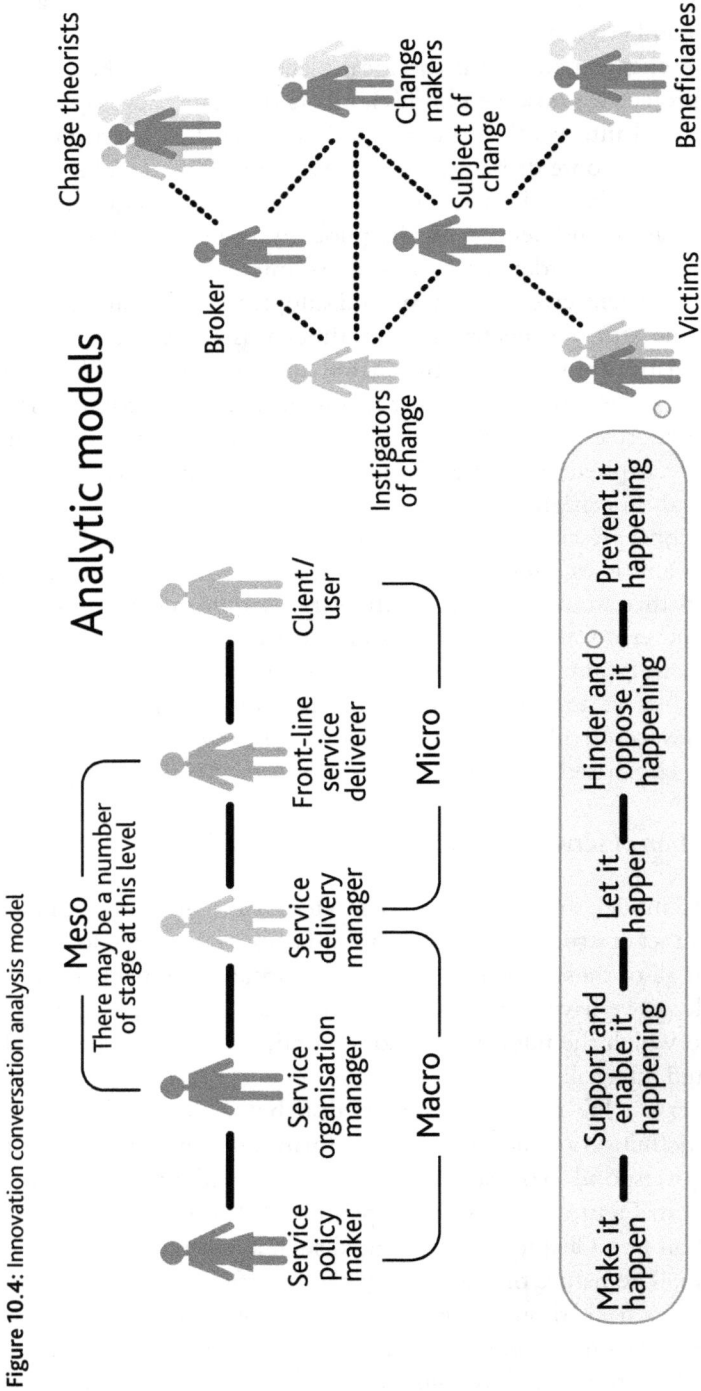

Analytic models

Change theorists

Change makers

Subject of change

Beneficiaries

Broker

Victims

Instigators of change

Service policy maker

Service organisation manager

Service delivery manager

Front-line service deliverer

Client/ user

Macro

Meso
There may be a number of stage at this level

Micro

Make it happen

Support and enable it happening

Let it happen

Hinder and oppose it happening

Prevent it happening

Figure 10.5: Co-creation of service model

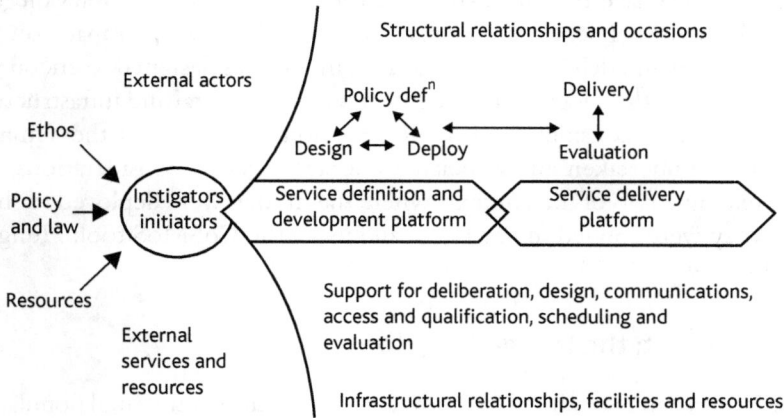

The reason for introducing these concepts is to encourage discussion about reusable infrastructure which can support and sustain successive initiative in co-creative service development which is an important element of sustainability through growth and diversification. Having identified an abstract, generic model of co-creation and of service, we have created the opportunity for shared resources between co-creation initiatives and services. Thus, below the platform we have a space in which to locate infrastructural capacities to support deliberation, design, communications, the means of access to different sorts of services and service components, and for the processes of qualification, scheduling and evaluation. The precise shape and nature of these resources will vary from pilot to pilot but there are some universal elements that are common requirements in many classes of wellbeing and developmental services. Many of these are concerned with the support of information management and communication, such as publication channels, registration services by which new actors and resources which join the service environment can be given identifiers and locators, catalogue publication and management, and recording and profiling tools.

The description so far has covered the right-hand part of the model in Figure 10.5. This represents elements that are within the co-creative ethos of a pilot's actions. The left-hand side of the model represents relevant external elements that are part of the initiation of such a process or have some ongoing impact on it.

First, we consider the instigators and initiators who may be driven by a combination of innate ethos and values, external matters of top-down policy or law or may be responding to opportunities created by local availabilities and resources.

Corresponding to the structural and infrastructural domains of the right-hand side, we have relevant external actors and agencies and relevant (and reusable) external services and resources which have an impact on the development and delivery processes. This model was designed to encourage its users to put their local initiative into a wider structural and infrastructural context and to consider the ongoing relationships between the activities they have undertaken and associated relevant external considerations. We now examine two of the contexts where the models were deployed to show how they were applied in practice – and using the CoSMoS tool: Hungary and Greece.

Case in point: the Hungarian pilot

The Hungarian pilot aimed to innovate the activation of the rural population in Hungary in the context of local food production. This was to be achieved via local government organisation and co-creation of new approaches to the economic activities of the citizens, moving rural communities from a service-oriented approach to a more entrepreneurial one (Csoba and Sipos, 2022). (See Chapter 3 for more information about this pilot.) The focus of the activity, linked to the national Social Land Programme, was to revive the culture of household economy by enabling families to utilise their own resources. The work took place in ten rural settlements drawing on grassroots initiatives within traditional communities, with the understanding that no two are same, by seeking improved engagement with local democratic mechanisms to improve resilience and contribute to sustainability. The Hungarian activity was both an early influence and an early adopter of the CoSMoS tool. Work undertaken in one village, Szolnok, intended to communicate the intentions of the Living Lab work package became the initial co-creation of service model. Figure 10.6 shows application of the model in this pilot. Subsequently, CoSMoS was used as a focal point for engagements inside the local context and to assist in the communication of reflection inside the pilots and we can see the mapping of the innovation environment was used through a range of co-creation activities to inform and animate stakeholder engagement.

The modelling process helped the Hungarian pilot bring stakeholders together to work with socially disadvantaged people to engage in conversations around the social innovation process. In Hungary, small-scale, domestic agricultural production is done within the framework of the family, usually in the backyard of private houses. The most important outcome of the project was the redistribution of power and authority among the actors in managing the social risks related to the household economy. For this reason, in executing the pilots, the main question is not 'what' was obtained through the pilot, but rather 'how' the pilot was conducted. One of the

Figure 10.6: Application of the co-creation of service model in the Hungarian pilot

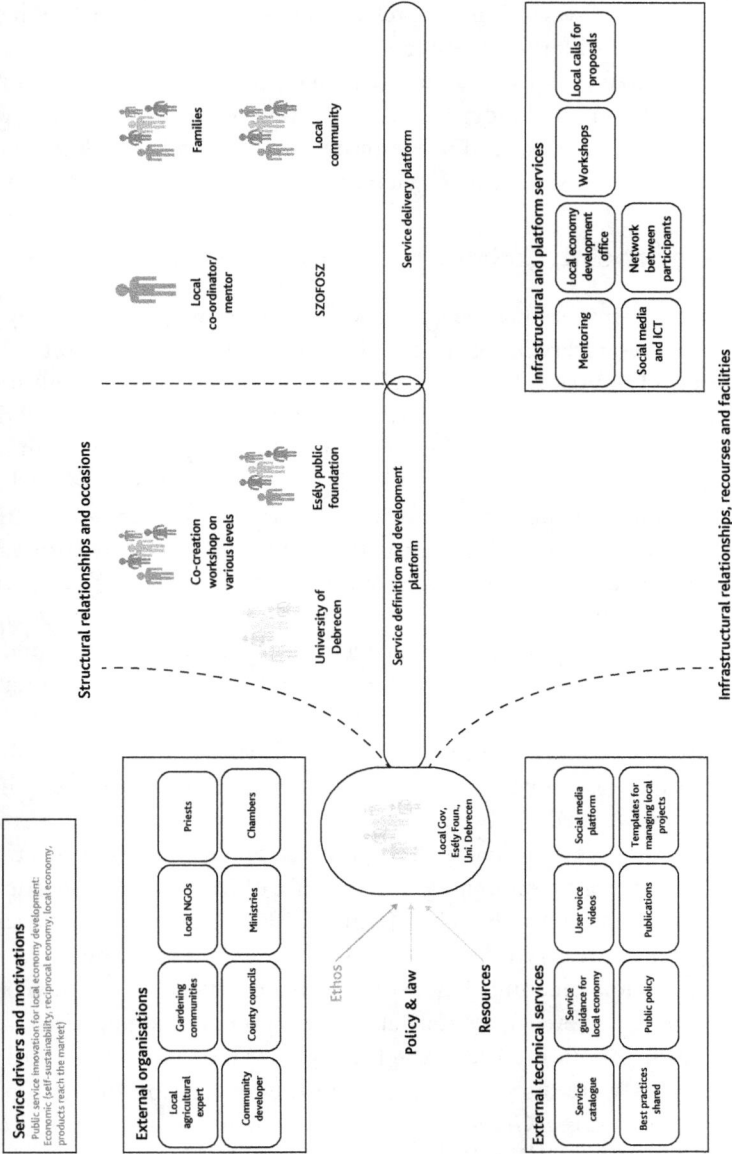

Co-creation of service model – Hungary – household economy in rural areas

Hungary ▬

Service drivers and motivations
Public service innovation for local economy development:
Economic (self-sustainability, reciprocal economy, local economy,
products reach the market)

Structural relationships and occasions

Families

Local community

Local co-ordinator/ mentor

SZOFOSZ

Service delivery platform

Co-creation workshop on various levels

Esély public foundation

University of Debrecen

Service definition and development platform

External organisations

| Local agricultural expert | Gardening communities | Local NGOs | Priests |
| Community developer | County councils | Ministries | Chambers |

Ethos

Local Gov, Esély Foun., Uni. Debrecen

Policy & law

Resources

External technical services

| Service catalogue | Service guidance for local economy | User voice videos | Social media platform |
| Best practices shared | Public policy | Publications | Templates for managing local projects |

Infrastructural and platform services

| Mentoring | Local economy development office | Workshops | Local calls for proposals |
| Social media and ICT | Network between participants | | |

Infrastructural relationships, recourses and facilities

main goals of the various projects is to change working routines during the formation and implementation of services: 'with the user' not 'for the user' but at the same time creating a balance between the actors and not leaving all the responsibility to the user. For the facilitators of the activity in Hungary the outcome was to innovate relationships to improve stakeholders' readiness to solve problems together and eventually evolve operating practices, professional codes and traditional paternalistic intervention models, which had represented the sociopolitical orthodoxy for many years. The CoSMoS activity helped the local programme to reflect on the scalability of activities to extend and sustain its service development and delivery platform.

Case in point: CoSMoS in the Greek test site

The Community Gardens pilot was a social innovation aimed at creating an alternative intervention in the depleted urban environment of the city of Aghios Dimitrios. It was not one of the original ten pilots but intended as a test site in which to trial tools and learning resources developed through the three 'waves' of CoSIE (see Chapter 1). Although many urban community garden initiatives exist worldwide this was a very new and innovative application in the Greek context, especially for local authorities. Aghios Dimitrios is a municipality situated about five kilometres from Athens city centre. It is densely populated with a significant lack of green spaces. The garden occupies an area of 2.5 acres that belongs to the municipality. This was unexploited land and outside the city urban plan, located in a fairly degraded neighbourhood on the edge of the urban area. The municipality of Aghios Dimitrios has set a priority for planning, organisation and exercise of innovative and inclusive social policies. The aim of the community gardens initiative was primarily to enable low-income households to gain access to fruit and vegetables. Longer-term goals were to improve the environment, enhance respect for nature and promote environmental education.

The emerging modelling method of CoSMoS was co-produced through engagement with the CoSIE pilots. The first meeting orientated the Greek pilot team to the tool, the final models and setting them up as users. The second meeting, based on the team reflecting on their situation in the pilot, covered questions about the potential applications and specific questions about the use of the functions of CoSMoS. The third and fourth meetings were discussions regarding the application of the CoSMoS tool to the emerging Greek pilot activity, which was significantly constrained by the local COVID-19 lockdown situation. However, the affordances of the CoSMoS tool were a significant support in the development of the pilot and the engagement of stakeholders unable to meet each other in the traditional way. The capabilities of the tool allowed a range of interactions, including synchronous interactive completion of models with stakeholders, asynchronous summaries to be completed of elements of the project based on online meetings and other co-creation actions (summarising the key results of the Community Reporting) and the basic linking of the pilot together for the local animateurs including the social media activity.

Within the Greek pilot, the community gardens project made extensive use of CoSMoS. By completing several models, the pilot has successfully integrated CoSMoS into the co-creative processes when developing and structuring delivery. The deployment of the models within CoSMoS was used to observe the co-creative inputs from a range of stakeholders. In the first workshop that was organised, the initial feedback was 'positive from the [participants] part – they thought this could be something that could be implemented in other occasions, not just this one'. It was noted that additional training could be implemented to support the completion of the models inside the application along with training and guidance around the theoretical underpinning of the models. The participants in the meetings comprised several members of the municipality, including the vice-mayor responsible for the project, a person responsible for the community gardens, a volunteer, and several social services representatives.

The co-creation of service model was completed remotely using web conferencing tools, screen-sharing and facilitated by the Greek pilot team. The use of the model helped to iteratively clarify the structure of the Community Gardens pilot, and explore preconceptions around the project. The process revealed that the full range of the interaction between the stakeholders assisted with the wider understanding and communication of the intentions of the project, including the relationships to the policy that underpinned it. The model was revisited and revised to ensure that, as it was discussed and revealed, stakeholders understood the project, its purpose and position. The use of the model allowed for a range of stakeholders to present their perspective as well as allowing for the space and occasion to discuss the project from each perspective.

The application of the analytical model for the community gardens pilot (Figure 10.7) made the relationships within the innovation explicit and easier to understand. This increased the transparency and openness of the innovation while allowing for an improved presentation to a wide variety of stakeholders in a political environment that is not ordinarily 'bottom-up'.

The intervention theory model was used to verify the input of the range of stakeholders throughout the municipality in terms of the aims of the pilot intervention bringing together with the perspective and feedback from the intended beneficiaries of the project. Additional perspectives of the beneficiaries were captured – and inserted into the model – to assert and assist with this. One of the more useful models for the innovation, the intervention theory model was effective in understanding the rich value identified in conversation with the beneficiaries and understanding how

Figure 10.7: Application of the analytical model for the community gardens in the Greek test site

Analytic model-community gardens, Aghios Dimitrios

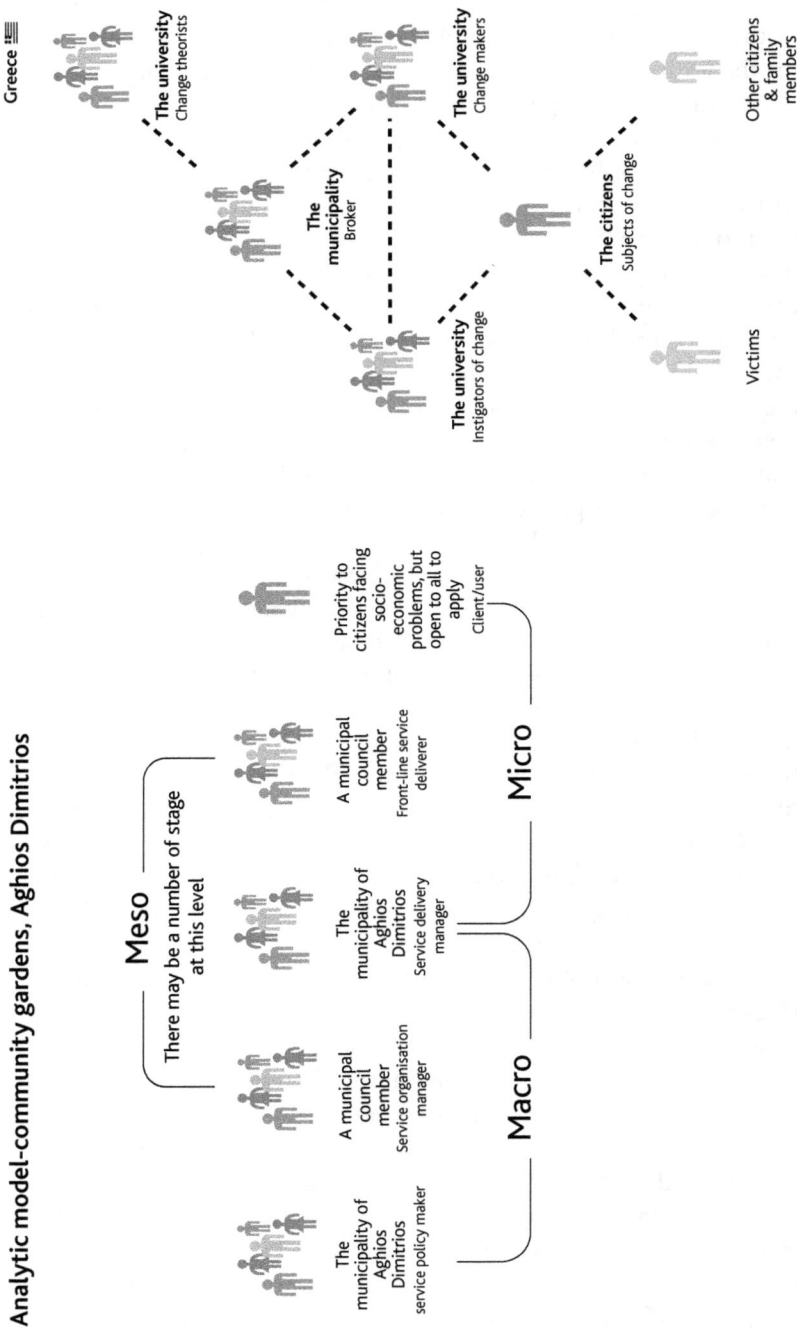

this was realised by them through the project, as one member of the project observed about their application of the model: "I think it's very interesting because the purpose of the model is, to, if you like, layout the complexity of human wellbeing ... so [there is a] match between the nature of [the] service and the utility of this model."

Conclusion

The modelling method of CoSMoS – with its origins in Living Labs – supports the concept and practice of co-creation. It offers a significant potential for stakeholders, service designers and participants to jointly improve their understanding of their environment, service provision and possible service platforms. This approach begins to address some of the weakness identified in the literature by means of an abstract modelling engagement which supports the necessary technical, management, governance and social processes required in the collaborative design and implementation of a service innovation. It achieves this by responding to the opportunity that the online cost-efficiencies and availability of multimedia-rich interactions offer to provide a more sustainable means of creating value in new forms of producer–consumer collaboration (see the call from Prahalad and Ramaswamy [2004] for new building blocks for co-creation).

CoSMoS emerged from the challenges of working with service innovation pilot projects that varied in terms of their sociopolitical, linguistic, technical and service contexts. It was an attempt to derive visual models that were sympathetic to various stages of maturity and co-creation approaches of the service and innovation environments, and to raise awareness of key external elements and factors that are relevant in any service development life-cycle. This type of deployment of a Living Lab approach, which seeks to improve collaboration in new ways, is challenging – particularly as such developments are often highly focused, tightly resourced and pragmatic. However, we see emerging evidence that the sort of modelling approach (exemplified in CoSMoS) scaffolds a wider range of collaborative possibilities between stakeholders involved in the co-creative process in relation to complex public service areas. It thereby makes these often short-lived yet cherished social innovations potentially more sustainable and scalable.

We reached the end of the project with a stable CoSMoS tool that provided the full range of CoSIE models and resources in the form of an interactive digital platform. The main outcome of our activities was firstly to position the CoSMoS tool as a source of co-creation-based reflective development activities for those seeking to innovate in heterogeneous complex social and welfare contexts. Moreover, it was clear that the models themselves represented a powerful way of mapping the stakeholders and comparing apparently very different settings and initiatives. The moral reordering, which is implicit in the shift to a co-productive approach, was evident and recognised by the project in both the conversational models and the transformation process models of the initial pilots. The models also provided a potentially very powerful framework for the organisation of and access to community storytelling (including the Community Reporting presented in Chapter 7). CoSMoS brought outputs from different sources together to provide a channel for the publication and dissemination of the learning that was taking place. Overall, the models within the CoSMoS tool enabled, supported and guided the many discussions that are required to identify and strengthen participation in the co-creation processes of service innovation in context. The provision of the range of models in the form of an interactive digital tool offers the means to apply explicit modelling processes in co-creation activities across diverse spatial, governance, practice and technical domains.

References

Bowker, G.C. and Star, S.L. (1999) *Sorting Things Out: Classification and its Consequences*, Cambridge, MA: MIT Press.

Brandsen, T., Cattacin, S., Evers, A. and Zimmer, A. (eds) (2016) *Social Innovations in the Urban Context*, Cham: Springer.

Brandsen, T., Trui, S. and Bram, V. (eds) (2018) *Co-Production and Co-Creation: Engaging Citizens in Public Services*, New York: Routledge.

Csoba, J. and Sipos, F. (2022) 'Politically-driven public administration or co-creation? On the possibility of modernizing public services in rural Hungary', *Public Money & Management*, 42(5): 314–322.

Dekker, R., Franco Contreras, J. and Meijer, A. (2020) 'The living lab as a methodology for public administration research: a systematic literature review of its applications in the social sciences', *International Journal of Public Administration*, 43(14): 1207–1217.

European Commission (2013) *Social Innovation Research in Europe: Approaches, Trends and Future Directions*, Brussels: Directorate-General for Research.

Gascó-Hernández, M. (2017) 'Living labs: implementing open innovation in the public sector', *Government Information Quarterly*, 34(1): 90–98.

Greve, K., Vita, R.D., Leminen, S. and Westerlund, M. (2021) 'Living labs: from niche to mainstream innovation management', *Sustainability*, 13(2): 791. https:// doi.org/10.3390/su13020791

Hakkarainen, L. and Hyysalo, S. (2016) 'The evolution of intermediary activities: broadening the concept of facilitation in living labs', *Technology Innovation Management Review*, 6(1), https://timreview.ca/article/960

Hamed, S., Lalanne, D. and Rogers, Y.(2020) 'The five strands of living lab: a literature study of the evolution of living lab concepts', *ACM Transaction on Computer-Human Interactions*, 27(2): 1–26. https://doi.org/10.1145/3380958

Hesselgreaves, H., French, M., Hawkins, M., Lowe, T., Wheatman, A., Martin, M. and Wilson, R. (2021) 'New development: the emerging role of a "learning partner" relationship in supporting public service reform', *Public Money & Management*, 41(8): 672–675.

Jamieson, D. and Martin, M. (2022) 'Supporting co-creation processes through modelling: the development of a digital modelling tool for complex service innovation environments', *Public Money & Management*, 42(5): 353–355.

Jamieson, D., Martin, M. and Wilson, R. (2020a) *CoSMoS User Guide: Co-creation Service Modelling System (COSMOS) Application of the Living Lab Platform*, https://guide.livinglab.org.uk/books/cosmos-user-guide

Jamieson, D., Martin, M. and Wilson, R. (2020b) *CoSMoS: The Co-creation Service Modelling System*. Open Source Software, https://doi.org/10.5281/zenodo.4058570

Leminen, S. (2013) 'Coordination and participation in living lab networks', *Technology Innovation Management Review*, 3(1): 5–14.

Martin, M., Jamieson, D. and Wilson, R. (2019) *Newcastle Living Lab*, 2019, [Software], Zenodo. https://doi.org/10.5281/zenodo.3383969

McLoughlin, I. and Wilson, R. (2013) *Digital Government at Work: A Social Informatics Perspective*, Oxford: Oxford University Press.

Meijer, A. and Thaens, M. (2020) 'The dark side of public innovation', *Public Performance & Management Review*, 44(1): 136–154.

Mulgan, G., Ali, R., Halkett, R. and Sanders, B. (2007) *In and Out of Sync: The Challenge of Growing Social Innovations*, London: NESTA.

Prahalad, C.K. and Ramaswamy, V. (2004) 'Co-creating unique value with customers', *Strategy & Leadership*, 32(3): 4–9.

Schumacher, J. and Feurstein, K. (2007) 'Living labs – the user as co-creator', *2007 IEEE International Technology Management Conference*, https://ieeexpl ore.ieee.org/abstract/document/7458680

Schuurman, D. and Tonurist, P. (2016) 'Innovation in the public sector: exploring the characteristics and potential of living labs and innovation labs', *Technology Innovation Management Review*, 7(1), http://timreview.ca/article/ZZZZ

Wilson, R., Baines, S., Hardill, I. and Ferguson, M. (2013) 'Information for local governance. Data is the solution … what was the question again?', *Public Money & Management*, 33(3): 163–166.

11

Moving towards relational services: the role of digital service environments and platforms?

Mike Martin, Rob Wilson and David Jamieson

Introduction

The Co-creation of Service Innovation in Europe (CoSIE) project's many explorations of co-creation in the context of public service development, which have been discussed in the chapters of this book, exhibit underlying commonalities and themes which became visible in cross-cutting work packages, particularly those associated with modelling pilot processes and contexts. In this chapter we will explore the sources – and observe some consequences of – what could be considered to be the 'theory of service' that emerged.

Our focus in this chapter is on the communicational and information related aspects of service development and the concept of the 'service platform'. The CoSIE project was initiated on the assumption that social media and web-based publication services provide opportunities for innovation in participation and co-creation in the public service domain (Jalonen et al, 2019; Jalonen and Helo, 2020). We will examine this assumption and explore some of the limitations and barriers that current commercial service practice places on the use of existing channels and media in some of the more sensitive contexts explored in the project.

The term 'service' is used in many different disciplinary settings and is treated from a number of quite distinct perspectives. It is an example of a sociotechnical concept which, to be explored with any thoroughness and rigour, must be examined in terms of empirical observation and also in terms of human experience and interpretation. In the following sections we will explore these dichotomies and present some models and conceptual framings that have proved useful in interpreting and understanding the work undertaken in the project.

An important conclusion of this discussion is that, in the case of wellbeing service environments, whether place-based or need/aspiration-based, co-creation is not simply a socially or morally desirable approach but rather a logical and practical necessity in responding to and coping with the inevitable complexity and emergence of the types of contexts presented by the CoSIE pilots.

Services and information and communications technology systems

In the face of complex health, care and welfare needs across Europe, there is a widespread appreciation that the information and communications systems ought to be a fundamental part of supporting service delivery. The question that remains seems to be the 'How?'. Vast amounts of political capital and national resource has been put into solving the 'problems' from the perspective of governments who have procured from vendors 'solutions' (ranging across simple to elaborate or from the institutional whole to the discrete task) with little real long-term impact or effect. It has become increasingly clear that the basis of digital government integration approaches has failed to deliver transformation of services, instead either arriving at 'disaster faster' or increasing the complexity, not reducing or even helping to manage it (Ciborra, 2000; McLoughlin and Wilson, 2013).

One rarely proffered explanation for the continuing issues of information and communications technology design and implementation in public service environments is that there is a fundamental contradiction in the architectural assumptions of current practice, in particular when applied to multi-agency, public service contexts. This chapter seeks to explore some hidden aspects of current information systems paradigms and sets out a third, architectural approach to the creation, operation and governance of collaborative sociotechnical information infrastructures and platforms for service innovation. This 'relational' approach explicitly supports mixed economies of provision in which public, private and third sector agencies coordinate to meet multiple and evolving objectives and interests in the delivery of services for and with people and communities.

The assumption of what we will call an 'integrationist' approach, which draws upon 'enterprise solution' practices, treats social relationships as transactional and creates silos which homogenise interaction, reducing it to workflow and data-points. This approach produces failed interactions for citizens, and a corresponding failure for organisations unable to cope with dynamic complexity beyond the boundary of the 'silo' they have created in, for example, health, *or* social care, *or* financial support.

As a result of some of the established problems of what we term the integrationist approach, there has been an understandable turn to the idea that Web 2.0 or social media could be used as an alternative vehicle for providing the means for mobilising citizen engagement with complex societal problems. After all, on the face of it, the platforms are apparently democratic with low barriers to entry and highly accessible through a range of devices including mobile phones. Moreover, they have attracted a critical mass of people and communities who have appropriated the tools for their own purposes. However, the values of what we term the 'universalist' system paradigm have been subverted for extractive and parasitic purposes, and there are significant difficulties in signalling the provenance of information and the identity and credentials of those publishing it. In highly sensitive contexts, it has become regarded as unsafe and ungovernable with limited utility beyond marketing services and initial invitations for engagement.

We now turn to propose and detail an alternative holistic, 'relational' approach to the information and communications infrastructure to support care and wellbeing service ecologies. In doing this we build on analysis of the problems of digital government in our previous research monograph (McLoughlin and Wilson, 2013) as well as the recent work of Lips (2019) on digital government and of Mohr and Ezra (2021) on integrated care. The approach proposed here involves a new form of ongoing sociotechnical 'conversation'. It represents an explicit recognition that innovation involves learning at the systems level which can often result in the creation of new conceptual frames and new shared language. Thus, it allows a more sophisticated and responsive approach to be applied to the negotiation (and renegotiation) of shared visions and intentions, closing the loop between design and implementation and replacing it with a system of ongoing collaborative evolution and governance. Adopting this approach affords new opportunities for the governance of practice and information, in tandem, fusing the hitherto distinct and usually poorly coupled activities of organisational culture change and development and technical systems design and development, making them mutually reinforcing and sustaining processes.

A digital government maturity model

The background to these assumptions has been a long and complex evolution of the relationships between public administration and electronic platforms and media in general. As an introduction to this discussion, we will outline the evolution of e-government over the last couple of decades. McLoughlin and Wilson (2013: 165) quote Martin's (2006) maturity model for e-government services (Figure 11.1). This represents the different strands of increasing complexity in the adoption of electronic media and

Figure 11.1: Digital government maturity model

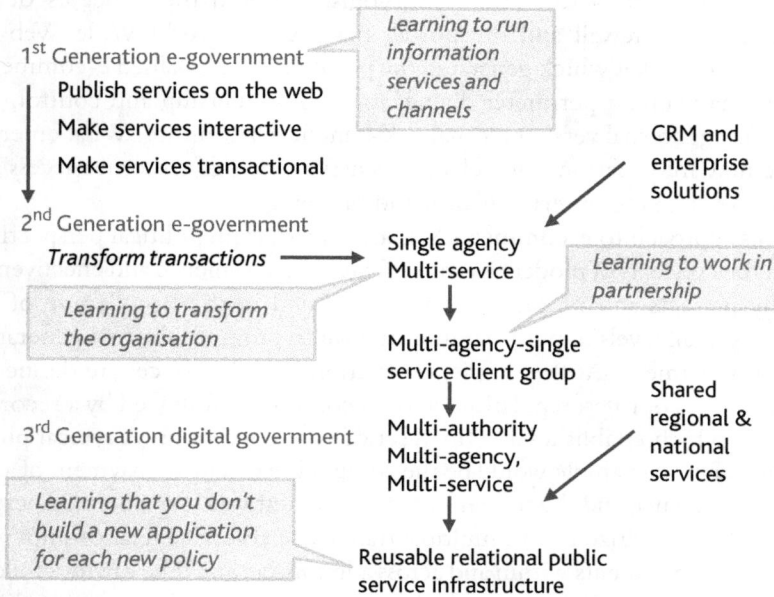

1st Generation e-government
- Publish services on the web
- Make services interactive
- Make services transactional

Learning to run information services and channels

CRM and enterprise solutions

2nd Generation e-government

Transform transactions → Single agency Multi-service

Learning to work in partnership

Learning to transform the organisation

Multi-agency-single service client group

Shared regional & national services

3rd Generation digital government — Multi-authority Multi-agency, Multi-service

Learning that you don't build a new application for each new policy

Reusable relational public service infrastructure

Source: Martin, 2006

channels to support the spectrum of interactions between the citizen and public administrations and services. This process of channel and media shift from paper and postage or direct contact to the electronic publication of information, which subsequently became interactive and then transactional, was initiated around the turn of the millennium. It was first applied to basic registration, licensing, taxation and reporting processes associated with single administrative departments of local, regional and national government.

The background and spur to these developments in the public sector was the progress that had then been made in the appropriation and adaption of the emerging internet technologies and services as a channel for e-business in the private sector. Initially, commerce rejected the Universalist Internet concept of every computer being connected to every other computer in a best effort network, as, at best, an academic toy. The fundamental tenet of the established, integrationist, enterprise solution approach was firmly maintained. This is the principle that, in all legal, physical and technological systems terms, there must be an explicit and clearly maintained boundary between the inside and the outside of the enterprise: the inside represents a domain of rational control with a single point of truth and recourse which is demarcated and separated from an external environment of opportunity and competition. The ability to physically, as well as contractually, manage the interface between these two domains was traditionally regarded as a mission critical aspect of doing business.

Very quickly, however, entrepreneurial opportunities were recognised and business innovators and technologists evolved the concepts of the intranet, the firewall and the portal, making the World Wide Web the channel to market which generated the possibility of globalised e-commerce, while maintaining perimeter demarcations of ownership and control, and redefining internal versus external risk-benefit relationships. What emerged were new information value chain business models of customer access and of market making, intermediation and brokerage.

This approach to e-commerce was associated, from political perspectives, with the concepts of modernisation, efficiency, convenience and effectiveness. Many projects and programmes were initiated in the first decade of this century at all levels of public administration to promote the first generation of e-government. At the simple, transactional level, services are defined in terms of sets of rules, regulations and preconditions, followed by a recorded process which establishes a defined set of post-conditions. A typical public administration example would be the completion of a form, payment of a fee, issue of a licence and the settlement of an account valid for a defined period. But individual citizens have multiple transactional service relationships with different departments within and across administrations. The obvious follow-on requirement, which represents the transition to second-generation digital government, involved identity and relationship management. With this, the citizen can avoid the need for separate credentials and access procedures for each electronically mediated service and the administration can correlate information across different service relationships. This entailed the adaptation and adoption of commercially derived customer relationship management tools and facilities and of a 'single front-office – multiple back-office' model of public administration. It entailed the creation of identity management schemes which operated principally as national level initiatives.

In the second generation of digital government evolution, an additional dimension of complexity came into play. This involved the progressive incorporation of electronic communications and coordination in the management and delivery of relational, as opposed to simple, self-contained, transactional services. At the operational level, the distinction between a transactional and a relational service is that the former is defined, as we have described, entirely in terms of pre- and post-conditions whereas the latter typically involves sequences of encounters as part of an ongoing, outcome-oriented relationship. These relationships may be delimited in the concept of an episode, with an explicit beginning and end, but they may persist over extended periods of time. This description of relationality, at the operational level, is only partial, however.

To be defined completely, a relational service must also be expressed in terms of the definition of the purposes and expected experiences of the providing and receiving parties: relationality implies shared intentionality;

the lived experiences of outcomes are essential in the definition, evaluation and governance of such services. This further implies that we are no longer exclusively in the world of empirical observation and measurement and have entered one where interpretation, social co-construction and culture are also significant. We will explore the implications of these added complexities the next section of this chapter.

Second generation service developments usually took place in the context of partnership working initiatives focused on the needs of particular client groups defined in terms of the experience of specific combinations of situation and of complex, long-term needs. Such needs often demand different combinations of specialist and generalist care, wellbeing and developmental services. These services, in practice, have varying capacities and availabilities, interact and interdepend on each other (sometimes detrimentally, sometimes synergistically) and have sources that represent multiple, independently governed agencies.

The initial attempts at supporting multi-agency working in the context of complex needs were essentially integrationist in approach. They involved the design and deployment of instruments, such as common assessment frameworks and shared electronic records, service directories and booking and referral systems. In these contexts, each multi-agency working initiative tended to generate its own, local 'integrated solution' and in effect, its own new silo, often unconnected even to its own members' existing integrated systems, and seldom, if ever, to each other. Alternatively, one member system, and service relationship, became dominant while others became subsidiary to it.

An observation that emerged clearly in this period was that the 'complex long-term condition' represents a universal problem shape: it applied to such diverse contexts as an individual with complex health and social care needs, the long-term unemployed, a family or household, a small or medium business or social enterprise organisation attempting to survive and grow in a regional economy or even a deprived community trying to improve its amenity and resilience (see McLoughlin and Wilson, 2013). In each case, any progress involves coordinated activities between different combinations of specialisms and resources, generating the need for creative improvisations, with dynamic learning and adaptation. These characteristics were strongly at odds with the predefined criteria of assessment tools and the standardisation of care pathway approaches, which are deeply embedded in the integrationist paradigm.

To summarise the argument so far, we have observed that in the complex social, economic, cultural and political contexts we are considering, services should be understood as components of wider service environments supported by development and delivery platforms that render them governable. While it is necessary that perhaps many of these service components are packaged as simply transactional, the individual, complex 'case', whether individual, familial or wider community, should not normally be exposed to the individual transactional service components but these should be intermediated and facilitated in the context of relational services. This is, in effect, a requirement on the development and delivery platform that it supports the process of 'joining thing up for others'. The joining up role may be formal or informal, some individuals are able to navigate and join up for themselves, but the outcome must always be a bespoke combination of service components constructed on the basis of presenting needs, preferences, availabilities and community experience and wisdom.

This structural requirement implies an infrastructural one: that all services exist as live publications, that their identity is registered within the community and that infrastructural brokers and intermediaries maintain catalogues that actively support the structural brokers and intermediaries (the human relational joining up service providers) in their care coordination activities.

A corollary of the infrastructurally supported service intermediation and brokerage communications platform is that each item of content it mediates must maintain a dependable link to a provenance which represents the means of linking data produced at the system level as an instance of a specific service process model, with the corresponding conversational model which indicates the norms and rules under which it was produced and is intended to be used

While the first set of attempts to support relational multi-agency services were based on the integrationist paradigm and/or the concept of shared applications, social media and exclusively monopolistic platforms have come to dominate global communications and personal information and relationship spaces. The optimistic interpretation of the emerged situation, embodied in the original conception of CoSIE (and in much policy around the role of information and communications technologies), is that the existing organisation-based integrationist enterprise systems and proprietary social media platforms can coexist and be mutually supportive in the delivery of better outcomes for society and the people and communities who live in it. The pessimistic interpretation is that the silo-based over-integration of the organisational systems and ungoverned, parasitic and exploitative underpinning of current social media renders it incompatible with the need for a relational public service which must be delivered in appropriately hybrid governable information spaces and contexts.

Through our involvement in the deployment of platforms (both technical and organisational) to support the evolution, delivery and governance of multi-agency relational public services and through the experiences of the

CoSIE project in the many different national contexts, we now have a deeper and more nuanced understanding of the need for change. In order to address the ongoing issues that are raised about safety, privacy and governance of the relationship between public administration and community-based relational services and the wider public information spaces we turn to the development of an emerging theory of service which conceptualises the relationality needed to address these challenges.

Towards a theory of service – conceptualising the relational

Now, we will consider more detailed aspects of the distinction and implications of the transactional and relational concepts of service. This will lead us to consider the concepts of service environments, infrastructures and platforms. We start with the concept of a simple individual service to address a specific need. Complex needs will always require a multiplicity of such servicers to be assembled and appropriately coordinated, on demand, so what we are considering is a service as a component to be incorporated in ongoing and evolving care plans. This idea of dynamic service coordination is a concept of integration that is quite different from that of data integration associated with integrated enterprise solutions which is achieved by amalgamation and homogenisation in the concept of the 'single point of truth'. It represents dynamic, situated integration as opposed to static pre-emptive integration. While the latter can, on occasion, respond to complication, only the former can respond to complexity.

While some of the CoSIE pilots, such as the UK initiative or the Swedish pilot, directly map onto this multi-service, complex and evolving problem solving and care planning approach, others, such as Spanish, Polish and Greek pilots, were more focused on the creation of community facilities. But even in these cases, the included activities and relationships complexify and evolve, numerous service elements emerge, combine and recombine in response to need and demand that is, itself, constantly evolving.

As indicated in the introduction to this chapter, we start our definition of a service component at the engineering or empirical level where it is defined in terms of a set of verifiable preconditions, a transactional process and a set of verifiable post-conditions. Service events, from this perspective, involve the verification of the preconditions, the performance of the transaction and the establishment of the post-conditions. A side effect of this may be a record or log which can be compared to the specification defined in a process model. In this analysis, we are not criticising transactional services as such. In complex service environments, many service elements are appropriately packaged as transactions. The challenge comes from the resulting need for intermediation and brokerage as a relational service.

Of course, the people who are actually involved in the delivery, reception and management activities of a transactional service experience feelings and reactions and the instigators of the service had certain purposes in mind in its definition, design and provisioning. Nevertheless, at the strictly transactional level, these remain implicit and, for transactional service definition purposes, irrelevant. Making a customer satisfaction survey part of the service protocol does not make it relational: it simply introduces another element of observation and measurement. This corresponds to the principles which are associated with the New Public Management approach: if you can't measure it, it cannot be performance managed and therefore you can't control or improve it (Lowe and Wilson, 2017). This entails an entirely empirical-realist stance that treats real-world processes simply as mechanisms. The objective of management, in this context, is to ensure that sequences of service events conform to the mandated process model by which the service has been defined. Whether the service process is fit for purpose or, indeed, what that purpose is, belong, as we have observed, to a different scope – the domain of policy not of service.

A relational service definition, in contrast, is not limited to the identification of observably verifiable conditions and processes but also includes the interpretation of proposes, intentions and experiences, both at the level of the individual participants in instances of service delivery and also of the wider service community. The intended experience is part of the definition of the service itself. This means that we must extend (not replace) the transactional service definition with a set of elements which belong to a different epistemic stance: they are idealist-constructivist rather than empiricist.

A consequence of this distinction is that an organisation that delivers a transactional service can only be held responsible for its operation – *what it does* – not for the consequences. A relational service provider accepts responsibility for both its operation and its outcomes, that is to say its effects and affects, costs and benefits, for all relevant stakeholders.

In Figure 11.2, we have called this extension to the service definition a 'conversational model'. The term 'conversation' is being used in a specific technical sense here as a definition and allocation of explicitly defined sets of rights and responsibilities between roles involved in the delivery and reception of a service, or any other human organisational context.

A conversational model captures the norms, rules and expectations which have been agreed and committed to as part of the governance processes of the service context. It thus represents the intentions and purposes of the service community. The flexibility and responsiveness of relational service contexts means that their process models must reflect this adaptability and cannot be defined with the same procedural strictness of a purely transactional model. It is as a result of these different approaches to the determination of the relational service that governance itself becomes an

Figure 11.2: Specifying a relational service

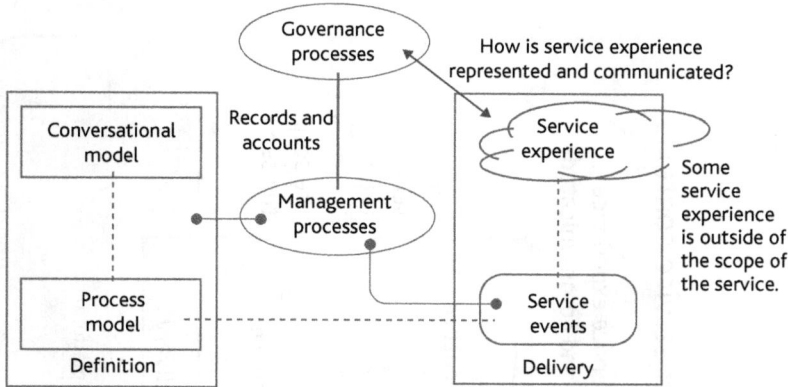

ongoing conversation which is addressing the relationships between what was intended, both at the level of the individual case and at the community level, what was experienced by the parties, and what was observed to happen and has been recorded.

Service definitions, in terms of both conversational and process models, are constructed and maintained on a development platform which supports the design, evaluation, maintenance and evolution of the service definitions while a delivery platform supports all aspects of service publication, access and qualification, delivery and recording. Both platforms support management, the purpose of which is to inform governance. Services also operate in a wider service economy, while platforms operate in the context of wider networks and infrastructures. Both of these operate in an inclusive sociopolitical context, as illustrated in Figure 11.3.

We are using the term 'platform' in the widest possible sense of infrastructure. Note that, in most circumstances, services are not delivered in isolation and that service coordination and brokerage is itself a necessarily relational activity especially for complex long-term situations and conditions.

To conclude this discussion about relationality, it is the fact that interpretation of the lived experience of the service is an essential element in its identity and evaluation that service user/client participation in governance is a logical and practical necessity. It is the participative, co-productive principle, extended to the whole life-cycle of the service that underpins and justifies the co-creative approach adopted in CoSIE.

The following section introduces a model which seek to represent a generic service creation process. It outlines of the theory of the architectural discourse of sociotechnical systems which underpins the Living Lab modelling methods and frameworks we used in Chapter 10 to facilitate the co-creation processes of the local innovation pilots.

Figure 11.3: Relational services and their contexts

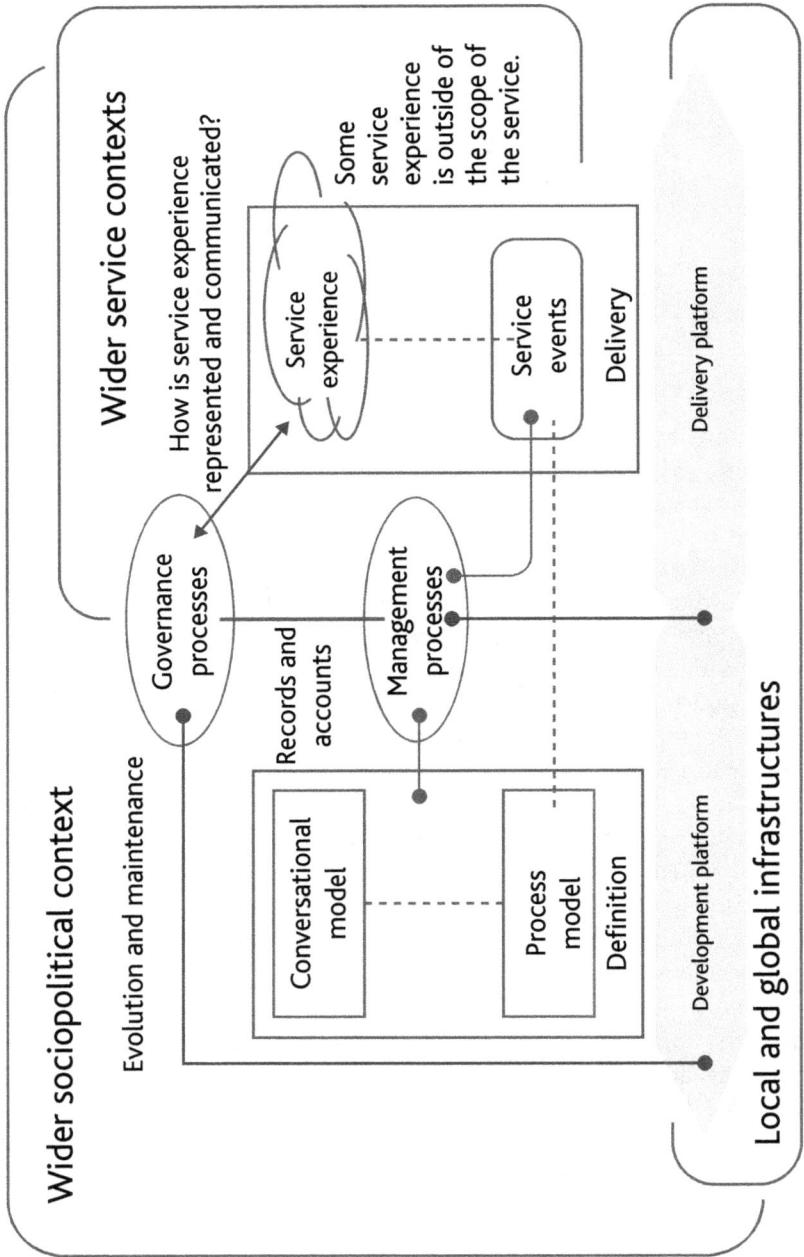

Wider sociopolitical context

Wider service contexts

Evolution and maintenance

How is service experience represented and communicated?

Service experience

Some service experience is outside of the scope of the service.

Governance processes

Records and accounts

Management processes

Service events

Delivery

Conversational model

Process model

Definition

Delivery platform

Development platform

Local and global infrastructures

The service life-cycle

In any service there is, whether implicit or explicit, a service development and delivery life-cycle. We observed this in each of the CoSIE pilots. The model we are using here is an adaptation and extension of a service life-cycle model originally developed through a series of projects on multi-agency collaborative working from 2000 to 2008 involving the authors of this chapter (reported in McLoughlin and Wilson, 2013).

This model (Figure 11.4) is initially articulated as a series of logically interdependent processes, each of which makes use of inputs and generates outputs to and from other processes. A consequence of this formal structure is the tendency to think that the actual processes are performed in logical sequence and that each is completed before the subsequent, logically dependent processes are performed. This is seldom the case in the lived experience of the stakeholders involved in the co-creation of the service. The articulation of a logical life-cycle model provides, on the one hand, an inventory of milestones and way points as an indicator of progress and completion and, in the case of a context in which participation and co-creation are important considerations, a template of the activities and processes which represent the 'what?' of the situation against which questions of participation, 'who?', can be posed. In a co-creative approach, each of the stages in the life-cycle is considered to be realised through a set of deliberative processes and the key question becomes who gets the right to participate in these conversations?

In the following section we define the stages of service creation abstracting from issues of who undertakes them and whether they are conducted co-creatively or not.

The definition of the service policy and objectives: it is at this level that many aspects of the intended ethos of the service itself and its mode of delivery are established. The intentionalities of wellbeing services can be categorised as palliative, rehabilitative, remedial, developmental and transformational. We must also include restorative and behavioural services (from the probation service pilot) to this list to cover the range considered in the set of CoSIE pilots. This is directly applicable to services with clients who are people and also applies, by analogy, to communities and locations as service innovation beneficiaries. Note that this classification includes both asset-based and deficit-based interventions and the different pilots exhibit a range of selection and combinations of these types of service and service component in their approaches. A core requirement on a service policy statement is that it identifies both the intended outcomes or benefits and the intended beneficiaries of the service. The envelope of financial and other generic resources, allocated for the delivery of an expected service capacity, are also an aspect of the service policy.

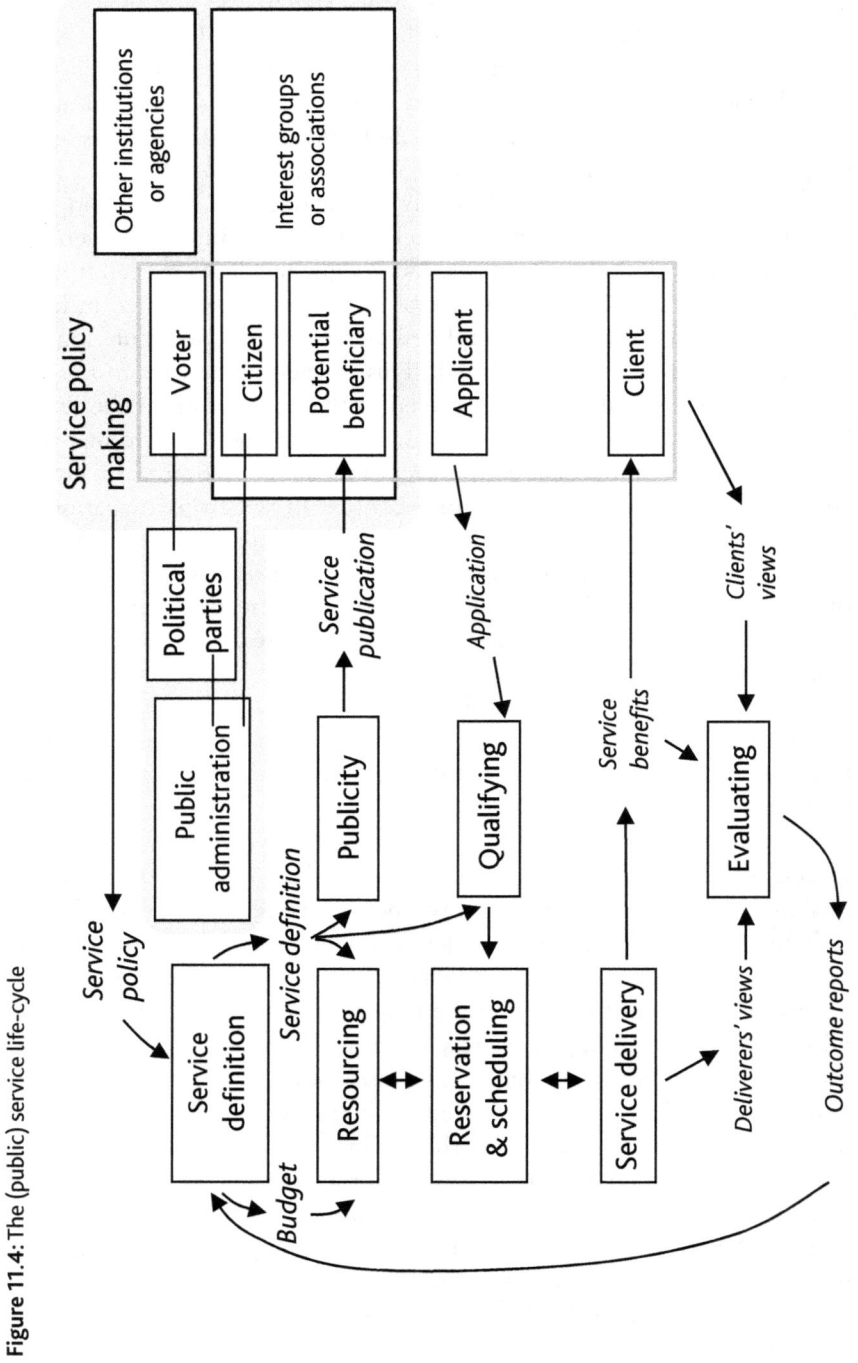

Figure 11.4: The (public) service life-cycle

Service policy making

Other institutions or agencies

Interest groups or associations

Voter

Citizen

Potential beneficiary

Applicant

Client

Political parties

Public administration

Service policy

Service publication

Application

Clients' views

Service definition

Service definition

Publicity

Qualifying

Service benefits

Evaluating

Budget

Resourcing

Reservation & scheduling

Service delivery

Deliverers' views

Outcome reports

Service resourcing and design: this activity is concerned with the conversion of the generic resources (budgets) into specific capacities to govern, manage and deliver a service design or plan.

Service publication/recruitment: this activity is concerned with establishing the relationship of awareness and accessibility between the service and its intended audience of potential beneficiaries.

Service qualification: the service policy has identified the intended beneficiaries of the service and a consequence of this is that any request or application for the service must be checked against these criteria, which may be narrow and specific or may be loose and inclusive.

Service reservation and scheduling: it is a characteristic of services that they require a balance between capacity and demand, which, in extreme cases, may amount to triage or rationing. In other situations, there may be a requirement for relaxation flow management in which a sufficient cohort is accumulated over a period and, when a threshold is reached, a collective delivery is initiated. There are many other modes of reservation and scheduling appropriate to different classes of service.

Service delivery: this also varies with the nature of the service from a simple transaction, collective occasions or series of events to an extended relationship making use of human and physical resources and facilities.

Service evaluation: this is a multilevel activity in which we distinguish between the evaluations of management and those of governance. The former involves a comparison between observed procedures and the rules, budgets and plans of the service design, while the latter involves the evaluation of the outcomes of the service with respect to the intentions and objectives articulated in policy. Both of these imply access to evidence in the form of data recorded as a part of the service delivery processes.

Service development and delivery platforms

All of the initiatives of the CoSIE pilots were, in one way or another, place-based and, inevitably, the situated facilities and amenities (or their lack) provides a key element of their respective 'platforms'. In this discussion, it is not these local contexts, critical as they are to the shape and outcomes of the pilots, that are the focus of our attention. Rather we are concerned with the communicational and informational aspects of the service development and delivery platform and, in particular, the identification of the common structures, resources and facilities which may be reusable and repurposable in the evolution or even redesign or replacement of the services that were the focus of the CoSIE pilots.

The rational and justification of this focus is the final learning stage in the maturity model (Figure 11.1), which is that the response to each new policy, priority or identified need should not be to build a new complete and specific 'application', in the conventional, integrated enterprise solution sense. The more effective and efficient alternative would be to repurpose, reuse and extend existing resources. This further implies that this reuse is not simply of the basic and lowest level infrastructural elements but should include relatively high-level structures, capacities and relationships.

In adopting this approach, we must remain aware that the processes we are dealing with are embedded in political cycles and processes. To survive and be effective in these contexts, the sunk investment in reusable and repurposable infrastructure must, itself, be depoliticised as far as possible. As long as the purpose of service investment is perceived as the maintenance of political power and influence of voters, then that investment becomes the symbol and monument of that policy and its makers, to be swept away and replaced by successors. Each of the CoSIE pilots exhibited elements of these political dimensions and tensions, to different extents and over different timescales.

Conclusion

At a fairly concrete and explicit level of abstraction, all the CoSIE pilots (and in fact any relational services) can be described in terms of a sequence of communication activities involving convenings, encounters and deliberations as seen throughout this book. Evidence-gathering and decision-making can be bureaucratic, participatory or a hybrid process where top down and bottom-up approaches are brought together in harmony or collision. The activities, in turn, were supported and mediated by a range of publication and communication channels and media, depending on the context, as well as locally available physical amenities and facilities.

In the conduct of all human affairs, whether social, political or economic, we have a need and propensity to demarcate and navigate spaces and memberships that create and maintain distinctions between internal and external relationships and participations. The more internal or intimate a conversation is perceived to be, the more it is expected to conform to norms, expectation and plans, in other words to be trusted. Thus, we are better able to conduct relational associations internally and tend to engage in transactional associations with what we regard as external. We all have roles, and participate in, many such overlapping and nested social and organisational spaces which we operate on a spectrum from the highly private and privileged to the entirely public and ungoverned. Participation in the co-creation of relational service is a clear example of this need to partition our communication spaces: some contexts may be quite public while others may exhibit high privacy and sensitivity.

So, in the case of care and wellbeing services, addressing complex need and demanding flexible responses from combinations of specialisms, the ability to configure and manage the information and communications aspects of dynamic relational and transactional 'spaces' becomes acute. They involve the creation, coordination and management of information flows across multiple formal and informal boundaries in the collective negotiation and pursuit of shared intentions of care wellbeing and development.

The structuration processes in which these associations and memberships are instigated and maintained are necessarily dependent on infrastructures. As we have observed in the case of the CoSIE co-creation pilots, these involve mechanisms and capacities for encounter, rendezvous, synchronous and asynchronous communications involving channels and media and the persistence of information, all configured to implement and maintain purposeful and evolving patterns of conversation and relationship. But infrastructure implies a horizontal boundary which demarcates 'below versus above' rather than 'inside versus outside', and, at all scales and distributions, our current information and communications infrastructures have come to be increasingly mediated by technological platforms and processes rather than by the more natural and instinctive affordances of our built environments and artefacts.

The core issue for a relational infrastructure to support relational services is governability, that is to say, the provision of all the facilities needed to ask and answer the following questions of governance, on the basis of reliable evidence:

- Have the activities and their outcomes that have been enabled and supported by the relational platform conformed to our expectations and intentions?
- If they have not, or our expectations and intentions have changed, what changes should we make to the platform and the activities it supports?

As indicated in the second query, the concept of governability being developed here requires that the implementation of the response must be a matter of the internal administrative actions and not require recourse to external technical support. So, the critical factor becomes one of participation in governance processes because, in the relational platform, it is through governance processes and publications that norms and expectations are conceived, defined, maintained and shared within the system.

So, our key conclusion in this chapter is that, if we are to support co-creation and participation in wellbeing services, whether these are aimed at individuals and families, communities or environments and ecosystems, we require information platforms that are trustworthy and governable in the interests of the whole service community. While the functionality implied has become familiar, the current contexts for the governance and use of social media render it inappropriate and, at times, positively dangerous in the more sensitive care and wellbeing contexts.

References

Ciborra, U. (ed) (2000) *From Control to Drift: The Dynamics of Corporate Information Infrastructures*, Oxford: Oxford University Press.

Jalonen, H. and Helo, T. (2020) 'Co-creation of public service innovation using open data and social media: rhetoric, reality, or something in between?', *International Journal of Innovation in the Digital Economy*, 11(3): 64–77.

Jalonen, H., Jäppinen, T. and Bugarszki, Z. (2019) *Co-creation of Social Innovation Policy Brief: Co-creation of Service Innovation in Europe (CoSIE)*, https://docplayer.net/200121040-Co-creation-of-social-innovation.html

Lips, M. (2019) *Digital Government: Managing Public Sector Reform in the Digital Era*, London: Routledge.

Lowe, T. and Wilson, R. (2017) 'Playing the game of outcomes-based performance management: is gamesmanship inevitable? Evidence from theory and practice', *Social Policy & Administration*, 51(7): 981–1001.

Martin, M. (2006) *E-Government Evolution: Technical and Organisational Trajectories*, Centre for Social and Business Informatics, Newcastle University, unpublished paper.

McLoughlin, I. and Wilson, R. (2013) *Digital Government @ Work*, Oxford: Oxford University Press.

Mohr, J. and Ezra, D. (2021) *Designing Integrated Care Ecosystems: A Socio-Technical Perspective*, Cham: Springer.

12

Conclusions: Moving beyond building sandcastles ... long-term sociotechnical infrastructure for social justice

Rob Wilson, Sue Baines, Andrea Bassi, Heli Aramo-Immonen, Riccardo Prandini, Inga Narbutaité Aflaki and Chris Fox

Introduction

This concluding chapter summaries the book's central premise, drawing from conceptual and empirical contributions of our collective experiences and reflection of enacting social innovation through co-creation. Throughout the volume we have explored current thinking and practices around co-creation and co-production. We have emphasised in particular the turn towards more asset-based and relational ways of thinking in the framing of individuals and communities as having their own assets, goals and means of change. This is allied to the need to be brought together in various combinations to form the sorts of mutuality envisaged by proponents of co-creation and co-production in policy and practice. In this final chapter we now turn to considering the transition needed from the current focus on pilot projects and interventions or experiments in co-creation, which almost always begin with a plan and end in what is an apparently concrete and impactful solution. The problem with these short-term investments, as many have come to realise, is that although we learn from them, we can rarely sustain or scale beyond the original resourcing. Or to put it another way - a world where pilots run aground, trailblazers burnout and pathfinders get lost.

We start with a reflection on the language of co-creation and then go on to dig a bit deeper into what is meant by 'scaling' co-creative social innovations. We pay particular attention to governance and the mixed success of digital tools. The need to cultivate a relational approach for social justice is emphasised. We further elaborate on the metaphor of the sandcastle and present a model that combines context-specific structures with reusable infrastructures able to support and sustain successive initiatives.

Co-creation: not as new as we think?

The need to work from the places and spaces where citizens and communities are aspiring to good lives is a key part of authentic approaches to co-creation. The language of participation has deep roots in the history and language of communities across the Europe. Multiple terms were used by partners and colleagues throughout the Co-creation of Service Innovation in Europe (CoSIE) project. These are illustrated in a simple visualisation (Figure 12.1). The data for this visualisation were provided by partners and colleagues at a Knowledge Exchange workshop in which all the CoSIE teams participated. As the word cloud (Figure 12.1) shows, our Italian and Swedish colleagues provide the largest number of terms for co-creation (five), followed by our Estonian and UK colleagues (four). Despite English being the most widely used language within the project, UK participants had four different terms for co-creation: co-production, personalisation, person–centred practice and

Figure 12.1: Word cloud of terms for co-creation

desistance (a term particular to the criminal justice context where the UK pilot was situated). So even to native English speakers there are multiple alternatives for the term co-creation, each with its own nuanced definition. Finnish and Dutch partners used three terms, and Hungarian colleagues two. Conversely, our Polish and Spanish colleagues used a single term for co-creation ('*wspoltworzenie*' and '*co-creació*', respectively).

Using just 'co-creation' adds even more complexity and prompts pertinent questions: Do we all share the same understanding of 'co-creation' when we discuss it among our colleagues and participants? Are our intentions of co-creation understood by the instigators of co-creation – and the users and (dis)beneficiaries of service innovation?

An example from a later discussion in a workshop in the Netherlands was the idea of 'Polder' or 'Poldermodel' (Woldendorp and Keman, 2007), which has its antecedents in the activities of the reclamation of land from the sea via the associated community construction and maintenance of dikes. The core aspect for our Dutch colleagues was the length of time and consensus-based process where all stakeholders need to be heard, often summarised as 'cooperation despite differences'. An environment that encourages co-creation is a powerful one (and the encouraging thing here is that all the languages represented were able to mobilise a response to the challenge). However, to leverage that power, we must ensure that all participants in a process understand the co-creation concept in their own terms. So is the term 'co-creation' doing a disservice in a multilingual community? The evidence suggests there is a need to address this further, understanding the roots of the terms with their particular historical implications which can then scaffold or provide social infrastructure for co-creation.

Learning from co-creating?

The activities (and empirical studies) described in this book and the wider literature of academia, policy makers, non-profits and think tanks are part of what is now over a decade of attempts to generate change by improving the means of social innovation through participatory and co-creation methods. There is evidence beyond CoSIE as well as within it that co-creation and social innovation can provide the methods for enacting initial engagements with socially excluded or seldom heard population groups. Eseonu (2022), for example, shows how this has been achieved with racially minoritised young people in a hyper-diverse British city. Yet there seems much left to do in terms of understanding how social innovation is propagated, the tools (including digital tools) that are utilised, relationships to existing institutional structures, and wider theories of social welfare and social policy.

In a very widely cited image Murray et al (2010) showed social innovation processes on a spiral path starting from the recognition of a need to change

Figure 12.2: The six stages of social innovation

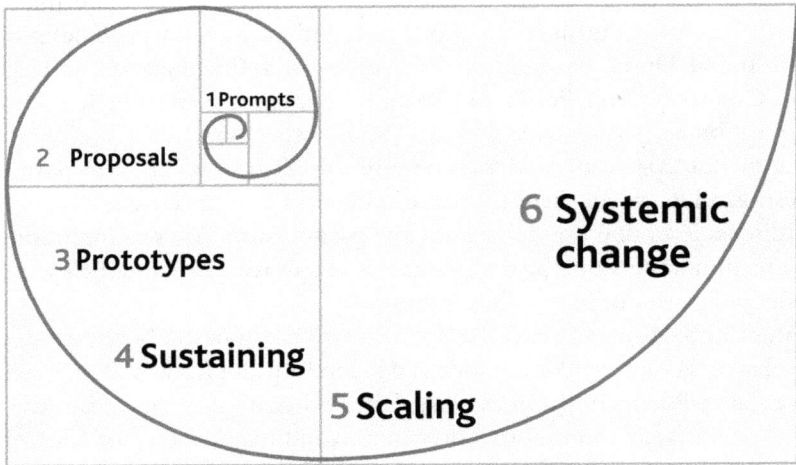

Source: taken from Murray et al, 2010: 11

(or an unmet demand) and eventually ending with a complete systemic change (see Figure 12.2). This path usually follows six steps (in a later version they became seven). However, most social innovations in practice fail to get beyond the third (prototyping) phase (Murray et al, 2010). Our language in the innovation context exemplified by the spiral has been typically borrowed from industrial and commercial innovation models in ways not entirely relevant to social innovation and this has perhaps inculcated expectations around the ways in which things ought to work, in particular thinking around scaling. Some of the prevailing optimism around citizen and community participation in designing and implementing social innovation seems to be grounded in misplaced confidence in a progressive spiral pattern.

Social innovations may not spread beyond their original context because they are not suitable for different conditions, or because their relevance is not recognised. This is a significant challenge. Having a strong evidence base can support scaling but is not sufficient. Equally important can be changing systems to support new ways of working, which in turn is often predicated on challenging existing values and building effective coalitions of people, communities and organisations with linkages across different scales (Kazepov et al, 2019). To do this, innovations must win the hearts and minds of key stakeholders (Barnett, 2021). Different routes not well represented in the spiral figure may lead towards wider system change. Typical scaling strategies that can be identified include:

1. increasing throughput to affect more people in need of the proposed solution (scaling up);

2. expanding the approach to another (geographical) context through replication and diffusion (scaling out);
3. enhancing the character and quality of the approach to increase effectiveness (scaling deep); and
4. broadening the framework and resources of the approach by building new partnerships (scaling wide) (Moore et al, 2015).

A combination of two (or more) strategies is also possible. This fourfold typology represents a more nuanced version of how social innovations may grow and change than the spiral model or linear notions of 'scaling up'. It needs to be said, nevertheless, that there remains a gap between the promises of social innovation and more widespread benefits. Indeed, this in and of itself is a significant understatement.

More recent takes on scaling of social innovation have critiqued the normative assumptions of the underlying political and economic rhetorics on scaling at the EU and national state level and the perversities these create for those undertaking such work (Ruess et al, 2023). Pfotenhauer et al (2022) identify three elements that in their analysis need to be addressed to provide a rebalancing of the dominant rhetorics: 'solutionism', 'experimentalism' and 'future-oriented valuation'. The first 'solutionism' refers to the problem of who decides, for whom, on what basis what is likely to work, thereby proscribing the boundaries of the solution to a problem. Second, the element of 'experimentalism' refers to the blurring of the boundaries of consent in the sorts of social innovation programmes and the ways in which both existing tools and technologies of social media and bespoke innovations gloss over moral issues of participation to foreground scalability as the key outcome of investments. The third element refers to the politics of scaling and the prevailing assumption that the 'future-orientated valuations' are economically dominated and privatised in the hands of a few powerful vested interests without wider considerations of the existing regulatory frameworks or norms of society. Considering a meaningful response to the challenges which these elements raise means '(we need) new visions of co-creation and for substantial deliberation on how participation and co-creation can be enabled in societies' (Ruess et al, 2023).

Certainly, the irony of being part of an EU Horizon project (and programme) attempting to co-create, evaluate and understand the dynamics of co-creation in local social innovation projects in order to co-create a set of generic tools and technologies scalable' for application at an EU level was not lost on us. We observed the ways that 'problems' and their attendant 'solutions' emerged to be addressed at the bid writing stage and for the pilots and project work packages on initiation of their work. This continued through the work, with extensive debates in the consortia about the role of technologies in and across the pilot activity, including the tension of applying commercial social media platforms with vulnerable citizens and communities on one hand (including evaluation of their use in situ) and the challenge of designing, building and evaluating bespoke tools with relatively small numbers of participants on the other. These debates persisted at the project level throughout as partners, work package leaders, and our project officer and reviewers, agonised over the contribution and scalability of the outputs of the both the pilots and the tools and technologies created (or not) and cross-cutting activities, in particular deliverables such as the Living Lab modelling tools, massive open online courses and the CoSIE Roadmap (see the CoSIE website and Jamieson and Martin, 2022).

The promise of co-creation and co-production as a sources of social innovation is that engagement of service users/citizens and wider stakeholders will both improve the design of what is offered as a service or product and its outcomes. Learning from CoSIE includes elements of an emergent alternative social system, for example, the co-creation methods deployed in the social hackathons in Estonia which instilled new contexts where experimentation and innovation were valued (Chapter 3; Kangro and Lepik, 2022). Other notable successes include facilitation of learning and development for personal assistance workers in Sweden (as discussed in Chapter 4). Capacity building through Community Reporting across all the pilot social innovations of the project co-created both insight and developing capabilities (Chapter 7). The work of the pilots in Italy (reported in Chapter 8) and Hungary (Chapters 3 and 10) began to show how specific interventions can lead to the emergence of new more inclusive stakeholder governance structures. There was evidence of potential to create the sorts of institutional structures envisaged by those who recognise the need to ingrain the ability to systematise engagement approaches more broadly (as outlined in Chapter 10).

Moulaert et al (2013), in the final section of their seminal edited collection on social innovation, proposed a holistic approach which bridges to collective action through long engagement and the production of knowledge. Brandsen et al (2018), in the concluding section of their widely read collection, propose a range of actions which basically imply the need to take a bespoke approach to the development of skills and relationships between the network of actors who have a role in initiating and sustaining co-creation efforts. Albury (2015) proposes a conceptual framework of three mechanisms for scaling and diffusion that research has shown to be promising in health and social care contexts, including organic growth, wide stakeholder engagement to mobilise demand and an enabling ecosystem (for example, appropriate leadership and investment approaches). Another stream of social innovation literature (Moulaert and MacCallum, 2019) refers to three dimensions to be achieved to make the innovation sustainable: the satisfaction of unmet needs; community empowerment; and governance transformations. There seems to be an emerging consensus that both the structure and process of co-creation requires the generative power and elasticity as well as the concrete outcomes required to engage stakeholders in the current policy environment.

A theme running throughout this volume is the extent to which the promise of digital tools and platforms was fulfilled, or not. There has been some optimism about the application of digital technologies, including social media and open data, as panaceas to support co-creation, despite a rather limited evidence base (Lember et al, 2019). Using the framework of Digital Social Innovation allows us to see that from a CoSIE-based perspective these approaches can be an input into bricoleuring interpretative multi-party co-creation conversations. One successful example was seen in the work of the Finnish pilot with its innovative application of social media for raising the voices of marginalised young people who did not normally interact with services (Chapter 5). Much less positive was the experience of the UK pilot (Chapter 6) where a proposed bespoke digital solution failed to deliver as proponents anticipated.

The cross-cutting work of the 'Living Labs' signposted how it is possible to bridge from a specific structural intervention in context to innovate *relationships* in the wider information systems infrastructures (soft and hard – or, as we would propose, sociotechnical). This is central to the possibility of cultivating through co-productive modelling processes both the system and the longer-term investments in shared components that produce the ability to sustain the system as platforms on wider sociotechnical infrastructure (see Chapters 10 and 11). However, such approaches need to develop both local social platforms as well as digital tools to provide the trusted governable platforms that we need to address the deep challenges faced by communities across the EU and beyond.

An emerging need for investing in a relational approach?

One thing we can be clear about is that the way forward is inherently relational and responses in a co-creative mode (innovative or not) require productive human relationships that are key to the delivery of services and the wider engagement with the wicked welfare challenges of contemporary society, such as ageing, immigration, climate change and inequality. Cultivating a relational approach potentially requires a reimagining of the co-creation and social innovation agendas from a fixed normative linear approach where interventions are treated as planned experiments with discernible outcomes to understanding these as processes of ongoing investment in learning as part of wider civic engagement in an inherently complex environment where the outcomes are almost always contingent (Lowe and Wilson, 2017; Charfe and Gardner, 2019; Bartels and Turnbull, 2020; Bartels, 2022; French et al, 2023).

Taking a relational frame of conceptualising and enacting co-creation and related capabilities for social justice allows to explore a new approach to change, improvement, learning and research endeavours as a basis to address the complex challenges of societies. More fundamentally, this 'relational turn' asks a deeper question of our understanding of value creation. Viewed through a relational lens, value is dependent on the quality of relationships between component parts of a system, be it a set of collaborating partners with a shared agenda or a looser federated community, rather than the efficacy of overspecified individuated interventions aimed solely at fixing particular individualised problems (such as obesity) rather than developing agency and improving relations in the local community context. The investment in capability over the long term plays into wider debates in social investment, public service reform and democratic/participatory deliberation essentially related to strengths-based, capability building approaches. It pushes this argument forward by drawing upon recent refinements of capability theory (as we outline in Chapter 2). It also questions the basis on which current technologies have been developed, for whose benefit and whether our existing service platforms are governable and governed by those who ought to be involved (see Chapters 1, 2 and 11).

For all the efforts of programmes such as these and the vast resources invested in a range of national and international social programmes (such as the Big Lottery in the UK and the European Regional Development Fund and European Social Fund in the EU), the evidence for change (as opposed to performance activity) materialised beyond the immediate resourcing appears relatively scant. In the seminal work *Theory of Justice* (1971), Rawls suggests that societies need to adopt the principles of social justice and enshrine them in systems with appropriate institutions whose role and responsibilities are to ensure the fair(er) distribution of social goods through 'social co-operation'. Later works on social justice emphasise the plurality of what counts as 'justice' in contemporary contexts, signalling the requirement for participative approaches such as co-creation to reach settlements within and between communities (Sen, 2005; 2006; Nussbaum, 2006). Arguments follow that social justice in order to be enacted should be redistributive in the development of the capacity building of capability (Pierik and Robeyns, 2007; Robeyns, 2017). Capability in these terms offers a way of making investments in humans and their environments which support the ongoing dynamic renewal of existing structures and communities in the face of complex issues (Teece et al, 1997; French et al, 2023; Ruess et al, 2023).

Taking such a relational approach breaks down the false dichotomy of the personal and collective and refocuses investments where the issues of resources and capabilities can be seen as an intention for the cultivation of agency (Claassen, 2016) in a wider framework of social pedagogy (Hatton, 2013; Charfe and Gardner, 2019). The argument that investing in the development of capability to provide the systems and cultivate relational human agency to enabling processes of social justice therefore feels generative in terms of the ways in which we might reposition the broader intentions of co-creation as a process of social innovation.

Towards concreteness AND elasticity?

Ultimately the question for any philosopher of social justice is what should this system and institutional form look like and how should it work? It is clear that the contemporary starting points for engagement are in the mode of linear projects with the challenges they bring in terms of explicit 'concrete' products and outcomes, constrained resourcing and associated evaluative frames (including what counts as evidence). What we have now (as the cover of our book implies) is a landscape of policy and practice 'sandcastles'.

The illusion that a sandcastle gives is one of concrete-ness. They are unproblematic in that they can be created efficiently using sand buckets (which act as moulds). People like creating them. Others admire them. They can be decorated with flags and shells. We can have competitions. We can protect and maintain them by building moats (Obrador Pons, 2009; Franklin, 2014). In the end, however, they are insubstantial, vulnerable to being washed away in social forces of the tide or kicked over by the policy careless or bullies leaving little trace of their existence. In spite of this critique concreteness matters both an imaginary and pragmatic exemplar for change and without the structure that process brings it is a significant challenge to engage the sceptical, whether they be policy makers or communities.

However, as well as the 'concreteness' we need the 'elasticity' to respond to the emergence and sustainability of innovation and change. As we have intimated, this requires investment in the social and technical (sociotechnical) infrastructures that support activity but also allow it to be cultivated and bricoleured through human capabilities into new process, mutuality and service. Such a generative approach potentially allow us to know and to learn and reflect; to govern and be governed; to manage and to steward; to lead and to collaborate.

Within our work we identified a range of core internal elements that are common to all the various approaches. They serve to make explicit certain key external elements and factors, which are relevant to any service environment if it is to be sustainable. The 'co-creation of service' model presented in Chapter 10 (Figure 10.5) derived from the modelling processes of the CoSIE project. It represents an attempt to present and interrelate a number of terms and categories to provide the basis for a language and framing of service innovation activities. It was adopted and utilised by some of the pilots to help them to visualise relationships between the actions they undertook locally and relevant external considerations. We return to that

Figure 12.3: Structural and infrastructural relationships

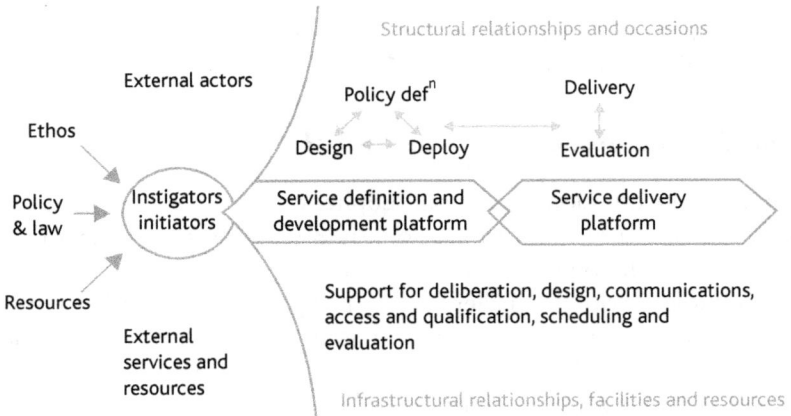

model here to draw attention to a key learning point from the project: the distinction between 'structure' and 'infrastructure' and the initiation of 'services' and 'service environments', and the 'delivery of service' and 'service platform infrastructure' (see Figure 12.3).

The top right of the model represents a set of structural relationships and occasions. Each structural process can be populated via some or all of these processes with the identities of stakeholders or resources. For example, as we know, external actors (top left) represent a range of input to which a co-creative innovation process has been instigated or had to respond, including 'Ethos', 'Policy', 'Law'. The service life-cycle processes are distributed over, and supported by, a service definition and development platform and a service delivery platform (bottom middle and right). As an example, a social hackathon (as a method and as an outcome) represents such a definition and development platform. The nature of the delivery platform for any service or service set defined in a hackathon is one of the outputs of the co-creation process. In another case, a social enterprise business development support facility has been both service definition and development as well as the delivery platform. Thus, below the platform (the soft and hard infrastructure) we have a space in which to locate the sociotechnical infrastructural capacities to support deliberation, design, communications, the means of access to different sorts of services and service components and for the processes of qualification, scheduling and evaluation necessary for investments in capabilities and also management and governance.

The aim here is to respond to the problem of emergent sustainability by proposing parallel investments in reusable infrastructures able to support and sustain successive initiatives in co-creative service development. Having married an abstract, generic model of civic participation and of service, we have created the opportunity for the shared resources between a broad co-creation initiatives and services and potentially improved the sustainability of both the concreteness and the elasticity required to support long-term coordination, collaborative governance and adaption. The precise shape and nature of these resources will vary from context to context but we believe there is a strong likelihood that there are some universal elements that are common requirements in many classes of relational services.

Final reflections

We opened this volume with the observation that co-creation in public services has become a widely accepted orthodoxy and in tune with the times (Osborne et al, 2016; Brandsen et al, 2018). Committed adherents view its further advance as inevitable. Yet some pilot experiences suggest aspects of service structures and policies that push against co-creation, most notably short-term planning, policy 'churn' and silo working.

In spite of today's pressing societal challenges (ranging from climate change to unmet care needs in an ageing population) that require significant collaborative effort, governments and those working in government seem reluctant to look beyond short-term goals, economic-based assumptions of innovation and/or reactive responses to events. We have observed this over many years watching projects fail like a set of sandcastles that are washed way. Fundamental challenges remain in the collaborative design and delivery of public services and mutuality with authentic and meaningful participation of citizens affected by those services. Many approaches continue to insist on mimetically adopting the architectures of commercial approaches of business cases, target-based measurement and return on investment tools. These practices have created an ecology in which collaboration has become increasingly difficult to justify without specific purpose and resourcing.

The challenge for public service is that large, long-term centralised programme investments, where one collaboration architecture 'size and shape' fits all, are meeting an increasing variety and innovation in architecture on the ground. Bottom-up approaches are appealing and can be successful, as detailed throughout this volume. However, they can be too reliant on local circumstances to meaningfully scale or sustain elsewhere.

It is time for a change. That means moving away from designing solutions to societal issues that reduce relationships to transactions and/or policies which have the effect of foregrounding a particular version of the problems that individuals or communities have been saddled with. This is compounded by the fact that those most in need often have complex and disjointed relations with services, coupled with the problem that those working with and in the services often have limited resources to mediate their relationships with each other. To respond to these needs effectively and begin to address the challenges set by taking a social justice approach, we must act differently. Most importantly, we must both innovate our public service architecture and invest in individual and collective capabilities as an ongoing infrastructural investment, thereby creating the potential for cultivating the heterogeneous possibilities in relationships that make the lives of people and communities worth living.

References

Albury, D. (2005) 'Fostering innovation in public services', *Public Money & Management*, 25(1): 51–56.

Barnett, S. (2021) *Scaling a Social Innovation? Share Your Learning*, Dublin: Genio Trust.

Bartels, K. (2022) 'Experiential learning: a relational approach to sustaining community-led social innovation', *Innovation: The European Journal of Social Science Research*, 1–20.

Bartels, K. and Turnbull, N. (2020) 'Relational public administration: a synthesis and heuristic classification of relational approaches', *Public Management Review*, 22(9): 1324–1346.

Brandsen, T., Steen, T. and Verschuere, B. (2018) 'How to encourage co-creation and co-production: some recommendations', in Brandsen, T., Steen, T. and Verschuere, B. (eds) *Co-Production and Co-Creation Engaging Citizens in Public Services*, London: Routledge, pp 299–303.

Charfe, L. and Gardner, A. (2019) *Social Pedagogy and Social Work*, London: SAGE.

Claassen, R. (2016) 'An agency-based capability theory of justice', *European Journal of Philosophy*, 24(3): 1279–1304.

Eseonu, T. (2022) 'Co-creation as social innovation: including "hard-to-reach" groups in public service delivery', *Public Money & Management*, 42(5): 306–313. https://doi.org/10.1080/09540962.2021.1981057

Franklin, A. (2014) 'On why we dig the beach: tracing the subjects and objects of the bucket and spade for a relational materialist theory of the beach', *Tourist Studies*, 14(3): 261–285.

French, M., Hesselgreaves, H., Wilson, R., Hawkins, M. and Lowe, T. (2023) *Harnessing Complexity for Better Outcomes in Public and Non-Profit Services*, Bristol: Policy Press.

Hatton, K. (2013) *Social Pedagogy in the UK: Theory and Practice*, Lyme Regis: Russell House.

Jamieson, D. and Martin, M. (2022) 'Supporting co-creation processes through modelling', *Public Money & Management*, 42(5): 353–355. https://doi.org/10.1080/09540962.2021.1996929

Kangro, K. and Lepik, K.-L. (2022) 'Co-creating public services in social hackathons: adapting the original hackathon concept', *Public Money and Management*, 42(5): 341–348.

Kazepov, Y., Columbo, F. and Saruius, T. (2019) 'The multi-scalar puzzle of social innovation', in Oosterlynck, S., Novy, A. and Kazepov, Y. (eds) *Local Social Innovation to Combat Poverty and Exclusion*, Bristol: Policy Press, pp 91–112.

Lember, V., Brandsen, T. and Tonurist, P. (2019) 'The potential impacts of digital technologies on co-production and co-creation', *Public Management Review*, 21(11): 1665–1686.

Lowe, T. and Wilson, R. (2017) 'Playing the game of outcomes-based performance management. Is gamesmanship inevitable? Evidence from theory and practice', *Social Policy & Administration*, 51(7): 981–1001.

Moore, M.-L., Riddell, D. and Vocisano, D. (2015) 'Scaling out, scaling up, scaling deep: strategies of non-profits in advancing systemic social innovation', *Journal of Corporate Citizenship*, 58: 67–84.

Moulaert, F. and MacCallum, D. (2019) *Advanced Introduction to Social Innovation*, Cheltenham: Edward Elgar.

Moulaert, F., MacCallum, D., Mehmood, A. and Hamdouch, A. (eds) (2013) *The International Handbook on Social Innovation: Collective Action, Social Learning and Transdisciplinary Research*, Cheltenham: Edward Elgar.

Murray, R., Caulier-Grice, J. and Mulgan, G. (2010) *The Open Book of Social Innovation*, London: NESTA.

Nussbaum, M. (2006) *Frontiers of Justice*, Cambridge, MA: Harvard University Press.

Obrador Pons, P. (2009) 'Building castles in the sand: repositioning touch on the beach', *The Senses & Society*, 4(2): 195–210.

Osborne, S.P., Radnor, Z. and Strokosch, K. (2016) 'Co-production and the co-creation of value in public services: a suitable case for treatment?' *Public Management Review*, 18(5): 639–653.

Pfotenhauer, S., Laurent, B., Papageorgiou, K. and Stilgoe, J. (2022) 'The politics of scaling', *Social Studies of Science*, 52(1): 3–34. https://doi.org/10.1177/03063127211048945

Pierik, R. and Robeyns, I. (2007) 'Resources versus capabilities: social endowments in egalitarian theory', *Political Studies*, 55(1): 133–152. https://doi.org/10.1111/j.1467–9248.2007.00646.x

Rawls, J. (1971) *A Theory of Justice*, Cambridge, MA: Harvard University Press.

Robeyns, I. (2017) *Wellbeing, Freedom and Social Justice: The Capability Approach Re-Examined*, Cambridge: Open Publishing.

Ruess, A., Müller, R. and Pfotenhauer, S. (2023) 'Opportunity or responsibility? Tracing co-creation in the European policy discourse', *Science and Public Policy*, 50: 433–444.

Sen, A. (2005) 'Human rights and capabilities', *Journal of Human Development*, 6(2): 151–166. https://doi.org/10.1080/14649880500120491

Sen, A. (2006) 'What do we want from a theory of justice?', *Journal of Philosophy*, 103(5): 215–238. https://doi.org/10.5840/jphil2006103517

Teece, D.J., Pisano, G. and Shuen, A. (1997) 'Dynamic capabilities and strategic management', *Strategic Management Journal*, 18(7): 509–533.

Woldendorp, J. and Keman, H. (2007) 'The polder model reviewed: Dutch corporatism 1965—2000', *Economic and Industrial Democracy*, 28(3): 317–347. https://doi.org/10.1177/0143831X07079351

Index

References to figures are in *italic* type; those in **bold** type refer to tables. References to endnotes show both the page number and the note number (231n3).

www.ingramcontent.com/pod-product-compliance
Lightning Source LLC
Chambersburg PA
CBHW070623030426
42337CB00020B/3891